For Jerry, Baby Alia and Steve

THE ENVIRONMENT IN INTERNATIONAL RELATIONS

Caroline Thomas

The Royal Institute of International Affairs

Published by The Royal Institute of International Affairs, 10 St James's Square, London, SW1Y 4LE

ISBN 0 905031 46 6 hardback
     0 905031 45 8 paperback

Cover by Twenty Twenty Design

Printed by The Chameleon Press Limited, on recycled paper

Contents

PART II: CASE STUDIES

Foreword

On the eve of the United Nations Conference on Environment and Development, it is appropriate to reflect on the growth of environmental awareness over the past two decades and to consider what may lie ahead.

I suspect that thirty years ago the environment was at best considered in isolation, and then only by a few farsighted people. For most it was not an issue at all. What a change from now, with our current recognition of how human activities affect the environment in so many ways. I believe that this awareness and its accompanying concern are positive developments. The raising of environmental consciousness has resulted in extensive and significant action to correct past mistakes and to provide a better path for the future. But much still remains to be done.

While some of the problems and their solutions are simple enough, many are far more complex; we rightly hesitate to act because in addressing one problem we may cause another. Global warming is an example. Here perhaps the evidence is sufficient to justify sensible remedial action, but not yet enough to sanction the more far reaching proposals with their attendant economic costs.

As we look ahead, it is clear that international relations will lose nothing in complexity as we adjust to the aftermath of the Cold War. Economic and trade issues are firmly on the agenda, but the environment is now their companion. Local concerns will remain a mainspring for many, acting also as a catalyst to the growth of environmental consciousness. And we now recognize, and are organizing to handle, issues which cross national boundaries, such as global warming, the ozone layer, the conservation of rainforests or the movement of waste. Acceptable standards of environmental performance are clearly now a matter for international concern and we only have to look at the legacy in the former Soviet Union to understand the point.

As the environment becomes part of the tapestry of the world's political, economic and security relationships it is all the more important that policy making is underpinned by well researched evidence and disciplined thinking. This can best be provided by multi-disciplinary studies undertaken by a variety of scientific, policy and other institutes.

For this reason I very much welcome this independent study commissioned by the Royal Institute of International Affairs. It assesses the impact of environmental issues on international economic, political and security relations; I am sure it will make a significant and timely contribution to this important debate.

Robert Horton, Chairman, British Petroleum, May 1992

About the Author

Caroline Thomas has a long standing interest in developing country issues in international relations and in non-military aspects of security. Her interest in the environment is a natural progression from these earlier concerns. Her publications include: *New States, Sovereignty and Intervention*, Wheatsheaf, 1985; *In Search of Security*, Gower/St Martin's Press, 1987; C.Thomas and P.Saravanamuttu (eds), *Conflict and Consensus in South/North Security*, CUP, 1989, and *The State and Instability in the South*, Macmillan, 1989. She is currently working on the politics of water sharing in an era of global environmental change (*Fresh Water Resources in International Politics*, edited with D.Howlett, Open University Press, forthcoming 1992).

Preface

This is an exciting moment to be publishing Chatham House's first major study on the environment and international relations. Previously the work of the Energy and Environmental Programme has concentrated on energy-related environmental issues. However, with the global environmental issues likely to feature even more centrally in the policy agenda of the 1990s, there was an urgent requirement for a text which clearly set out the issues for a general audience. This is likely to be particularly important in the aftermath of the June 1992 United Nations Conference on Environment and Development which will be seen as a landmark in international environmental diplomacy, even if commitments to sustainable development policies turn out to be less than were originally hoped.

Given that the enormous public interest in environmental issues has yet to translate into major funding for research in this area, the Programme is particularly grateful to British Petroleum for supporting this project so generously.

The study groups which considered draft chapters of the book were among the most interesting meetings held by the Programme and thanks are due to all of those who gave their time and expertise.

Finally, more than usual thanks are due to Caroline Thomas for taking on such a huge canvas and completing the task to a demanding schedule made immeasurably more complicated by the birth of her daughter during the time she was completing the manuscript. Anybody running a research programme is greatly appreciative of authors who accept a task and then show grim determination to fulfil their commitment. To have produced this book to such a tight deadline at such an important time in the international political process is a major achievement.

Jonathan Stern, May 1992

Acknowledgments

Many people have been generous in offering their time to help me research this book. Colleagues on the Energy and Environmental Programme at Chatham House provided a working environment characterized by unique energy and enthusiasm. Jonathan Stern, whom I hold in the highest regard, displays the rare quality of knowing how to get the best out of those who work with him. He leads a first rate team in Nicola Steen, Rosina Pullman, Michael Grubb, Matthew Tickle and Silvan Robinson. Without their individual and concerted drive, understanding and effort, this book would have not seen the light of day. Lis Parcell in the Chatham House library has been extremely helpful. Colleagues at Southampton provided vital support and encouragement. Matthew Paterson stepped into the breach and wrote Chapter 5, when the delivery of a baby competed for my time with the delivery of the manuscript! Study group participants too numerous to mention by name, provided lively debate on the book at various stages in its evolution. I owe a particular debt to James Mayall. Norman Myers, Peter Wilkin, Bob Rowthorn, Sally Morphet, John Gordon, Neville Brown, Marc Williams, Owen Greene, Jacky Karas, Anil Markandya, Jim Rollo, Julian Saurin, Peter Lloyd, Alan Ingham and Darryl Howlett have been most helpful. So too were my friends and colleagues in India and Nepal. Family and friends have provided the emotional and physical support to see this project through in difficult circumstances. My mother, brother and Jerry deserve special thanks. So do Rona Thurston and Sheila Fox. Finally I thank Helle Amin for her example.

Caroline Thomas, May 1992

Acronyms used in text:

ACC	Administrative Committee on Coordination
AfDB	African Development Bank
ANEN	African NGOs Environmental Network
ANGOC	Asian NGO Coalition for Agrarian Reform and Development
AOSIS	Alliance of Small Island States
AsDB	Asian Development Bank
CERDS	Charter of Economic Rights and Duties of States
CFC	Chlorofluorocarbon
CIDA	Canadian International Development Agency
CIDIE	Committee of International Development Institutions on the Environment
CILSS	Permanent Inter-State Committee on Drought in the Sahel
CIS	Commonwealth of Independent States
DOEM	Designated Officials on Environmental Management
EBRD	European Bank for Reconstruction and Development
EC	European Community
ECOSOC	Economic and Social Council of the United Nations
EIB	European Investment Bank
ELC	Environmental Liaison Centre
ELCI	Environmental Liaison Centre International
EPA	US Environmental Protection Agency
FAO	United Nations Food and Agriculture Organization
FDAUS	US Food and Drug Administration
FOEI	Friends of the Earth International
GARP	Global Atmospheric Research Program
GATT	General Agreement on Tariffs and Trade
GCED	Global Coalition for Environment and Development (known as ECLI)
GEF	Global Environment Facility

GEMS	Global Environmental Monitoring System
GET	Global Environment Trust Fund
GRID	Global Resource Information Database
HABITAT	United Nations Habitat and Human Settlements Foundation
HEALS	Human Expose Assessment Locations Programme
IAEA	International Atomic Energy Agency
IBRD	International Bank for Reconstruction and Development (World Bank)
ICC	International Chamber of Commerce
ICSU	International Council of Scientific Unions
IDB	Inter-American Development Bank
IFC	International Finance Corporation
IGO	Inter-Governmental Organization
IGY	International Geophysical Year
ILO	International Labour Organization
IMO	International Maritime Organization
INC	Intergovernmental Negotiating Committee for a Framework Convention on Climate Change
INFOTERRA	International Referral System for Sources of Environmental Information
IPCC	Intergovernmental Panel on Climate Change
IRPTC	International Register of Potentially Toxic Chemicals
ITTA	International Tropical Timber Agreement
ITTC	International Tropical Timber Council
ITTO	International Tropical Timber Organization
IUCN	World Conservation Union (previously International Union for the Conservation of Nature)
MRL	Maximum Residue Level
NFAP	National Forestry Action Plan
NGO	Non-Governmental Organization
NIEO	New International Economic Order
OAU	Organization of African Unity
ODA	Overseas Development Agency
OTF	Ozone Layer Protection Fund

PEC	Primary Environmental Care
SAARC	South Asia Association for Regional Cooperation
STAP	Scientific and Technical Advisory Panel
SWCC	Second World Climate Conference
SWMTEP	System-Wide Medium-Term Environmental Plan
TFAP	Tropical Forestry Action Plan
UNCED	United Nations Conference on Environment and Development
UNECLA	United Nations Economic Commission for Latin America
UNCTAD	United Nations Conference on Trade and Development
UNCTC	United Nations Centre on Transnational Corporations
UNDP	United Nations Development Programme
UNEP	United Nations Environment Programme
UNESCO	United Nations Education, Scientific and Cultural Organization
UNGA	United Nations General Assembly
UNHCR	United Nations High Commission for Refugees
UNICEF	United Nations Children's Fund
UNIDO	United Nations Industrial Development Organiaztion
WCP	World Climate Program
WCS	World Conservation Strategy
WEDNET	Women, Environment and Development Network
WHO	World Health Organization
WICEM	World Industry Conference on Environmental Management
WIF	Worldview International Foundation
WMO	World Meteorological Organization
WRI	World Resorces Institute
WRM	World Rainforest Movement
WWF	World Wide Fund for Nature
WWW	World Weather Watch

PART I: THEMES

PART I: THEMES

1.1 The environmental crisis identified

The environment is in crisis. The atmosphere, oceans and land are all beset by problems resulting from human activities, the ultimate effects of which remain uncertain. Problems range from the global, such as greenhouse warming and ozone depletion, to regional, such as acid rain and desertification, to national, such as deforestation, and even to local, such as urban pollution and contamination of freshwater resources. Cause and effect linkages are complex, and operate in both directions: from local to global, and from global to local. The environmental crisis covers a huge and shifting canvas. Pollution is growing; scientific knowledge of it is expanding; community and public awareness are increasing. The stated positions of concerned actors, ranging from governments to industry and non-governmental organizations (NGOs), are changing rapidly.

Many of the problems have been bubbling away and increasing in strength for decades, and some can be traced back to the Industrial Revolution which began in Europe 200 years ago. The premium placed on economic development, defined in terms of industrialization and the promotion of intensive agriculture, has been responsible for widespread damage. The result is that the future sustainability of such development is doubtful, unless the environmental dimension is incorporated. At the opposite end of the spectrum, the population increase, especially among the world's poorest people, has resulted in pressures leading to environmental devastation. Slash-and-burn agriculture has played a major part.

Environmental degradation is not limited by time or place: even localized actions such as national energy or transport policy may have repercussions regionally or globally, and over time periods far in excess of their duration. The international political system, based on the pursuit of state interest tempered by a very limited recognition of global interdependence, is ill-equipped to deal with such global problems. Nevertheless there is some evidence that small steps are being taken to address aspects of the global environmental crisis. While the situation is critical, all is not yet lost.

Urgent action is required if environmental decline is to be slowed, halted, and ultimately, where possible, reversed. This is necessary not only for preservation of intrinsic environmental value, but also for sustainable economic development, and of course for political stability within and between states and regions. Moreover, it is necessary for security at all levels: from the individual, through the state to the international political system. The quality of life, and long-term habitability of the planet, are in question.

The environmental crisis differs from other political crises because while it is all around us, many important aspects of it are invisible. We do not receive continual reminders of the danger from our everyday experience. This makes it more difficult to comprehend than one in which governments perceive that they have to act urgently under pressing time constraints. Hence the environmental crisis demands a different basis for political action than the more familiar military or diplomatic crises. The crisis is with us, and whatever action we take now to address it, it will not be resolved completely in our lifetime.

In global terms, this situation has arisen largely due to three underlying factors, and it continues to be grounded in them: the competitive states-system, the international economy and demographic trends. (The range of specific, overt influences affecting particular local environmental problems is huge, and each such problem must be examined on its own merits.) The high profile of environmental issues in international diplomacy in the late 1980s thrust these underlying factors onto the diplomatic agenda. The UN Conference on Environment and Development (UNCED), or Earth Summit, to take place in Rio in June 1992 and any subsequent protocols, will be indicative of the degree to which initiatives to transcend traditional individual state interest are going to be met. How will global responsibility fare? Will population growth be subjected to international bargaining? Will the long-term global perspective needed to meet the environmental challenge win over the short-term vision of politicians? What will have the greatest impact: environmental issues on the conduct of international affairs, or traditional inter-state concerns on the fate of environmental issues?

The challenge for international relations and diplomacy is to take us back from the brink of disaster by promoting the principle of global sustainability over parochial state interest. This will require grassroots organizations, governments, scientists, diplomats, bureaucrats, intergovernmental organizations, non-governmental organizations, and business to learn from one another and to cooperate in a spirit of mutual interest. The situation calls for unprecedented levels of cooperation and finance, sometimes in the face of scientific uncertainty. Sir Crispin Tickell remarks, 'Uncertainty may be part of the human condition. We must always look at the cost of doing nothing'.[1] In essence, the structure of the international political system and the processes which reinforce it may need to change, for the states-system itself is a major part of the environmental problem.

What follows is a brief look at how the environmental crisis relates to the three underlying factors which continue to drive it.

The competitive states-system

The global political system based on the primacy of sovereign states has created conditions detrimental to environmental protection. Sovereignty in theory allows governments to pursue domestic policies of their choice, without fear of external intervention. In practice this has been modified by economic interdependence and international law. However, in terms of states' external affairs, sovereignty has lent an anarchical quality to the international system. Traditional international relations scholars have for the most part understood state behaviour in terms of the pursuit of the national interest, defined in terms of power.[2] States have been portrayed in perpetual competition for power as the means of defence against external threats. This competition explains the adoption by

---

[1] See F.Pearce, 'The Green Diplomat: Sir Crispin Tickell', *New Scientist*, 21 March 1992, pp. 38-40.
[2] For a realist interpretation of state behaviour, see H.Morgenthau, *Politics Among Nations*, Knopf, New York, 1955; and for the place of this approach in the international relations debate, see M.Wight, 'Why is there no international theory?', in H.Butterfield and M.Wight (eds), *Diplomatic Investigations*, Allen and Unwin, 1966.

governments of short-term policies aimed at enhancing the relative power of their respective state. At best, the effect on the natural environment has been disregarded. At worst, the natural environment has been perceived as something to be exploited in this competition;[3] it has been regarded as an expendable resource, and often as an unlimited one. There has been little scope for the political cooperation advocated by less fashionable international political analysts who noted the environmental crisis twenty years ago.[4]

Until the end of the Cold War in the last years of the 1980s, ideology fuelled inter-state competition, and to that extent it contributed to environmental degradation. Yet it is important to note that the particular ideology holding sway in various parts of the world made little difference to local attitudes to environmental degradation. In recent years the environment has fared better in developed capitalist countries than in socialist ones, but this has been the product of the desire for a better quality of life in the richest countries rather than an inherent respect for nature in capitalist societies.

Political pragmatism has tempered the anarchic characteristic of the states-system. It has prompted cooperation by various combinations of states on specific issues, and even the pursuit of regional and global balance of power policies. However, attempts at whole-hearted global cooperation in support of shared values and an international interest (eg. via collective security during the interwar years), have rarely been undertaken, and where they have, they have usually failed dismally. In the post-World War II period the record of the United Nations in promoting collective action on global issues has not been impressive. The interdisciplinary challenge presented by the environmental crisis has arguably been preceded by a number of others, such as the specific problems of women and population, and the wide-ranging problems associated with discussions on the law of the sea. None of these has met with much success in terms of a positive global response to deal with them. On these issues at least, the UN does not appear to be bigger than the sum of its parts, and failure to make real headway rests with its

---

[3]See A.Westing, (ed), *Global Resources and International Conflict*, SIPRI/Oxford University Press, Oxford and New York, 1986; and R.Lipschutz, *When Nations Clash: Raw Materials, Ideology and Foreign Policy*, Ballinger, 1989.
[4]R.Falk, *This Endangered Planet*, Random House, New York, 1970.

member states. The UN has often been used by them to pursue their own self-interest, rather than in support of international interests.

The environmental crisis overwhelming the planet requires collective action on a global scale. No one country acting alone can solve the problems, though that is no reason for unilateral action being rejected where cooperation has proved impossible. Indeed, unilateral national action can precede agreement on cooperation, as happened with CO_2 emissions. In a sense the requirement of collective action to meet the environmental challenge has moved from the realms of idealism to the realms of pragmatism in international affairs; it is necessary for the long-term sustainability of our planet in all senses - environmental, economic, political and strategic. This has not been fully comprehended by politicians in the developed or the developing countries, for they are preoccupied with the short-term. The former are concerned with their re-electability, and respond to the dictates of public opinion, while the latter have far more pressing immediate problems to deal with, ranging from hanging on to power to promoting short-term survival strategies for their people.

When President Gorbachev came to power in the Kremlin in 1985, glasnost and perestroika in the domestic context were accompanied by a foreign policy based on cooperation rather than confrontation. He championed a new conception of security based on the recognition of interdependence of all peoples and of economy, environment and security both at the domestic and the international levels.[5] Yet his vision was not powerful enough to hold together the disparate areas of the Soviet Union. Similarly, there is scant evidence that such a vision is likely to be powerful enough to pull together all corners of the globe. While international interest may capture people's imaginations, national interest is still popularly perceived as the best practical route to achieve and/or protect material and physical well-being. The surge of nationalist sentiment in the former Soviet Union and in eastern Europe, as well as in many parts of the developing world and even in some parts of western Europe, testifies to this. Nations want states through which they expect to promote the interests of their individual group. The appeal of

---

[5] See 'Mikhail Gorbachev's Address to the UN General Assembly', *Soviet News*, 14 December 1988, No.6455; and 'Mikhail Gorbachev's Address to the Participants in the Global Forum on Environment and Development for Survival', *Soviet News*, 31 January, 1990, No.6511.

nationalism, the mystique of statehood and the power of domestic politics pose formidable challenges to the elaboration of cooperative responses to global problems. Yet while we are unlikely to witness a rush of enthusiasm for dealing with global environmental problems by world government, limited cooperation on specific issues is feasible. Indeed it is already apparent. Institutions are evolving to tackle certain facets of the environmental crisis. Perhaps states are edging very slowly towards the recognition that over the long-term, national self-interest and the common global interest merge.

The international economy

The international economic system, the philosophy informing it and the culture accompanying it undermine the natural environment and pose further obstacles to cooperation to meet global environmental challenges. They have resulted in unsustainable production and consumption in the North, and the adoption of inappropriate, and similarly unsustainable, development paths in the South.

Most countries, including the former socialist states now classified as 'economies in transition', function within the context of what has come to be known as the global economy. Within that system, the neo-classical assumptions informing economic policy have resulted in costs to the environment being externalized, in other words, disregarded. No value has been put on the environment, and thus the pursuit of profit has left the environment a victim. Production has continually moved to parts of the world where costs are lowest. These tend to be where labour is cheap, local expertise and finance for environmental clean-up lacking, and environmental legislation weak or absent. The economic growth achieved by such policies cannot be sustained over the long-term, not least because it undermines the natural capital resource base on which it depends. In 1987, the Brundtland Report[6] undertaken for the UN argued that growth was a prerequisite to environmental protection and sustainable development, and advocated that sustainability be taken to the heart of growth-oriented policies.

The Bretton Woods system established at the end of World War II supported the development of a liberal international economy based on the free market philosophy. Institutions and mechanisms were set in place to free international trade, to provide conditional support for

---

[6]World Commission on Environment and Development, *Our Common Future*, (The Brundtland Report), OUP, Oxford and New York, 1987.

short-term balance-of-payments problems, and to provide aid for the war-torn economies. Free trade was seen as the key to growth, and it was believed that riches would trickle down to the poorer countries and to the poorer people within them. The liberalization of trade would provide a spur to international peace, in contrast to the politically destabilizing beggar-thy-neighbour policies pursued in the interwar period.

However, the operation of this system has not always worked to the advantage of the majority of countries. In the 1980s, the impressive economic performance in terms of GNP per capita of many developing countries in preceding decades was eroded. The power of the market developed unfettered. There was a serious regression, with tragic consequences for millions of people. It has been argued that the behaviour of the rich states was responsible for the severity of the crisis, for example by supporting structural adjustment packages at the IMF[7] and by insisting on debt repayment at floating rates of interest.[8] By worsening the lot of the poor, such policies have extended the adverse impact on the environment as more and more people have been pushed onto marginal land. Developing countries portrayed themselves as being at the mercy of external forces: floating interest rates, an unstable market for their commodities, deteriorating terms of trade and an international financial system that was completely outside of their control.

Whilst there is much truth in this, it should not be forgotten that Southern states bear some responsibility for their environmental predicament. Misuse of agricultural land, rural overpopulation and urban pollution are particular problems. While the situation varies widely between countries and is often dependent on the stage of development, in much of the developing world the distribution of resources is heavily skewed. Such distribution patterns, which are in the control of local elites, have a profound impact on the environment. In their daily struggle for survival, the growing numbers of landless peasants must degrade the environment; they are offered no alternative. They may well realize that they are eroding tomorrow's base for survival, but they have no option. While the Northern countries have helped make the South what it is today, and in this respect bear an historic responsibility, Southern elites must take responsibility for the environmental repercussions of the

---

[7] See G.Cornia, R.Jolly and F.Stewart, *Adjustment with a Human Face*, OUP, 1987.
[8] C.Payer, *Lent and Lost: Foreign Credit and Third World Development*, Zed Press, London, 1991.

domestic maldistribution of land and wealth. It is their responsibility to reform domestic distribution patterns to the benefit of the majority. This would add weight to their call for a reversal of international resource transfers which currently flow in an absurd direction, from the South to the North. It would also further their call for democratization of international institutions.

The perception of imposed economic policies and unfair debt leading to further social deprivation in already impoverished countries heightens international tension and reinforces a confrontational atmosphere in the international arena, thus lessening the possibility of negotiated agreements to tackle global environmental change.

Conventional wisdom suggests that the centrally planned economies fared even worse than the market economies in terms of environmental degradation. However, this has been challenged recently by Hughes who compares the general degradation in eastern Europe in 1991 with that of western Europe twenty-five years before.[9] Functioning around the notion of a labour theory of value, development in the centrally planned economies occurred in a context where the environment was perceived as bereft of inherent value, as a free resource to be exploited or as a sink in which waste could be dumped and forgotten.[10] It suffered in much the same way as it had done in the market economies.

With the passing of the Cold War and the opening of the former eastern bloc to western economic policy, the international economy has been truly globalized. With the state being rolled back there and throughout the world, the global homogeneity thus produced is lessening the options for discussion of different economic philosophies, and largely determining that the debate remains within the context of tinkering with the present liberal system rather than transforming it. The opportunities for environmental improvements are being couched in terms of market instruments rather than the traditional standard-setting or more radical transformation. These are presented as the cheapest and most efficient way to address environmental decline.

---

[9]G.Hughes, 'Are the Costs of Cleaning Up Eastern Europe Exaggerated? Economic Reform and the Environment', *Oxford Review of Economic Policy*, Vol.7., No.4, Winter 1991.

[10]Z.Wolfson, 'Natural Resource Development: An Economic and Environmental Problem in the USSR', *Communist Economies*, Vol.1, No.1, 1989, pp.79-88.

The demographic structure

The importance of the global demographic structure as a factor in environmental degradation has been stated clearly by Myers who writes that:

As the 20th century draws to a close, the world is confronted by a daunting challenge: to bring growing human numbers and their growing needs into balance with the natural resource base that underpins much development. Choices made during the next ten years will determine, to a large extent, the future habitability of the planet. The collision between human numbers and the resources needed to sustain them will become more acute in the remaining years of this century and beyond ... The search for sustainability must be addressed within the context of population and natural resource issues.[11]

As population increases, the population-environmental resource balance deteriorates. Since the early 1800s, world population has quintupled. Over the past three decades, the population of many developing countries has doubled. While the global *rate of population growth* has been falling over the past few decades, the *absolute numbers* of people added to the global total each year is increasing. In the 1990s it is estimated to be over 100 million annually. World population is expected to increase from 5.4 billion in 1991 to 10 billion in 2050. Currently 96% of population growth takes place in developing countries.[12] Fifty per cent of the projected increase is expected to take place in seven countries: India, China, Nigeria, Pakistan, Bangladesh, Brazil and Indonesia. The highest rate of increase occurs amongst the world's poorest peoples who have no option but to degrade the natural environment in their daily struggle for survival.[13] By 2020, 84% of people will live in the poorer countries.

The population issue will figure in the Earth Summit. The UN's World Health Organization (WHO) sponsored an independent report entitled *Our Health, Our Planet* for its submission to the UNCED. The report claims that environmental destruction resulting from overpopulation is killing millions of people every year, largely as a result of the

---

[11]See UNFPA/Norman Myers, *Population, Resources and the Environment: The Critical Challenges*, UN Population Fund, New York, 1991, p.5. This book provides the most up to date presentation of figures and the most comprehensive analysis of the linkages between population growth and environmental degradation.
[12]ibid, p.iv.
[13]ibid, p.4.

contamination of water, soil and air. It argues that unless population growth can be reduced drastically, the resources needed to support the human race will be overwhelmed.[14] The report looks to improvement in the health and education of poor people, plus family planning, to reduce fertility rates.[15]

While increasing pressure of population causes environmental degradation, the precise contribution of this factor to global environmental decline is the subject of intense debate. Many developing country commentators regard emphasis on the population factor as a Northern ploy to remove responsibility from their own massive per capita consumption of resources. The North, with 20% of world population, uses up 80% of world resources, has a per capita income 15 times higher than the South[16] and accounts for 85% of the world's gross national product.

Both poverty and wealth degrade the environment in different ways. Clearly the search for environmentally-sustainable development will have to address consumption patterns and lifestyles, not simply gross numbers of people. However, this in no way eliminates the need to tackle the population explosion in the South, which poses an enormous environmental problem. Measures taken now to control pollution and other environmental problems will be equivalent to swimming against the tide if population continues to expand. The population explosion in the South already poses enormous problems for the people concerned, and the associated difficulties will become more acute as the expansion continues. It also poses severe moral dilemmas for the rich states. Undoubtedly it will become a source of political instability within and between states, and a cause of friction between regions of the world. The inability of the land to support growing numbers will prompt migration. Indeed it is already becoming difficult in some cases to distinguish between economic and environmental refugees.

Unless there is a major shift in emphasis in development policy internationally as well as nationally, we can expect the major impediments to population growth to come not from effective public

---

[14]See *The Environment Digest*, February 1992, No.56, p.15; and *The Guardian*, 5 March 1992.

[15]See *The Environment Digest*, op.cit, p.15.

[16]M.Khor Kok Peng, 'UNCED Must Reform North Economy, South Development and World Economic Order', *Third World Resurgence*, No.14/15, October-November 1991, Third World Network, Penang, Malaysia. p.11.

policies but rather from the limitations imposed by the carrying capacity of the land, natural disasters, war and disease.

A note on UNCED

Given the purposeful timing of publication of this book immediately before the UN Conference on Environment and Development in June 1992 in Brazil, a few words on this are in order. The UNCED and the process leading up to it provide a microcosm of the international environmental debate, both in terms of actors and arguments, and reflect the basic North/South diplomatic divide on this issue.

The UNCED grew out of the Brundtland Commission's report, *Our Common Future*.[17] The findings were clear: sustainable development had to be promoted. Thus the UN called for the Earth Summit to address the global environmental crisis. That crisis was inseparable from the crisis of development. Sweden was a major state sponsor of the conference, and the largest donor government. Several big businesses contributed to the cost of the Summit, for example ICI, and so too did the large foundations such as MacArthur and Rockerfeller. NGOs played an important role during the preparatory committees (prepcoms) procedure in pushing the parameters of the debate forward.

The negotiating environment in which the UNCED prepcoms operated has been far from favourable. The atmosphere has been confrontational.[18] Massive differences emerged on the fundamental questions of how much emphasis should be given to development as opposed to environment, indeed whether the two can be separated, and what constitutes sustainable development. Developing countries saw the environmental crisis as a long-term developmental crisis, while the developed perceived it in more strictly short-term technical environmental terms. The former called for discussion and negotiation of the underlying causes of the environmental crisis, which they perceive as being rooted in an unfair international economic system. They accuse the developed countries of being interested only in symptoms of the crisis (and more particularly in the symptoms which most affect the rich countries), and unwilling to tackle fundamental causes which would demand a change in lifestyles and consumption patterns in the rich countries. The arguments put forward by the developing countries at the

---

[17]The Brundtland Report, op.cit.
[18]For an excellent presentation of Third World positions in the UNCED prepcom process, see the special double issue of *Third World Resurgence*, op.cit.

prepcoms resemble those championed by them in 1974 with the call for a new international economic order. They are using UNCED to put their economic requirements back on the international agenda. In 1992 one notes that the debate has barely moved on. It remains to be seen whether UNCED will be any more fruitful in terms of real change than was the 1974 resolution.

Southern countries perceive the environmental agenda to have been set by the rich industrialized countries. They regard it as a luxury which they can ill-afford, and as an impediment to development. Indeed, they are suspicious of the developed countries intentions, fearing environmental imperialism. The environmental problems which have received greatest attention tend to be those of most immediate concern to the developed countries, including the greenhouse effect, whaling, and the forest conservation issue. Specific environmental problems of most immediate concern to developing states, such as the provision of freshwater resources and the encroachment of deserts, have received far less attention.[19]

Major differences have arisen over particular principles and policies such as sovereignty over natural resources, burden-sharing, equity issues, democratization, funding, the role of multilateral institutions, technology transfer, biodiversity and biotechnology, deforestation and climate change. Developing countries have been especially keen to protect their sovereignty, which they see as potentially under attack. The emphasis on tropical deforestation has been seen as another face of imperialism, especially in view of the discussion of the creation of global commons which would effectively remove sovereign territory from national control. This conflicts with Article Two of the 1974 Charter of Economic Rights and Duties of States (CERDS), which asserts the right of every state to exercise permanent sovereignty over its natural resources and economic activities. Europe destroyed forests as it industrialized, and countries like Brazil regard it as their right to do what they will with their forests without foreign interference. Also, developing countries perceive a clear double standard when developed countries call upon them to stop cutting trees which provide a sink for carbon dioxide, without themselves being willing to make great efforts to reduce the production of carbon dioxide by the development of more efficient energy options.

---

[19]P.Chatterjee, 'Action to Limit Deserts', *New Scientist*, 21 March 1992, p.11.

The entrenchment of attitudes in the prepcoms has done nothing to allay the fear that state interest will carry the day. Indeed, the opposite is suggested: that the threat of global environmental change is throwing up all the old inter-state frictions that have characterized the North/South debate over the past two decades. Just as the threat of oil power in the early 1970s, and the leverage it was expected to carry with it, have proved illusory, the idea that global environmental change will also give developing countries new leverage in international relations has yet to be translated into reality with concessions by the rich states. The evidence from the prepcoms suggests that rich states would prefer to pay the price of protecting themselves against the adverse consequences of such change rather than transfer resources and technology to help developing countries take environmentally-friendly paths to development. We need only consider the US position in the run up to the UNCED conference. Inevitably since he is responsible to a domestic electorate, domestic politics is of more concern to President Bush than the long-term fate of the planet. Hence, while giving $75 million to help developing countries produce data on their greenhouse gas emissions and how they may abate them, the US, the biggest producer of those emissions, has refused to give a clear commitment to reduce its own emissions. Its government will not set a target of any percentage reduction by any date.[20] This gives strength to the developing world's argument that those countries most responsible for creating global environmental problems are unwilling to make real sacrifices themselves to address the problem. Instead, they appear to want developing countries to make disproportionate sacrifices.

While transformation of the underlying structures which have created the environmental crisis cannot be expected from the UNCED process, it appears that there are possibilities for the groundwork to be laid there for reform within the system. While these do not add up to a final solution, they do suggest a way forward out of diplomatic deadlock. This amounts to edging away from the abyss, a necessary but not sufficient condition for the sustainability of our planet.

1.2 Aims and organization of the book

The book aims to explain the changing profile of environmental issues in international diplomacy in recent years; and to examine how international collaboration and the formulation of international

---

[20]P.Chatterjee, 'US Offers Cash for Carbon Cuts', *New Scientist*, 7 March 1992.

agreements in the environmental area have fared. In the course of the study it is revealed whether, and if so how, environmental issues are challenging and changing the conduct of international relations. The intended audience is concerned lay people and students of international relations, economics and environmental studies.

The book is structured around two parts. Part One analyses environmental issues separately in their political, economic and security contexts. By so doing it emphasizes the relationship between environmental and other issues in international relations. The need to be aware of all the potential consequences of international environmental action - or lack of it - is clearly identified. The priority here is to highlight important linkages between environment, economy, politics and security at the international level.

Part One explains how environmental issues have won a place on the agenda of international politics, economics and security, and attained the high diplomatic profile they enjoy today. It is widely believed that the nature and extent of global environmental change means that failure to act is likely to result in irreparable harm to our planet. Yet the imperative of urgent action implicit in such knowledge cannot alone explain the new place of these issues in international discourse. After all, knowledge of the severity of implications of other problems, such as the nuclear arms race, has not resulted in immediate, meaningful global action. The sudden prominence of environmental issues in international diplomatic fora has less to do with the enormity of those problems themselves than with the coalescence of certain political developments.

This study argues that the current diplomatic profile of environmental issues derives largely from the activities of NGOs who took advantage of the political space provided by the fortuitous ending of the Cold War. Indeed the ending of the Cold War provided a real window of opportunity, without which the environmental cause would not have been promoted so successfully at the international level. This coincided with greater awareness on the part of international lenders such as the World Bank and other branches of the UN of the links between economic development and environmental degradation, itself partly the result of NGO campaigning. The environment had not been an issue in the Bretton Woods system. However a consensus had emerged amongst NGOs by the early 1980s that environment and development were inextricably linked, and this idea was given credibility by the Brundtland Commission which advocated further growth as a prerequisite of environmental protection and sustainable development.

It is undoubtedly the case that the reduction in tension between the superpowers in the second half of the 1980s, the associated lessening of ideological conflict between the two blocs of developed states, and the practical arms reduction agreements negotiated and on-going between them, presented an opportunity for environmental concerns to attain high diplomatic profile. The passing of the Cold War facilitated discussion of global problems that depend on international cooperation if they are to be addressed with any possibility of success. With the creation of this political space, the superpowers themselves were quick to seize the opportunity and express primary interest in environmental concerns which had been building up support at the NGO and IGO level for two decades. President Gorbachev in particular gave an important push to environmental issues by calling for international cooperation to tackle fundamental transnational problems, the resolution of which would form an integral part of a more secure world. His international stance directly reflected his domestic position: he wanted to ensure that particularist interests in the USSR did not compromise the interest of the state as a whole, and similarly he wanted to ensure that the global interest was not sullied by particularist, self-seeking state-interest.

The experience of the Gulf War prompted greater recognition of the relationship between the environment and security, previously the concern mainly of academics. It gave further momentum to the international debate on the environmental crisis, and increased the role of NGOs in an area of environmental concern which they had hitherto neglected.

Through case-studies, Part Two of the book sets out to bring together all the different issues addressed in Part One. It underlines the need to be aware of the wider implications of environmental behaviour when making policy. It examines the development of international collaboration to deal with global warming, ozone depletion and deforestation.

The way in which these particular issues have won a place on the international diplomatic agenda deserves a mention, for there is a certain pattern which may be repeated with other environmental problems, or indeed even with other interdisciplinary problems. How have specific global environmental issues which have received most international attention been taken up at the international level? Firstly, NGOs and/or radical scientific opinion raised them. They were told by the political and commercial establishment either that the problem didn't exist, or that too much scientific uncertainty remained, or that billions of dollars would be required to fix the problem and hence such action was not worth taking. Thereafter the NGOs accused the establishment of being greedy, tight-fisted and uncaring, and the establishment accused the NGOs of being ignorant hotheads. The arguments became empty and very predictable, along the lines of: 'they would say that, wouldn't they?'. Ozone, climate change and acid rain all display this pattern. Generally, as time has progressed, NGOs and scientific activists have won, as has happened with ozone and acid rain. This pattern may well be followed with climate change and deforestation. We have yet to see whether it will occur with issues such as desertification, sea-level rise and freshwater resources. To date these issues have not received so much attention from the Northern NGOs which have become so talented at promoting their chosen causes.

The case studies suggest that while radical reform of the three underlying factors driving environmental degradation is unlikely, specific, limited cooperation is possible. They reveal also that the range of issues confronting us demands a flexible response; there can be no blueprint. Some issues lend themselves to regional solutions, others require the participation of a select group of countries, while others require a global response involving many different types of international actors. For some problems, grassroots involvement is the key. Education seems to be a primary requirement, both in developed and developing countries.

The North/South divide reflects the major diplomatic division on the environmental crisis. Hence while this book has not been written systematically from a North/South perspective, inevitably that perspective has permeated much of the study. This has influenced the material for discussion. It has resulted in emphasis being given to global as opposed to local issues, even though the latter have in certain cases been very effective consciousness-raisers in a range of countries, particularly the rich ones, and have resulted in politicians taking notice and jumping on the environmental bandwagon. Our primary concern is with the environment in international relations at the global level.

1.3 Key issues and motifs

Various key issues and motifs run through the book. They establish the questions to be asked by students of international relations, though not necessarily the answers. Readers may bear these in mind, and come to their own conclusions. Here, some of the most important are outlined as pointers for consideration.

Short-term, long-term

In the long run, the book argues that we will only be saved from environmental catastrophe if fundamental political, economic and demographic structures, and ways of thought and action, are modified. Whether this is to happen is unclear, but if it is to happen, it will require a sustained educational campaign of the kind on which many NGOs have already embarked. Such consciousness-raising to the point of fundamental reform is a long-term proposition. In the meantime, the immediate question is what can be achieved within the constraints of the states-system and the fact that politics, above all democratic politics, is a short-term affair.

Justice and equity

The present evidence is overwhelming that justice is not a problem awaiting a solution, but is likely to remain an essentially contested concept. If this is right, the various positions are not going to be resolved. The question becomes whether it is possible to work towards a consensus which will be accepted as broadly fair, even if it does not correspond to the conception of justice urged by a particular party. At issue here is the feasibility of international collaboration and international agreements in the environmental field.

Valuing/pricing the environment

For the time being, it is no good looking for a solution - even if this were desirable - to the transformation of capitalist economies, since it is their system which is the beneficiary of the collapse of the command economy and central planning. It follows that the various proposals that have emerged within the profession of western economics must be given serious consideration. Market instruments seem to have won the day as economists plan for environmentally-sustainable growth.

North/South bargaining and burden-sharing

Despite the emergence of interest coalitions which straddle the old North/South divide (such as the unusual marriage between China, Saudi Arabia, the USA and the former USSR to protest against reduction of carbon emissions), that divide still reflects the major division on the environmental crisis. The crucial question, therefore, is what kind of leverage Southern countries can acquire which will persuade the industrial world that as the original polluters, they will have to pay if the South is to cooperate in effective environmental control.

The role of NGOs

Perhaps the most noticeable change in the conduct of international relations visible in the environmental arena is the central role of NGOs. These actors have played a crucial part in getting environmental issues onto the international political and economic agenda. Over the past decade they have changed in character from being principally consciousness-raising flagwavers to organizations with significant research capability producing authoritative reports. Whereas national positions have often not been extensively articulated in accessible literature, NGO views are in the forefront of public discussion. The scale of their involvement in the whole UNCED process is unprecedented in the history of international negotiations.

Science and policy

The relationship between science and policy is important. Science can drive public policy, even where it is uncertain. In the case-studies we see how diplomatic agreements can be forged even before scientific evidence is watertight. It is also clear that scientists tend to step back from urging specific policies. It has often been left to NGOs to publicize scientific research and findings relevant for public policy, and to canvass particular policies.

Empowerment of local communities

While problems may be global in scope, it is clear that the empowerment of local communities whether in the developed or the developing world is essential for the success of solutions. Education and community management of local resources are vital to their preservation. Collaboration for sustainable usage is imperative.

Knowledge-based networks

Cooperation to tackle certain environmental issues, such as ozone depletion, seems to have been the result not of traditional bargaining between states, but of the activities of states plus 'transnationally-organized networks of knowledge-based communities',[21] or 'epistemic communities'. These refer to technical experts, in this case ecologists. In areas which require a high level of technical expertise for their management, as is the case with many environmental problems, this type of cooperation may become more widespread. Where such networks are politically empowered, they may be highly influential in policy-formulation.

---

[21]P.Haas, 'Obtaining International Environmental Protection through Epistemic Consensus', in I.Rowlands and M.Greene (eds), *Global Environmental Change and International Relations*, Macmillan, London, 1992.

The Environment on the International Political Agenda

In the two decades since the 1972 Stockholm intergovernmental
Conference on the environment, governments have taken both concerted
and unilateral action on the environment. At the same time, international
actors concerned directly or indirectly with environmental issues have
grown enormously in number and in political significance. Also, the
range of problems has mushroomed. In the latter half of the 1980s,
environmental issues moved firmly to the centre stage of international
politics. This chapter charts and explains the changing fortunes of
environmental issues in world politics, and accounts for their position
in contemporary international political discourse.[1]

The Stockholm Conference represented a milestone in the recognition
of environmental issues in international relations. The chapter begins by
outlining international interest in environmental matters prior to
Stockholm. The significance of the Conference itself is addressed.
Attention then is turned to the post-Stockholm era. The growth of interest
in environmental issues is identified and examined at two main levels:
international institutions, and grassroots politics. In the case of the
former, particular attention is paid to the often overlooked importance of
the United Nations Environment Programme (UNEP) as a catalyst.
Regarding the latter, attention is focused on four main factors which have
influenced the rise in public awareness globally: the role of
non-governmental organizations (NGOs), green protest movements,
green parties, and environmental accidents. Finally, the chapter considers

---

[1]For a general overview of the growth of interest in the environmental in international
relations, see J.MacNeill, 'The Greening of International Relations', *International
Journal*, Vol.XLV, Winter 1989-90, pp.1-35.

the sudden interest in the environment evident in superpower relations in the late 1980s. This development is explained against the background of domestic changes in the former USSR and changes in the superpower relationship. The passing of the Cold War presented a window of opportunity for environmental debate. Pragmatic conjecture about the future of environmental issues in international politics must be formulated in a wide political context, giving necessary attention to other possible inputs such as strategic or ideological considerations.

2.1 Pre-Stockholm

While the Stockholm Conference is seen as a watershed in the history of environmental concern and organization, environmental awareness and cooperation dates back much further. Sand has encapsulated this experience succinctly:

> Conventions on marine pollution control were already drafted twenty years earlier [than Stockholm] by the International Maritime Organization (IMO). The constitutional mandate of the UN Food and Agriculture Organization (FAO) for the 'conservation of natural resources' was formulated in 1945. Standards to protect workers against occupational hazards in the working environment were adopted by the International Labour Organization (ILO) as early as the 1920s. Transboundary agreements for the protection of migratory birds and for the management of shared water resources date to well before World War I, as do international arrangements for the sharing of atmospheric data by nineteenth century precursors of the World Meteorological Organization [WMO]. The first serious, if unsuccessful attempt at global environmental management was probably Theodore Roosevelt's initiative in 1909 to convene at The Hague a world conference for natural resource conservation.[2]

In the 1960s and 1970s prior to Stockholm, interest in environmental issues was expressed both inside United Nations (UN) agencies and by non-governmental groups and protest movements mainly in the west.[3]

---

[2]P.Sand, 'International Cooperation: The Environmental Experience', in J.T.Matthews (ed), *Preserving the Global Environment*, Norton & Co., London and New York, 1991, p.237.

[3]M.Bookchin, *Toward an Ecological Society*, Black Rose Books, Montreal, 1980; and W.Hulsberg, *The German Greens*, Verso, London, 1988.

Both, however, exhibited a limited and partial vision: neither perceived the environment in a holistic manner, and global connections with economy, society and the international political community were lost to all but a few advocates.

The blossoming environmental NGOs in the west in the mid-1960s and beyond concerned themselves primarily with national issues and in many respects were parochial in outlook.[4] They were reacting against the environmental impact of industrial development, especially contamination of land, air and water from industrial and agricultural chemicals. They were particularly effective in mobilizing public opinion on energy issues such as the effects of coal-fired power stations. In most cases, however, their vision was limited. Few of these environmental groups concerned themselves with environmental issues in the developing world, and those that did - such as the International Union for the Conservation of Nature (IUCN) and the World Wildlife Fund[5] (WWF) - were interested in wildlife and wildlife habitat preservation. In contrast, developmental NGOs took a great interest in the poorer parts of the world, but omitted to integrate the environmental dimension into project design, delivery and implementation.[6] Yap suggests this was 'a generalized institutional failure to undertake, support, or learn from scientific research'[7] on the part of the NGOs, and points to their responsiveness to local requests as a failure to acknowledge the interdependent relationship between provision of basic needs and the quality of the environmental base. Western environmental NGOs did not concern themselves with environmental problems in the eastern bloc in the 1960s; indeed little information was available on this matter.

There was a certain amount of overlap between ecology groups and peace groups as the 1960s progressed, with both being part of the larger social protest movements developing in the west at that time. Interestingly, however, the links which have been established more recently between the Vietnam War and environmental devastation by

---

[4]N.Yap, 'NGOs and Sustainable Development', *International Journal*, Vol.XLV, Winter 1989-90, pp.77-8.
[5]Renamed World Conservation Union in 1990 and World Wide Fund for Nature respectively.
[6]Yap, op.cit, p.87.
[7]ibid, p.88.

chemicals and defoliants were not a major focus for concern in the anti-war or environmental movements of the 1960s and early 1970s.[8]

Interest at the UN at this stage concentrated narrowly on the environmental effects of pollution caused mainly by industrialization. Thus attention was focused on developed countries. A growing concern within the UN Economic and Social Council (ECOSOC) resulted in that agency calling upon the UN to convene a conference on the human environment, largely the result of a Swedish initiative supported by the US. It was agreed that such a conference should be held in Stockholm in 1972.

In 1969 the Secretary-General of the UN issued a report on preparations for the conference which called for the environment to be seen in global terms.[9] This presented a real challenge to policymakers who were trained to protect the national interest, narrowly defined, and to regard the environment and development as two separate concerns. It also presented a challenge to NGOs to broaden their horizons. There was a dawning realization that environmental protection and economic development had to be integrated; the pursuit of either one in isolation would be essentially flawed. There was also a growing awareness that multilateral cooperation was essential. In many issue areas, unilateral actions by states, while useful, could not address problems which transcended international boundaries.

As part of the preparations for Stockholm, the Founex meeting[10] in 1971 brought together thirty people, mainly from the developing world, to discuss the relationship between environment and development (see Chapter 3). For the first time semi-formal recognition was given to this critical link.

2.2 The Stockholm Conference

The Stockholm Conference had both symbolic and practical significance. Some of the major subjects of debate and division at Stockholm remain at the centre of the environmental debate today, for

---

[8]See A.Westing, *Herbicides in War: the Long-term Ecological and Human Consequences*, Taylor and Francis for SIPRI, London and Philadelphia, 1984.
[9]*The United Nations Yearbook*, United Nations, New York, 1969, p.389.
[10]See 'Development and the Environment: the Founex Report', in *In Defense of the Environment: the Basic Texts on Environment - Founex, Stockholm, Cocoyoc*, UNEP, Executive Series 1, 1981.

example, the question of funding.[11] The Conference is important because of the legitimacy it lent to environmental concerns in international affairs[12] and the clear link it established between environmental and developmental matters, and also because of the practical developments which ensued from it. These included the setting up of UNEP and the Environment Liaison Centre (ELC). UNEP has developed to play a pivotal role in facilitating the discussion of an ever-growing range of international environmental problems between governments, UN agencies and, to a lesser extent, NGOs. The ELC, a coalition of environmental NGOs, was to provide a mechanism for inter-NGO communication.[13]

The Stockholm Conference is rarely remembered for the discussions held on particular issues, yet these represented embryonic concerns which have been taken up regularly thereafter by various UN agencies, individual governments and NGOs. The Conference addressed a variety of problems, from the planning and management of human settlements to the identification and control of pollution.[14] It also provided a forum for the voicing of several themes which have increased in importance with the passing of time, such as the inadequacy of sovereign states in dealing with environmental issues which often traverse state boundaries. Developing countries voiced their belief that environmental matters could not be tackled in isolation from the divide between rich and poor countries.[15] In other words, the link between environment and development in a North/South context was being formally elaborated in an intergovernmental forum probably for the first time, and by implication the perceived inadequacies of the prevailing international economic and financial systems to deal with these issues were being highlighted. Developing countries argued that the level of cooperation needed to tackle environmental problems would require a philosophy of

---

[11]For a very useful analysis of the Conference, see, I.de Lupis, 'The Human Environment : Stockholm and its Follow Up', in P.Taylor, and A.J.R.Groom, (eds), *Global Issues in the United Nations Framework*, Macmillan, London, 1989.

[12]Representatives from 114 countries attended, but the eastern bloc states were largely absent because of non-recognition by west of GDR rather than lack of interest.

[13]On ELC, see Yap, op.cit, p.79.

[14]See United Nations, Report of the United Nations Conference on the Human Environment, Stockholm, 5-16 June 1972, UNGA Document No. A/CONF.48/14/Rev.1, UN, New York, 1973.

[15]ibid, p.46.

mutual aid based not on the pursuit of profit but on an idea of the common good.[16]

The general approach of the Conference was to look for technological solutions to environmental problems. Criticism has been expressed since by ecological movements such as the Social Ecologists and the Deep Ecologists in the US and the German Greens, who stress that technological response can never adequately address the current environmental crisis. They perceive fundamental flaws in industrial society which are beyond the scope of technological management.

Assessing the overall impact of the Conference, it has been remarked that:

> The Stockholm UN Conference on the Human Environment in 1972 signalled the institutionalization of the problem of environmental disruption, and therefore, the subject of explicit management.[17]

Certainly thereafter the problem of environmental management became well entrenched in international political discussions not only at the level of governments and intergovernmental institutions but also, very importantly, within the NGO community.[18]

2.3 The growth of public awareness

The 1970s and 1980s witnessed the worldwide spread of 'green' ideas at the level of citizenship. The number and membership of NGOs rose enormously. Green movements were established in developing countries, often campaigning around single issues such as the destructive potential of dams or logging. In the former USSR, Baikal was the first focus for environmental protest at the beginning of the 1970s, and surprisingly this protest was tolerated by the authorities. Environmental protests have blossomed in the context of the political transition of eastern and central Europe, and the disintegration of the USSR. In western Europe, green political parties made inroads into the political process of several countries, notably The Greens in Germany. In North

---

[16] ibid, p.46.

[17] M.Colby, 'The Evolution of Paradigms of Environmental Management in Development', *Strategic Planning and Review*, Discussion Paper No.1, The World Bank, Washington DC, October 1989, p.15.

[18] For a general discussion, see M.Soroos, 'A Theoretical Framework for Global Policy Studies', in *International Political Science Review*, Vol.11, No.3, 1990, pp.309-322.

America, the disparate ecology movement made a big impact, but not in terms of electoral politics. In the 1980s, already heightened sensitivities were further shocked by a series of environmental disasters (see below, p.32), and these too have played a significant role in securing a place for environmental matters in standard political discourse within as well as between countries.

Non-governmental organizations

There exists a vast, worldwide network of NGOs concerned primarily or partly with environmental issues. In the 1980s, many of these developed from being principally consciousness-raising flag-wavers into organizations with significant research and project-management capability, focused on the environment, development, or on wildlife. A common feature seems to be the expansion of the interests of individual organizations from specific areas or issues to encompass the wider issue of sustainable development. WWF, for example, has expanded its domain from species protection, to habitat conservation, to international financial structures and the broader question of sustainability. IUCN has undergone a similar shift, from scientific interest and nature concerns to socio/economic/political questions. Developmental agencies like Oxfam are expressing interest in the environmental dimension to poverty. The interlinkages between all forms of life on the planet are pervading the thinking of many NGOs which are increasingly perceiving that they have a common cause.[19] In organizational terms, this is still at an embryonic stage.

Two major and interconnected developments concerning NGOs occurred as a result of the Stockholm Conference. Firstly, the intergovernmental conference was mirrored for its duration in Stockholm by a group of environmental NGOs. The pattern of parallel NGO monitoring has gone on ever since at all major meetings concerning the environment. Thus alternative views are given expression. This broadens the base of information and analyses from which public opinions can be formed. Secondly, the Conference led to the establishment of the ELC in Nairobi. This has been central to networking between NGOs worldwide.

ELC was established in 1974, and in 1987 'I' for international was added to the end of the acronym, reflecting the global nature of its membership. The recognition of the interdependent concerns

---

[19]See L.Starke, *Signs of Hope*, OUP, 1990, Chapter 4.

represented in this coalition is clear from the fact that the group now identifies itself as the Global Coalition for *Environment and Development.*[20] ELCI has over 340 members, at least half of which are located in developing countries. It maintains connections with over 8,000 NGOs worldwide. The Board of Directors, elected annually, is dominated by representatives from developing countries.

ECLI has helped promote contacts between wide-ranging NGOs, and has facilitated common statements on such issues as climate change. In December 1988 it arranged a meeting in Tunisia for NGOs to discuss their responses to the Brundtland Report. Not surprisingly, a wide spectrum of opinion emerged, with some seeing the findings as a great opportunity for environmentalists while others saw them as a threat because of the stress on the need for growth to assure sustainability.[21] ECLI publishes a bimonthly magazine, *Ecoforum*, for the exchange of information and ideas. It offers limited financial sponsorship to grass-roots groups in developing countries especially at a regional level, has helped to set up the Pesticide Action Network, and launched WEDNET (Women, Environment and Development Network) in 1989.

Some regional NGO networks were in place from the early 1980s. The African NGOs Environmental Network (ANEN) was established in 1982 in Nairobi on the 10th anniversary of the Stockholm Conference. The Asian Coalition for Agrarian Reform and Rural Development (ANGOC), based in the Philippines, was set up in 1979 following a meeting in Bangkok of several groups to discuss recommendations for a forthcoming UN conference on agrarian reform. In 1989, ANGOC and ELCI co-sponsored a meeting in Manila of thirty-one NGO leaders from around the world. The resulting 'Manila Declaration on People's Participation and Sustainable Development' stressed the necessity of NGOs working with governments and donor agencies towards a people-centred development.[22] These NGO networks have collaborated with governments and UN agencies on a variety of projects.

Looking to the future, the effectiveness of NGOs would be greatly enhanced if they were given some status under international law. WWFI

---

[20] ibid, p.82.

[21] ibid, p.83. Starke presents Lloyd Timberlake's analysis of the array of views. He felt that it was a good thing, in that it would prompt NGOs to clarify their positions.

[22] Declaration adopted at the 'Inter-Regional Consultation on People's Participation in Environmentally Sustainable Development', Makati, Metro Manila, Philippines, 6-10 June 1989, cited in Starke, op.cit, pp.80-1.

has been given observer status at certain UN meetings, and several NGOs were granted observer status for the UN Conference on Environment and Development (UNCED) in 1992. This in itself enhances their status significantly. Nevertheless, recognition of NGOs could go further. Sands has argued that:

NGOs have shown themselves to be willing and able to act as guardians of the international environment. In that context the time has come to expand the role of NGOs under general international law by giving their guardianship role formal legal expression.[23]

He argues that not only would this increase the power and influence of NGOs; it would also enhance the role of international law in environmental protection.

Green movements

Many green movements do not take on the institutionalized form of NGOs. Nevertheless, they may play a very important role in raising awareness. This has certainly been the case in India. Bandyopadhyay and Shiva, while noting the historical importance of green-related protests in colonial India,[24] argue that the number and range of ecology movements in the post-colonial state has increased enormously. They believe that this relates directly to the intensification of exploitation of natural resources to feed the process of development, which has resulted in the narrowing of the resource base available for the poor and powerless. They see ecology movements as the peoples' response to the threat to their survival. They identify the common property resources of water, forest and land, as well as clean air following the Bhopal tragedy, as being the areas which have evoked the greatest protests.

The Chipko movement is undoubtedly the best-known ecology movement in India.[25] Chipko loosely means to hug, and the movement began when the hill people in Uttar Pradesh literally hugged the trees to save them from exploitation by contractors from outside the forest area. The movement developed into a struggle for the maintenance of

[23]P.Sands, 'The Environment, Community and International Law', *Harvard International Law Journal*, Vol.30, No.2, Spring 1989, p.417.

[24]J.Bandyopadhyay and V.Shiva, 'Development, Poverty and the Growth of the Green Movement in India', *The Ecologist*, Vol.19, No.3, 1989, p.111.

[25]For a full account, see T.Weber, *Hugging the Trees: The Story of the Chipko Movement*, Penguin Books, 1989. See also J.Bandyopadhyay and V.Shiva, 'Chipko: Rekindling India's Forest Culture', *The Ecologist*, Vol.17, No.1, 1987, pp.26-34.

ecological stability in the major upland watersheds of India. It provided a huge demonstration effect for the rest of India, and inspired protest movements far beyond forest protection.[26]

Bandyopadhyay and Shiva believe a growth in such movements is inevitable while the problems inspiring them remain unaddressed:

> They are an expression of the universal socio-ecological impacts of a narrowly conceived development strategy based only on short-term commercial criteria of exploitation. The impact of ecology movements cannot be assessed merely in terms of the impact of the particular development projects they originate from. The impact in the final analysis is on the very fundamental categories of politics, economics, science and technology which together have created the classical paradigm of development and resource use.[27]

They argue that in developing countries generally, ecology movements are usually a response to a threat to survival, and thus they embrace poor people. This stands in contrast to the developed countries, where such movements are often middle-class based. Certainly this argument applies in Brazil, where the rubber tappers in the Amazon have responded to the threat to their survival by organizing themselves to protest and call for extractive reserves.[28]

In the changing political context of the late 1980s, green movements developed in the USSR and eastern Europe, often in response to a specific pollution problem. Before the disintegration of the USSR, Hilary French wrote:

> The country is now experiencing an environmental awakening on a par with that triggered by Earth Day in the United States in 1970. Seizing the opportunities presented by glasnost, local citizens' groups across the country are demanding government action to combat the legacy of the country's ruinous industrialization drive.[29]

---

[26]For example, against limestone quarrying, see J.Bandyopadhyay and V.Shiva, 'Conflicts over Limestone Quarrying in Doon Valley', *Environmental Conservation*, Vol.12, No.2, pp.131-39; and a series of protests about dams, such as the Silent Valley Dam in Kerala and the Tehri Dam in Uttar Pradesh. Most recently protests have occurred in response to the planning and implementation of the Narmada Dam project in Gujarat, see O.Sattaur, 'Greens in Muddy Water over Indian Dam', *New Scientist*, 5 October 1991, pp.16-17.

[27]Bandyopadhyay and Shiva, 1989, op.cit, pp.113-4.

[28]C.Mendes, *Fight for the Forest*, Latin American Bureau, London, 1989.

[29]H.French, 'The Greening of the Soviet Union', *Worldwatch*, May/June 1989, p.22.

The protest movement to fight the pollution of Lake Baikal, the world's largest freshwater lake which supplied 80% of Soviet freshwater, has gathered momentum. Pollution of the Aral, Baltic and Black seas has also prompted protest movements. In September 1988, for example, 50,000-100,000 Latvians, Estonians and Lithuanians linked hands along the shore of the Baltic sea to protest against its dismal condition. With the break up of the USSR, more information has become available to local people about the extent of environmental degradation, and this has given a spur to protest.

In eastern Europe, some environmental movements have played a role in pushing for domestic political change.[30] In Bulgaria, for example, the Ecoglasnost environmental movement joined the Union of Democratic Forces, calling for political pluralism.[31] Since the political changes that swept the region, environmental protests have become more common. In Hungary in 1989, for example, protests against the Nagymaros Dam, which was part of a joint hydroelectric scheme with Czechoslovakia and Austria, were successful in stopping work on the dam following over a year of growing street demonstrations about possible adverse environmental consequences for the Danube River ecosystem. The project was ultimately scrapped.[32]

Green Parties

Green movements have in some instances developed into green political parties. They are mainly a feature of west European democracies, and their popularity increased dramatically in the 1980s. The most successful in electoral terms was the German Green Party, which enjoyed a meteoric rise.[33]

---

[30] See the RIIA series of publications, 'Environmental Issues in East and Central Europe: the Energy Dimension', on NGOs, especially Duncan Fisher, *Paradise Deferred: Environmental Policymaking in Central and Eastern Europe*, RIIA, June 1992.

[31] See *Keesings Record of World Events*, Vol.XXXV, Bristol, December 1989, p.37110.

[32] Fisher, op.cit; *Keesings Record of World Events*, Vol.XXXIV, Bristol, September 1988, p.36166.

[33] Formed in 1980, the party won 27 seats in the Bundestag in 1983. By 1987, they had captured 8.3% of the vote and 42 seats in the Bundestag, see Hulsberg, op.cit. Elsewhere in Europe, in 1987 Greens won seats in the Italian parliament, taking 2.5% of the national vote and 13 seats in the Chamber of Deputies. In 1988, the Swedish Greens entered parliament, with 5.5% of the vote and 20 seats. In the 1989 elections to the European parliament, the Greens did very well. Belgium, France, West Germany, Italy, the Netherlands and Portugal all returned Green members. In the UK, due to the particular electoral system of first-past-the-post, the Greens won 15% of the vote but no seats.

Ideologically the west European Greens are heterogenous both within and between countries, despite the common cause engendered by the proximity of the nuclear threat and the consequent development of the peace movements. Hulsberg suggests that an understanding of the historical development of post-war Germany is essential for understanding the shape and complexion of green politics and the Green Party within Germany. Any attempt to export the model of the German Green Party is destined to fail. Looking to the future, it is unclear whether green movements in the European context will make a greater impact on politics through entering the electoral competition themselves or through prompting the greening of the more traditional political parties. The latter is more likely, given that ecological questions are not regarded by many as the central political issue. Hulsberg attributes the success of the German Greens partly to the fact that the party today is not a purely ecological phenomenon but has embraced the left.[34]

The roots of a Green Party in Poland go back to 1981 when the Polish Environmental Club was formed. In 1989, a Green Party drew up a 26-point programme of environmental action.[35] For such a party to have any hope of electoral success in the Polish context, it would have to embrace other political groupings. Poland is an exception in eastern Europe, where the rule is that the former Green NGOs have been 'captured' by taking them into government.

Disasters

During the 1980s a series of environmental disasters and incidents occurred in the developing and the developed world with devastating human consequences. These heightened public awareness of environmental issues both locally and internationally.[36] Public confidence in government and industry was severely eroded in many areas. It became apparent that conventional notions of progress have omitted to attach a value to the environment and ultimately therefore to life. Some of the most influential of these incidents are outlined below.

Accidents associated with nuclear power have had a huge impact on the perceptions of populations and governments in the industrialized world, yet the debate over its acceptability as a form of power is far from

[34]Hulsberg, op.cit, pp.218-20.
[35]*Keesings*, Vol.XXXV, 1989, op.cit, p.36783.
[36]For an interesting account of how disasters become 'normal', see A.Cockburn, 'Ordinary Disasters', *New Statesman and Society*, 21 April 1989, pp.18-19.

over (see Chapter 5 on Global Warming). In March 1979, the cooling systems failed at the Three Mile Island nuclear reactor at Harrisberg in the US. Miraculously, a major disaster was avoided, but the safety aspects of nuclear power generation were held up for public scrutiny. Seven years later, the world was not so fortunate. Explosions in a nuclear reactor at Chernobyl, north of Kiev in the former USSR, killed 31 people at the plant, and caused radioactive fallout across much of Europe. In April 1992 the Ukranian government revealed that 6-8000 people had already died as a result of the accident and the long-term health effects elsewhere in the former USSR and Europe are daunting,[37] and largely still unknown. Hence this is likely to remain an issue over the next several decades as the epidemiological data unfolds over the generations.

These disasters strengthened the anti-nuclear power lobbies throughout the world. For example, in October 1988 in Lithuania, 600,000 people signed a petition condemning the Ignalina nuclear power station, a Chernobyl-type RBMK.[38] All work on nuclear power stations in the former USSR came to a halt, and many were abandoned in various stages of construction or, like Chernobyl, closed. The incident at Sosnovy Bor in March 1992 showed that the threat is still significant.[39] The building of nuclear power stations has been cancelled in some other regions, such as the USA. While nuclear power may be cleaner and contribute less to global warming than fossil fuel energy, the potential costs - both human and financial - of an accident are enormous. The debate on future sources of energy is of the utmost importance. As the states of eastern Europe opened up politically, it became clear that the likelihood of further nuclear incidents was extremely high. In Bulgaria, for example, 40% of the electricity is derived from the plant which remain operational at the Kozlodui nuclear power station. These are riddled with design faults, in a very bad state of repair, and, now that the Soviets have left, are operated

---

[37]'Chernobyl death toll put as high as 8000', *Financial Times*, 24 April, 1992. See also J.Perera, 'Headless Calves Betray the Legacy of Chernobyl', *New Scientist*, 4 March 1989, p.27; and V.Rich, 'Concern Grows over Health of Chernobyl Children', *New Scientist*, 21 April 1990, p.23. Also M.Bojcun, and V.Haines, *The Chernobyl Disaster*, Hogarth Press, 1988, and D.Marples, *The Social Impact of the Chernobyl Disaster*, Macmillan, London, 1988.

[38]French, op.cit, p.27.

[39]A cloud of radioactive gas leaked from a nuclear power station outside St.Petersburg on 24 March 1992. See *The Times*, 25 March 1992, p.11; and *The Independent*, 25 March 1992, p.16.

by under-qualified staff. It has been suggested that the closure of the rest of the plant, with all the implications this would have on domestic electricity supply, would result in the fall of the government and a return to authoritarianism,[40] though some analysts would regard this as too dramatic a prediction.

In October 1984, pictures of the Korem refugee camp in Ethiopia were shown widely on European and North American television. While Africa had suffered drought and deforestation on and off for several years, media coverage had never before been so extensive, creating an enormous impact on the conscience of people in the developed world. Local groups sprung up to raise financial support for the area, and these continued to flourish throughout the decade. Band Aid and Sport Aid became household terms in the UK for example. The involvement of several pop stars such as Bob Geldof helped mobilize interest among young people. These initiatives are all the more significant when seen alongside the limited efforts of governments which have chosen to lend little practical support to the UN anti-desertification plan.

In December 1984 attention turned to the question of safety standards at chemical plants, and the thorny issue of corporate and government accountability and liability. A leak of cyanide gas at a pesticide plant in Bhopal, India, caused the death of over 2,800 people, and the injury of thousands more. A legal battle has been raging ever since between Union Carbide, the owner of the plant, and the government of India.[41] The former denies responsibility for the accident, arguing that the incident was a result of sabotage, while the latter portrays it as an industrial accident resulting from irresponsible behaviour by the multinational company. The ramifications of the case are huge, not just for the people of Bhopal, but for others throughout the world. The question of the universalization of safety standards is critical. While it could be argued that each state should be free to set its own standards, there is the very real problem that multinationals may transfer their activities to countries where standards are the most lax. Thus the choice for a government which is both concerned about the welfare of its citizens and wishes to attract foreign investment is very difficult. From the human rights perspective, the problem of corruption in government is particularly

[40]For further details on the Bulgarian example, see P.Godwin, 'Europe's Nuclear Timebomb', *The Guardian*, 4 October 1991.
[41]See S.Hazarika, *Bhopal: Lessons of a Tragedy*, Penguin Books, Delhi, India, 1987.

worrying, and lends weight to the argument for universal standards. The problem of chemical pollution was raised again in November 1986, when the river Rhine suffered pollution by the discharge of mercury and phosphorous in water used to fight a fire at the warehouse of the Sandoz chemicals company near Basle.[42]

Issues of nuclear weapons testing, nuclear power and radioactive waste came to the fore in the mid-1980s. Most noteworthy, of course, was the Chernobyl incident already cited. In July 1985, the Greenpeace ship *Rainbow Warrior* was sunk in Auckland Harbour, New Zealand, by French government agents in order to stop the boat being used in protests against French nuclear weapons testing in the Pacific.[43] One crew member was killed. The action was revealing in that it indicated the level of threat perceived by a government from an NGO. In September 1987, the focus shifted to Brazil, where radioactive caesium chloride powder was found on a dump in Goiana. It came from a cylinder which had been stolen from a hospital radiotherapy unit and sold as scrap. It was handled by children playing on the dump. The official death toll of four cannot take account of an unknown number of others who will have long-term effects from radioactive pollution in the area.

Over the period 1985-88, the publication of scientific findings on the depletion of the ozone layer were alarming. The British Antarctic Survey team published compelling evidence of a hole in the ozone layer above the Antarctic, while an international group of scientific experts recorded a 6% loss per annum of the general ozone layer. The potential health effects of increased ultra-violet radiation at the earth's surface are immense, as are the possible effect on terrestrial and aquatic animal and plant life. Much research needs to be done to assess likely damage (see Chapter 6).

In 1988 a spate of incidents and disasters gave the impression of impending crisis. Drought hit many agricultural regions of the world, including the mid-western states of the US where the impact was great and resulted in a significant drop in food production. It was an exceptionally hot year. Also in that year, Chico Mendes, a leader of the

---

[42]'Pollution Following Factory Fire in Switzerland', *Keesings Record of World Events*, Vol.XXXII, Bristol, 1986, p.34784.
[43]See M.King, *Death of the Rainbow Warrior*, Penguin, Harmondsworth, 1986; J.Dyson, *Sink the Rainbow*, Gollancz, London, 1986; and R.Shears, and I.Gidley, *The Rainbow Warrior Affair*, Centerpoint/Unwin Paperbacks, 1986.

Brazilian rubber-tappers union who had fought for the preservation of the Amazon rain forests and their indigenous peoples, was assassinated.[44]

In March 1989, major oil pollution from the grounded *Exxon Valdez* caused extensive damage to coastline wildlife and habitat in Alaska. The enormity of the ecological disaster caused by the spillage must be placed in the context of the ease with which the company was able to use profits to cover the cost of the clean-up.[45] Yet no amount of money can repair the damage that has been done to the regional ecosystem. Corporate damage has been significant. Exxon was heavily criticized within the industry and in other fora, both for allowing the disaster to happen and for its attitude following the accident. For a while afterwards, when TV coverage was at its heaviest, the company became a pariah within the US and suffered a much reduced market share at the petrol pump. Damages were increased from lower to higher amounts. The incident placed the Arctic National Wildlife Range off-limits to companies for the foreseeable future and as far as Exxon is concerned, possibly for ever. Other offshore drilling in California was similarly set back. Oil companies worldwide made strenuous efforts to learn from the event and subsequent spillage incidents have benefited from the Valdez affair.

In 1991, the sabotage of Kuwaiti oil wells by retreating Iraqis caused a major environmental disaster, the full extent of which has yet to be revealed. Scientists differ on whether the burning of the oil wells will contribute to global warming and affect the Asian monsoon. Nevertheless, even those who do not predict this do not underestimate the impact on regional ecology. Small, for example, while denying any global warming impact, remarks that:

> Nevertheless, the amount of smoke produced would be large and cause a massive pollution event. It would impact the ecology of the Persian Gulf and fall out on a wide swathe across southern Iran, Pakistan, and possibly northern India. Because the fires could continue for prolonged periods, the particulate fallout would persist. In the worst case, human population would be exposed to persistent

---

[44]See Mendes, op.cit. Also, for an interesting account of the personal risks associated with green activism, see A.Cockburn, 'Cut Down in their Prime', *New Statesman and Society*, 29 June 1990.
[45]M.Walker, 'Why Green Policies are Now a Threat to US National Security', *The Guardian*, 23 August 1990.

air pollution; grazing herds may be affected by accumulated ingestion of soot; agricultural and ecological systems impacted by a covering of soot; and water systems polluted by the fallout and accumulations in runoff. The impact on human and animal populations and regional ecosystems from such prolonged effects is unknown.[46]

It has also been suggested by some scientists that allied bombing resulted in widespread atmospheric pollution and spillage of oil into the Gulf before the retreating Iraqi troops set fire to the oil wells.[47] These claims have not yet been substantiated.

Disasters concentrate public attention on environmental problems, albeit for short periods. There is no doubt that the range of environmental accidents and incidents that occurred in the 1980s, coupled with heightened general public awareness of environmental issues, have had a cumulative effect on the interested public in the developed countries. Yet the trade-offs are not necessarily about to be resolved in favour of safety as against jobs or availability of energy. The Bulgarian risks in continued operation of defective nuclear plant makes this all too clear. In developing countries, the disasters have focused attention on safety standards of multinational corporations and the perceived inequality of standards of operation between southern and northern countries. This perception of inequality has been heightened by the scandals concerning the trade in toxic waste. While the educated middle classes may adopt positions similar to those of their counterparts in the developed world regarding such issues as nuclear power and oil pollution, there is no doubt that incidents like Bhopal, wherever responsibility lies, have resulted in greater resentment against perceived northern exploitation. Such feelings are strong in India and have been fuelled by the recent Gulf crisis which had a significant impact on the sub-continent's economy, even without taking into account potential effects on its climate. Perception is all-important, and what is seen as a disaster by one may be regarded as an opportunity by another. Hence charges of eco-imperialism have emanated from Brazil, in relation to external requests for it to stop cutting down the Amazon rainforest.

---

[46] R.Small, 'Environmental Impact of Fires in Kuwait', *Nature*, Vol.350, 7 March 1991, p.11-12.

[47] B.Tokar, 'Disaster in the Gulf and Poison at Home', *Z Magazine*, December 1991, pp.57-9.

For the majority of peasants trying to eke out a living in the poorer countries, accidents are of little note. Their lives are a constant struggle in hostile, degraded environments. Life in such circumstances is cheap. Environmental issues are not new on their agenda, nor are they fleeting. They are fixed and overwhelming.

2.4 Consciousness-raising in intergovernmental institutions

Over the past two decades, most UN agencies and many other Inter-governmental Organizations (IGOs) have tried to promote environmental assessments in their operational procedures. UNEP must take some of the credit for this.[48] UNEP was established by UN General Assembly Resolution 2997 (XXVII) of 15 December, 1972, following the Stockholm Conference. In two decades, UNEP has come to play an international role and exercise influence out of all proportion to the very limited means at its disposal.[49] It is a major actor in the field of international environmental affairs, yet its profile internationally remains fairly low-key. Through its achievements in the fields of environmental public policy and consciousness-raising, UNEP has become a catalyst for change in other intergovernmental institutions. UNEP merits greater attention than it has received to date, and a small contribution will be made here to redressing the balance.

UNEP as a catalyst

UNEP was not conceived as an executing agency within the UN, nor as a major funding body for environmental projects. Rather, it was intended to be 'a focal point for environmental action and coordination within the UN system'.[50] It has played the primary catalytic role in mobilizing interest, awareness and concern within UN agencies. Outside the UN

---

[48]On the role of international organizations - particularly UNEP - in the context of environmental degradation, see M.Untawale, 'Global Environmental Degradation and International Organizations', *International Political Science Review*, Vol.11, No.3, 1990, pp.371-383. For an excellent account of how the environment has been taken up in different international organizations, see Lee A.Kimball, *Forging International Agreements: the Role of Institutions in Environment and Development*, World Resources Institute, Washington DC, April 1992.

[49]On official statements indicating UNEP's evolving role, see Mostafa Tolba, (ed), *Evolving Environmental Perceptions: From Stockholm to Nairobi*, Butterworths, London, 1988.

[50]General Assembly Resolution 2997 (XXVII) 15 December, 1972.

system it has fostered teaching, training and research on a host of environmental topics. All this has been achieved on a small budget. In the Annual Report of the Executive Director, 1984, it was remarked that UNEP:

> ... was envisaged as a small focus of global know-how, charged with stimulating effective global environmental action through the coordination of independent activities, leadership and efforts to catalyze and stimulate action by others. UNEP was not funded to address major environmental concerns by itself; it was mandated to mobilize the concern of a much wider circle.[51]

Unlike most of the UN programmes which have their headquarters in the industrialized countries, UNEP's headquarters are in Nairobi.[52] Membership is identical to membership of the UN. Every two years the Governing Council (GC), whose fifty-eight members are elected on a rotating basis every four years, meets in Nairobi to formulate policy. The GC reports through the Economic and Social Council (ECOSOC) to the UN General Assembly (UNGA). The Executive Director, nominated by the Secretary-General and elected by the UNGA to a four-year term of office, heads the small secretariat.[53]

Funding comes primarily, but not exclusively, from voluntary contributions which are usually small, often late, and sometimes unreliable. Moreover, some contributions are made in soft currencies. (It also receives a small allocation from the regular budget of the UN - $6.05 million in 1989). All of these factors make planning more difficult. This is a common problem throughout the UN system, but due to the particularly meagre resources of UNEP the late arrival of funds is even more problematic for the programme. Even at the Stockholm Conference, it was pointed out by Israel that the voluntary Environment Fund to be attached to UNEP would be totally inadequate to meet the

---

[51] United Nations Environment Programme, *Annual Report of the Executive Director*, 1984, p.17.

[52] Regional offices are located in Nairobi (for Africa), Bangkok (for Asia), Geneva (for Europe), Mexico (for Latin America and the Caribbean) and Bahrain (for west Asia). Liaison offices are located in Washington DC and in New York. The latter two are vital for the huge diplomatic networks which exist in those cities on account of the UN, its specialized agencies the IMF and World Bank, and diplomatic missions to the US, as well as the profusion of NGO headquarters.

[53] For these and further institutional details, see 'Institutional Profiles:UNEP', *International Environmental Affairs*, Vol.1, No.1, Winter 1989, pp.65-7.

challenge posed by environmental problems.[54] (However, UNEP was never intended to provide resources for the implementation of major environmental programmes; its original role was to promote environmental policies). The programme operates on a two-year budget, averaging a total of $29.5 million per annum. While much has been achieved by UNEP on a small and insecure budget, this is an argument for more funding rather than less. Its achievements could be even more widespread and significant if its activities were not so hampered.

UNEP activities are guided by the System Wide Medium Term Environment Plan (SWMTEP). This plan is drawn up by representatives of the heads of UN agencies, referred to as Designated Officials on Environmental Management (DOEM). The plan is assessed by the coordinating mechanism of the UN system, the Administrative Committee on Coordination (ACC). Once accepted, it guides the environmental policy not only of UNEP but of all the other UN agencies in terms of environmental matters.

Nevertheless, UNEP's areas of interest are not all predetermined by SWMTEP. Indeed, UNEP itself plays a major role in developing SWMTEP as a coordinating mechanism. UNEP's interests have evolved over the past two decades and are still evolving in line with changing perceptions of the most pressing and important environmental problems. The role of the Executive Director has often been crucial. UNEP's changing focus has been reflected in other UN agencies, which is not at all surprising given the central role played by UNEP of facilitator. It has also been reflected in international conferences, reports, research projects and conventions on particular issues which UNEP has played a leading role in instigating and/or co-sponsoring. Most UNEP activities are carried out with other UN agencies and sometimes with NGOs. Thus UNEP has played a major role in shaping the agenda of international discussion of environmental issues.

At the first meeting of its Governing Council in Geneva in June 1973, three main items were discussed: firstly, an Action Plan for the human environment, consisting of 109 recommendations for international environmental cooperation, which had been drawn up at Stockholm; secondly, the functioning of the voluntary fund established by the General Assembly on 15 December 1972; and thirdly, a UN conference

---

[54]*Report of the UN Conference on the Human Environment, Stockholm,* op.cit, p.62.

on human settlements. Since that first meeting, UNEP's interests and activities have increased exponentially.

UNEP's programme has been classified under ten broad groupings:

1. Environment and development

2. Environmental awareness (including INFOTERRA, a system of information exchange based on national clearing houses)

3. Earthwatch, covering monitoring and assessment activities including the Global Environmental Monitoring System or GEMS

4. Oceans, which includes the regional seas programme

5. Water

6. Terrestrial ecosystems

7. Arid lands and desertification control

8. Health and human settlements, including the International Register of Potentially Toxic Chemicals (IRPTC)

9. The environment and armaments

10. Regional and technical cooperation.[55]

Many of these categories overlap, and knowledge gained in one is often vital for policy formulation in another. The range of categories reflects the concern of UNEP to investigate environmental issues not in a vacuum but rather in their social and political context. Ever since the call for a New International Economic Order in 1974, UNEP has been at pains to point out that environmental issues must be located within the framework of the prevailing international economic and financial structures and also national and local economic systems. Effective environmental policies may only be possible in the context of a revised international economic order or a changed national or local order. At the time of the second session of UNEP's General Council in March 1974, ECOSOC reminded UNEP's Executive Director of the importance of UNEP activities working in line with the Second UN Development Decade's international development strategy.[56] Indeed UNEP has come to represent an unusually holistic stance among the UN agencies and programmes.[57]

---

[55]*International Environmental Affairs*, op.cit, p.66.

[56]*Yearbook of the UN, 1974*, United Nations, New York, 1974, p.435.

[57]It has worked closely with the UNDP, UNCTAD, FAO, UNESCO, WMO, ECOSOC, UNIDO, HABITAT, plus many other arms of the UN.

UNEP has played a vital role in consciousness-raising, information-gathering, networking and coordination. The results are evident not only in cases of particular environmental problems but also in terms of centralizing information. UNEP has developed a wide-ranging data-base on the state of the environment in the 1980s. The Global Resource Information Database (GRID), the International Referral System for Sources of Environmental Information (INFOTERRA), and the International Register of Potentially Toxic Chemicals (IRPTC) combine information from governments, inter-governmental organizations, NGOs and companies. They are evolving all the time with the growth in our understanding of environmental science and the development of more sophisticated techniques of evaluation. Access to such information is vital to the successful management of the environment, especially for countries which are poor.

UNEP has often taken up an issue well before the problem has reached the centre stage of international discussion, and has helped to transform global perceptions of its gravity. This has certainly been the case with ozone deletion, global warming and deforestation. These particular problems are discussed in detail in separate chapters later in the book. Here, attention is turned to UNEP's less well-known, but very important, activities.

UNEP's efforts regarding desertification illustrate the instrumental role it plays in information-gathering, monitoring, coordination, consciousness-raising and mobilization. UNEP has been concerned about the spread of deserts since its foundation, and as early as 1974, it passed a resolution calling for international cooperation to counter this problem.[58] It emphasized the need for the UN system to coordinate data on the topic, calling especially upon the FAO and UNESCO to join the effort. Under UNEP's auspices, the UN held a special conference on desertification in Nairobi in 1977. The UNGA adopted a Plan of Action on 9 September 1977 to combat desertification and to reclaim land by the target year 2000.[59] Actions to this end were to be carried out within the framework of the UN. Two years later, in April 1979, the GC of UNEP adopted a resolution calling upon governments to contribute to a special fund set up by the Secretary General a month earlier to counter the spread

---

[58]*Yearbook of the UN, 1974*, Resolution 3337 (XXIX), United Nations, New York, 1974.
[59]*Yearbook of the UN*, 1977, United Nations, New York, pp.509-510.

of deserts. UNEP's Executive Director was authorized to coordinate activities with the Organization of African Unity (OAU) and to pursue a joint project with the UNDP in the Sudanian and Sahelian regions of Africa.

UNEP pursued collaborative efforts on desertification vigorously in the 1980s. In 1984, partly with UNEP encouragement, a four-year drought and desertification control programme for the Sahel was announced by the Permanent Inter-State Committee on Drought Control in the Sahel (or CILSS), the UNDP and the UN Sudano-Sahelian Office.[60] The widespread famine in Africa in 1984-85 helped increase international interest in desertification. In 1985, the Cairo programme for African cooperation was launched. This called for cooperation to prevent environmental degradation and to move towards continent-wide sufficiency in food and energy.[61]

Before the 15th session of UNEP's GC in 1989, Africa's Environment Ministers met in Nairobi to review the problem of drought and desertification.[62] Mostafa Tolba, the Executive director of UNEP, urged them to start implementing the Cairo Declaration which was already four years old. He urged Africa to take 'the main responsibility for its own environment through the Cairo plan'.[63] At the UNEP meeting itself, he pointed out that although one-third of the earth's land surface was threatened by desertification, the governments concerned had not taken serious measures to address the problem.

The 1977 Plan of Action has never received adequate financial support to stand a chance of success. While UNEP played the major role in getting the desertification issue onto the international agenda, it has been unable to galvanize the international community into action to meet this huge environmental challenge. The primary reason for this is that those who suffer most from the problem live in the poorest regions of the world, and the developed countries have been largely unaffected by their plight. The latter have offered little in terms of financial contributions to the 1977 Plan. Yet since the late 1980s, some of the world's developed country crop-producers, such as the US, former USSR and Australia,

---

[60]*Keesings Record of World Events*, 'Africa: Drought and Famine', Vol.XXXI, 1985, p.33380; and 'CILSS Ministerial Council Meeting', Vol.XXXII, 1986, p.34212.
[61]*Keesings Record of World Events*, Vol.XXXV, No.6, 1989,op.cit, p.36796.
[62]'Nairobi Conference', in ibid, p.36796.
[63]ibid, p.36796.

have been suffering drought. (Other major crop producers like India, Latin America and China, have suffered likewise). In these new circumstances of developed-country affliction, the problem may receive more attention.

UNEP has played a similar, but more successful role, in relation to maritime pollution. It has stimulated data-gathering, remedial action and good management practices through its regional seas programme. UNEP's activities follow the London Dumping Convention of 1972 which provided a framework for the control of waste-dumping at sea. UNEP has taken a greater interest in near-shore pollution by run-off from land and shoreline development. It has been particularly concerned about the effect of pollution on near-shore hatcheries and nurseries for many species of fish.[64]

There are now well over 130 countries bordering twelve shared seas which have been brought together under the UNEP programme, and sometimes with the collaboration of other regional organizations such as the United Nations Committee on Latin America (UNCLA) in the case of the Caribbean. Regional action plans are drawn up, and these are followed by conventions which form the basis for remedial action. The first regional seas action plan was drawn up for the Mediterranean region in 1975,[65] and the signing of the convention followed in February 1978, with additional protocols in 1980 and 1983.[66] UNEP announced in July 1980 that 80% of the region's beaches were clean and safe, compared with 65% in 1975. Thus the Mediterranean regional sea programme seems to have been a success thus far, but there is no room for complacency as pollution remains a serious problem in some places such as parts of the south of France and the Bay of Naples.

Reaching an agreement on a convention is the very first step on the road to addressing the problem of maritime pollution. Political will must be however to translate the conventions into practical action for the environment. Other regional agreements have also been signed but not

---

[64] ibid, p.36790.
[65] Other regional plans followed in quick succession. Action plans were drawn up for the Red Sea and the Gulf of Aden in 1976; the Kuwait region in 1978; west and central Africa in 1981, and in the same year the wider Caribbean, east Asia, and South East Pacific; the South Pacific in 1982; eastern Africa in 1985; and in 1989 south Asia. Most were followed by conventions within a couple of years.
[66] See P.Haas, *Saving the Mediterranean: the Politics of International Environmental Cooperation*, Columbia University Press, New York, 1990.

directly under the instigation of UNEP.[67] Undoubtedly UNEP's efforts in raising international awareness regarding maritime pollution, and the example of the regional seas programmes, gave a big impetus to cooperation in these other regions.

Many of UNEP's activities go unnoticed. Here we will mention just a few to illustrate the huge range of issues under its umbrella. UNEP's early interest in the question of human settlement, added to the concern of ECOSOC, provided a push for the establishment of the UN Habitat and Human Settlements Foundation (HABITAT). This programme has received little attention in the developed world, and it is funded mainly by developing states. It often works in association with ECOSOC and UNEP. UNEP sends numerous technical experts throughout the world each year, and these sometimes work on projects with HABITAT. UNEP and HABITAT frequently hold joint meetings to monitor collaboration and discuss possible future ventures.

UNEP has been instrumental in bringing the question of water onto the international stage. As well as carrying out its own studies, UNEP supported the 1977 UN conference on water in Argentina which gave top priority to water resources development. Water has been marked out as a future cause of instability in regions such as the Middle East.

Another area of concern has been human health. Here, UNEP has worked closely with the World Health Organization (WHO). For example, they jointly monitor health in industrialized and developing countries under the Human Expose Assessment Locations Programme, or HEALS.[68] The UNEP-inspired IRPTC has also assumed international importance.

UNEP has intensified its activities regarding hazardous wastes. In February 1989 it undertook the task of modifying a draft treaty that had been produced by representatives from developing and developed countries in Dakar, Senegal, in that January.[69] The final agreement, the Basle Convention on international transport and disposal of hazardous waste, was signed in March 1989 by 34 countries.[70] It required written

---

[67] The North Sea in 1984, *Keesings*, Vol.XXXII, 1986, op.cit, p.34525; the Baltic Sea in 1974 but effective since 1980, *Keesings*, Vol.XXVI, 1980, p.30425; and the Pacific, effective since 1986, *Keesings*, Vol.XXXII, 1986, op.cit, p.34526; Vol.XXXI, 1985, op.cit., p.33855; and Vol.XXXV, 1989, op.cit, p.36703.

[68] *Yearbook of the UN, 1985*, United Nations, New York, 1985, p.803.

[69] *Keesings*, Vol.XXXV, 1989, op.cit, p.36789.

[70] ibid, p.36541.

assent from waste-importing governments. Again, however, the signing of the convention amounts to a first step, albeit a vital and difficult one. It remains to be seen whether governments and companies interpret and implement it according to the spirit of the drafters.[71] The *New Scientist* reported on 1 April 1989 that the treaty's controls were very weak, and that the necessity of generating foreign income might result in poor countries accepting hazardous waste. The role of UNEP in getting the issue accepted internationally is an example of its efficacy among international agencies.

Apart from its interest in specific environmental issues, UNEP has played an important role in bringing the concept of sustainable development to the attention both of UN agencies and concerned individuals throughout the world. Starting in 1975, UNEP and WWF provided funding for the preparation of the *World Conservation Strategy* (WCS) drawn up by the IUCN. Five years later, and with the help of UNESCO and the FAO as well, the final strategy was published. It was concerned mainly with the maintenance of genetic diversity and sustainable utilization of species and ecosystems. While it highlighted the problem of sustainable development, it was criticized by some developing countries for urging the adoption of National Conservation Strategies which they felt amounted to an instruction to keep the environment intact at the expense of meeting basic human needs. A second WCS was published in 1991 which took some of these criticisms into account and offered a much broader perspective on environment, conservation and development.[72]

Further refinement of the concept of sustainable development was achieved by two independent reports which were both in different ways associated with UNEP. The first, the Brundtland Report, *Our Common Future*, resulted from discussions at a special session of UNEP's GC held in 1982 to assess achievements since Stockholm. It was concluded that long-term environmental planning was needed, and the UNGA accordingly in 1983 called for two reports. The independent commission under the leadership of Gro Harlem Brundtland was complemented by *Environmental Perspective to the Year 2000 and Beyond*. The latter was prepared by governments through UNEP's GC, and it provided a

---

[71] See, *New Scientist*, 1 April 1989, pp.24-25.
[72] IUCN, UNEP, WWF, *Caring for the Earth: A Strategy for Sustainable Living*, Gland, Switzerland, October 1991.

framework for national and international action to translate the Brundtland Report into practical action. Both reports are significant for the context in which they locate the environment problem: that of the structures of the international economy which allow inequality in terms of trade to be perpetuated and capital transfers from the poor countries to the rich in the form of debt repayment. They argue that real progress on the environment will only be achieved when these fundamental structures are changed. When the UNGA had considered these two reports in 1987, it urged the UN agencies to integrate the proposals into their programmes and report back on progress made to UNEP. (For a detailed examination of the Brundtland Report, see Chapter 3).

UNEP's role of international facilitator of environmental discussions and inter-agency coordinator has been criticized from certain quarters. The issue crystallized in 1985 when the UNGA called upon UNEP to widen its contacts with other UN agencies further in an effort to promote environmental awareness and harness resources and information, and avoid duplication and ignorance within the unwieldy UN structure.[73] The resolution was opposed by the US (although that country abstained at the vote), which argued that UNEP had no need to study the arms race and could not do anything about it anyway. This position was supported by the UK, France and Israel as well. The developing countries and those of eastern Europe took the opposite view. This general political alignment reflects similar alignments that had developed in the GA on such questions as that of a new international economic order, the Palestinian issue and South Africa.

Certainly the developing countries themselves place great importance on UNEP. After all, given their lack of resources and information, and the poor scientific base many of them have, UNEP is seen as a focal point for information, advice, technical assistance and small-scale funding on environmental matters, as well as an inter-agency coordinator. Since UNEP takes an integrated view of environmental and developmental concerns, the poorer states naturally feel comfortable with it.

For the developed states, especially those of the west, UNEP's stance on many issues conflicts with their own, as UNEP presses on all possible fronts for international dialogue on environmental and resource

---

[73]*Yearbook of the UN*, 1985, United Nations, New York, p.789. Vote details: Against - 0; abstained - France, West Germany, Israel, Portugal, UK and USA; in favour - 149 states.

management issues transcending international boundaries. While the western states in general are happy with some of these activities, some of them are less happy with the idea of broadening the debate to encompass general issues associated with the structures of international trade, finance and aid. The US, for example, was particularly unhappy with the way UNEP and other agencies like ECOSOC jointly mobilized support for specific policies such as the banning of trade abroad of goods deemed harmful domestically.[74] The US alone had voted against this at the GA on 17 December 1982.[75] The US went further in 1984 when it alone voted against a resolution calling for the publication and annual update of a list of products harmful to human health and the environment. The stated reasons were finance and problems of clarification within the list.[76]

Undoubtedly the US perceives UNEP, if only to a limited degree, as having been over-influenced by developing countries and by 'radical' scientific opinion. Since the issues that UNEP tries to bring to the centre stage of international diplomacy are vital to the well-being of the planet it is very important that the political wranglings that have tainted the workings of various UN bodies do not get transferred onto UNEP, for they will certainly inhibit its future functioning.

UNEP is in a unique position to influence the policy debate, since it has affected not only the choice of issues discussed and the form the discussions take multilaterally, but also the profile of certain issues in the perceptions of UN agencies, certain governments and NGOs. Moreover, UNEP has been open to advice from those actors, and has learnt from them. UNEP has been dismissed as being 'far from the corridors of power, financial resources and decision-making'.[77] Given this, its achievements are all the more remarkable. Its future, however, remains somewhat uncertain, given that the important mandate for climate change discussions was taken out of its hands in late 1990 and transferred to the UNGA. (See Chapter 5 on global warming.) This represents a real loss of potential influence given the centrality of the problem. The issue of whether there should be a new UN agency to deal with the environment, or whether UNEP's strengths should be built on,

---

[74] See *Yearbook of the UN, 1982*, United Nations, New York, 1982, pp.1011-1012
[75] ibid.
[76] *Yearbook of the UN, 1984*, United Nations, New York, 1984, p.752-755
[77] Colby, op.cit, p.15.

or even whether the UN Trusteeship Council should turn its attention to the environment will greatly influence the agenda and the outcome.

2.5 The environment on the superpower agenda

The second half of the 1980s witnessed the arrival of environmental concerns on the diplomatic agenda of the most powerful countries in the world. Undoubtedly the reduction in tension between the superpowers facilitated this, as did the associated lessening of ideological conflict between the two blocs of developed countries and the practical arms reduction agreements and on-going negotiations between them. The passing of the Cold War presented an opportunity for discussion of global problems that depend on international cooperation if they are to be addressed with any possibility of success. With the creation of this political space, the superpowers themselves were quick to seize the moment and express primary interest in environmental concerns which had been building up support at the NGO and IGO level for two decades. Their conceptions of security, at least at the rhetorical level, paid far more attention to the importance of international cooperation. Their involvement was welcome, being crucial for the negotiation and success of critical agreements, and also because of the extent of their respective land masses. Yet rightly it was treated with caution by observers. Motivated hitherto by geopolitical and ideological concerns, it would have been premature to assume that such priorities had permanently disappeared. They might resurface, or others, such as domestic political problems, might replace them. It has transpired that the former USSR has disintegrated, and the uncertainty associated with this may result in the environment being put on the back burner once more as governments adopt more traditional security concerns. Clearly the events unfolding in the former USSR add a huge element of uncertainty to the picture.

Nineteen eighty-five was a propitious year. Reagan entered his second, and necessarily his last, term of office at the White House. While his first term had been characterized by real Cold War rhetoric such as the evil empire language, the tone of his second term was set to be different. History will judge him on his later achievements. Aspects of his foreign policy moderated noticeably. The US adopted a softer approach in its dealings with its chief adversary. In the former USSR, the arrival of Mikhail Gorbachev as President in 1985 heralded a new era of openness in the Kremlin and some huge shifts in domestic and foreign policy.

Glasnost and perestroika in the domestic context were accompanied by new thinking in foreign policy and by new personnel, sympathetic to an approach based not on confrontation but on cooperation.[78] Gorbachev and Foreign Secretary Shevardnadze re-examined the Soviet position vis-a-vis the west, and pushed a new conception of security based on the recognition of the interdependence of all peoples and of economy, environment, and security both at the domestic and international levels. Reagan, and later Bush, were willing to respond in a reasonably positive manner to the Soviet overtures. The US had a long-standing history of domestic environmental legislation and had played an important role in the negotiations prior to the 1985 Vienna Convention on the Protection of the Ozone Layer. There was a real concern in US society and in certain sectors of government about the global environmental problem.

During the late 1970s and first half of the 1980s, the superpowers had increased the political tension in Europe especially but also internationally by their build-up of intermediate range nuclear arsenals in Europe. Schmidt had first drawn attention publicly to Soviet SS20s in Europe in 1976, and Nato decided to respond in 1979 with its 'dual track' policy. This referred to the simultaneous modernization and build-up of intermediate nuclear forces, notably the Pershing 11 and the Grand Launch Cruise missiles, and the continuation of negotiations with the former USSR for an arms control agreement. By the mid-1980s, the superpowers were ready, each for their own reasons, to begin bargaining in arms reduction in earnest.

Negotiations for an intermediate nuclear force reduction agreement began in the late 1970s, but only really got underway in 1981/2. In 1983, they were broken off, only to be re-opened in 1984/5. The period 1985-7 saw a profound change in attitude in the Kremlin, accompanied by sweeping peace proposals. In a sense the former USSR at this time called the west's bluff, by suggesting more far-reaching measures than the west had hitherto put forward, for example in the field of on-site inspection. Following intense negotiations carried out with remarkable speed, the superpowers signed the Intermediate Nuclear Forces (INF) Treaty in 1987.

---

[78]For a general discussion see M.Light, *The Soviet Theory of International Relations*, Wheatsheaf, 1988, chapter ten.

The INF Treaty represented a major step forward in international cooperation.[79] For the first time, the superpowers agreed to the eradication of a complete weapons system. All intermediate range nuclear forces within the range 500kms to 5500kms, were to be dismantled in Europe. Moreover, the treaty allowed for intrusive on site inspection and verification procedures. Recognition of the interdependence of global security underlay this agreement. The nuclear threat, while far from over, seemed to be receding somewhat, at least from the standpoint of the Europeans who had been faced with the massive build-up of nuclear arsenals on their soil. Of course, in other parts of the world the nuclear threat was increasing, leaving no room for complacency.

The domestic and international imperatives of Gorbachev's policies were clearly linked. The Soviet economy was in complete disarray, and the cost of sustaining the military competition with the US was a burden the former USSR could ill afford to carry. Domestic loss of faith in government policies had reached the point of crisis proportions. The policies of perestroika and glasnost went hand-in-hand with an international position supportive of peace and an enhanced role for the UN as the expression of the community of mankind. Presenting the UN as the body which would serve international interests, an analogy was drawn with the domestic situation of the former USSR where Gorbachev was at pains to ensure that particularist interests did not compromise the interest of the state as a whole. The entry of the environment into Gorbachev's domestic and international political thinking can be interpreted in this wider context.

In his book published in 1988, Gorbachev called for a new international political thinking, on the basis that: 'We are all passengers aboard one ship, Earth, and we must not allow it to be wrecked. There will be no second Noah's Ark'.[80] Interdependence was at the heart of his world view. At the UNGA in December 1988, Gorbachev proposed the creation of a special centre for ecological aid under the auspices of the UN. Recognition of the appalling state of the Soviet domestic environment, its clear links with the internal economic and political situation, and the

---

[79]However, some commenters have pointed to loopholes in the agreement which could seriously undermine its effectiveness. See, for example, P.Rogers and D.Plesch, 'Less Means More', *New Statesman and Society*, 21 October 1988, pp.8-9.
[80]M.Gorbachev, *Perestroika*, Collins, 1988, p.12.

psychological as well as physical effect of the Chernobyl accident, undoubtedly fuelled his awareness of and conception of international environmental issues, and probably his attitude to international standard-setting and verification also. The help the Soviet Union received after the Chernobyl accident lent weight to Gorbachev's conversion to multilateralism. Economy, ecology and the international political community were becoming increasingly interconnected in his thinking. He noted that:

> International economic security is inconceivable unless related not only to disarmament but also to the elimination of the threat to the world's environment.[81]

At the 44th session of the UNGA in September 1989, Eduard Shevardnadze, heading the Soviet delegation, reported on the talks with President Bush and Secretary of State Baker. While emphasizing the environmental threat that the world faced, he stressed that the greatest threat to the world still came from nuclear weapons. He stated a word of caution:

> ... the world community has as yet no reason for complacency or euphoria. The nuclear threat has only been reduced by the Soviet-US treaty eliminating intermediate and shorter-range missiles.[82]

He called for a moratorium on nuclear explosions, real discussion of a complete test ban, and cessation of production of fissionable material for nuclear explosions supported by an agreement to this effect by all nuclear powers.

Shevardnadze acknowledged the new place which environmental issues had suddenly acquired in international politics, and located them within a holistic conception of security. His statement is instructive: it reveals a dramatic sea-change in government thinking in the former Soviet Union. Accordingly it is quoted at length:

> Before the eyes of just one generation the sphere of politics has linked up with environmental conservation to give mankind the science of political ecology. No one can master it alone, entangled in the fetters of narrow interests.

---

[81]M.Gorbachev, 'Address to the UN General Assembly', *Soviet News*, 14 December 1988, p.461.
[82]'Eduard Shevardnadze's statement at the United Nations General Assembly', *Soviet News*, 4 October 1989, p.342.

Political ecology requires urgent planetary decisions at the highest political level and an internationalization of national efforts through the UN, by consolidating its leading environmental branch, the appropriate branch of this organization. And since we are speaking of a major component of international security, political ecology requires the involvement of the Security Council in solving problems and activating such tools as transparency and monitoring.

The United Nations Conference on Environment and Development to be held in 1992 will undoubtedly become a watershed in establishing universal cooperation and working out a code of civilized ecological behaviour. We call for holding this conference at the level of Heads of State and Government.

Defining for itself the main principles of the concept of ecological security, the former USSR considers disarmament, the economy and ecology as an integral whole. While participating in implementing conservation strategies, the Soviet Union has programmes for speeding up the integration of its economy, on an equal and mutually beneficial basis, into the world economy, modern international division of labour and international exchanges in science and technology.

To that end we would like to participate actively in the work of international economic organizations and to establish contacts with the IMF and the World Bank, being convinced that our cooperation with them, as well as with GATT and FAO, will be useful for us and the community as a whole.[83]

This statement is extremely interesting. It is characterized by tones of cooperation, not confrontation. The former Soviet emphasis on class struggle is completely absent, as is any notion of peaceful co-existence. Different paths of social development take a back seat to the primary responsibility for the future of mankind, which is threatened not just by weapons but by new forms of destruction. Environmental issues are placed alongside disarmament and economic questions, and indeed it is suggested that the three cannot be separated. The central role which cooperation must play in the international community, especially through the UN, is stressed. Regarding the environment, the status of UNEP is underlined. The idea that the Security Council should be

---

[83] ibid, p.343.

involved with environmental issues lends weight to the notion of their centrality in international affairs, especially with regard to peace and security. The seriousness of environmental issues is also reflected in the call for the 1992 Conference to be attended by Heads of State and Government. The intention of the former USSR to work with the major economic institutions of the world is critical in terms of environmental issues receiving global treatment, for many of their concerns, such as the rules governing trade, will have a great impact on the environment. It remains to be seen the extent to which the constituent parts of the Community of Independent States (CIS) inherits the new philosophy.

Shevardnadze expanded on this conception in some detail in November 1989, when he called for the formulation of an international strategy and a common system of law on environmental protection. He repeated Gorbachev's proposal made at the UNGA in December 1988 for the creation of an ecological fund under UN auspices. Resources should be forthcoming from the developed western states, and similarly those who have advanced technologies should share them with those who do not under favourable terms.[84] He also suggested that machinery for reducing military danger be used to prevent ecological danger. Here, he may have been thinking both of technology for information gathering, such as satellites, and also institutions such as verification procedures like those developed by the International Atomic Energy Authority (IAEA). Linking the environment and security once more, he suggested adding an ecological dimension to the 'open skies' concept, to cover the earth, sea and space. This concept had first been formulated by the Eisenhower administration in the 1950s. The idea had been that both military/political blocs should have access to the air space of the other bloc for observation purposes, without risking interference from its national defence forces. This was promulgated as a confidence-building measure for the superpowers. The idea was never adopted, but has reappeared at various intervals ever since, and especially over the last few years.

At the Global Forum held in Moscow in January 1990, as well as reiterating former proposals, Gorbachev made further proposals of a

---

[84]The article appeared in *Literaturnya Gazeta*, No.47, 22 November 1989, and is reported in 'Environmental Pollution in the USSR', *Background Brief*, Foreign and Commonwealth Office, London, July 1990, pp.4-5.
[85]See M.Gorbachev, 'Address to the Participants in the Global Forum on Environment and Development for Survival', *Soviet News*, 31 January, 1990.

substantive nature and offered a clear explanation of the new change in Soviet thinking on the environment.[85] He admitted that his country had only recently come to understand the importance of ecological problems, saying that the reason for this was that 'The war danger stood in our light'.[86] He acknowledged that perestroika had played a formative role in altering Soviet views on ecology. He stressed that the ecological crisis represented proof of the interdependence of the world, and that only a concerted international policy could avert catastrophe. He underlined Soviet support for the environmental protection policies of the UN, for the UNCED, and for the formulation of a binding code of international ecological ethics. He supported the idea of international laws to protect unique natural zones, such as Antarctica. He emphasised the need for technological cooperation on nature conservation and monitoring, and called for the exchange of 'ecologically clean technologies effectively accessible to all nations without any limitations and under the most-favoured-nations regime.'[87] He called for regular reporting by states on ecological accidents, and the limiting of military activities on ecological grounds as well as to reduce world tension. He promised that the USSR would allow inspections on its territory to ensure that the technology involved was not being misused. He suggested that 'ecological confidence-building measures could be based on the methods, procedures and instruments similar to those used in arms control.'[88] He called for the participation of individuals and groups in the drafting of ecological policies. The statement amounted to a revolution in Soviet thinking on the conduct of international cooperation.

Even though the USSR no longer exists, the attention given here to the Soviet position is necessary for several reasons. Firstly, Gorbachev was the prime mover in the second half of the 1980s in terms of raising environmental issues at the highest level of diplomatic discussion. Secondly, President Bush's vision of a new world order and hence the possible place of the environment within it, is not yet clear. Thirdly, information on the former USSR as compared with the US is very limited.

Gorbachev's stand represented a complete break with the Soviet past, and is all the more remarkable because of this. It also represented a

---

[86]ibid, p.33.
[87]ibid.p.34.
[88]ibid.

diplomatic victory of a sort. The US response was positive if cautious, but lacked the vigour of the Soviet representations. However, it must not be forgotten that the US had exhibited a far stronger commitment to environmental protection at the domestic level than the former USSR (even though environmental deregulation in the 1980s suggested that its progress in this regard was not linear).[89] It had also played an active role in international negotiations, such as on the ozone question,[90] and in bilateral negotiations such as with Canada over acid rain.[91] However, the new approach to security, based on the interdependence of actors in the world community and also of the sectors of economy, environment and security, had not gripped the imagination of the policymakers or academics in the US to the same extent as in the former USSR. Bush's vision of a new world order had yet to be fully expounded, but to date there has been no significant statement suggesting the interdependence of concerns or the elevation of the environment into a primary security issue in this vision. The ecological devastation of the Gulf War might have been expected to prompt a change of emphasis, but this has not happened.

In trying to assess whether environmental issues will remain on the international agenda of the world's most powerful states, it is useful to consider the circumstances under which a regime evolved to manage the threat of nuclear holocaust. Undoubtedly the biggest impetus for the acknowledgment of the deadly global threat and for the formulation of management techniques to deal responsibly with this came from the Cuban missile crisis in 1962 which brought the world to the brink of nuclear war. Starting with the hotline in 1963, a whole series of memoranda of understanding on how to deal with accidents, incidents at sea and so forth have been developed over the years. Even during the height of Reagan's 'evil empire' rhetoric and his increased defence budget in his first term of office, at lower levels of communication hotline updates were introduced. Joseph Nye believes that a nuclear regime has

---

[89] A.Cockburn, 'The Green Racket', *New Statesman and Society*, 13 April 1990, pp.22-3.
[90] See R.Benedick, *Ozone Diplomacy: New Directions in Safeguarding the Planet*, Harvard University Press, Cambridge, Mass., and London, 1991.
[91] For elucidation of the acid rain issue in North America, Europe and the developing world, see McCormick, *Acid Earth: The Global Threat of Acid Pollution*, Earthscan, London, 1989; and articles by Carroll, McMahon, Rosencranz and Persson in J.E.Carroll, (ed) *International Environmental Diplomacy*, CUP, 1988.

developed over the past three decades.[92] As conflictual situations have developed, cooperative policies and mechanisms for restraint have evolved out of perceived common interest.

If we regard this as a model, then the question facing us is what sort of near-catastrophe of an environmental sort could elicit this kind of cooperative management response? Unlike the nuclear example, where there have been two major players, the environmental example would require a genuinely multilateral response. There are indications that single issues, such as Chernobyl, awakened greater awareness and more enthusiasm for international institutions to set standards and verify compliance. However, on-going disasters, such as desertification, have elicited no effective institutional response. The problem now is how we can work towards institutional management to prevent further single issue disasters before they happen. To the extent that certain issues, such as CFCs and climate change, have been discussed - and in the case of CFCs, addressed - by the international community before scientific proof of their role was absolute, there is a degree of hope. To carry such action into all spheres of international environmental concern remains a challenge in the 1990s. While the former USSR remained intact, there was always the possibility that hitches on the arms reduction agenda of the superpowers, such as rumblings of US and UK dissatisfaction over the Soviet implementation of the CFE agreement and differences of opinion within the USSR itself concerning this, might undermine international efforts toward cooperation on environmental matters.[93] However, the superpowers did make small steps forward in terms of environmental cooperation before the disintegration of the USSR. In 1989 we witnessed the rekindling of a US/USSR agreement on environmental cooperation covering eleven areas of ecological enquiry, and in December 1988 the national science academies of the two countries formed a Committee on Global Ecology Concerns.[94] The break-up of the USSR throws the whole area into disarray, and adds great complexity to the process of negotiating arms reductions.

---

[92]J.Nye, 'Nuclear Learning and US-Soviet Security Regimes', *International Organization*, Vol.41, No.3, Summer 1987, pp.371-402.
[93]See, for example, H.Pick, 'West Warned of Red Army Trap', *The Guardian*, 21 March 1991. On Soviet differences of opinion, consider the resignation of Shevardnadze and his disagreement with the army over the implementation of the treaty.
[94]French, op.cit, p.29.

2.6 Other diplomatic fora

Aside from the superpower agenda, which is now in a state of transition due to the disintegration of the USSR, environmental issues have captured a place in the diplomacy of other international groupings. A few of the most noteworthy are mentioned here briefly. The interest in environment and development displayed by some of these groups may be more enduring than that exhibited in the superpower relationship. While the latter is critical, we must not loose sight of the fact that progress can be - and has been - made outside of that diplomatic arena.

It is in the context of the European Community (EC) that environmental concerns have been addressed in a serious, systematic and ongoing manner by a group of states. No mention was made of environment policy in the Treaty of Rome which established the EC in 1957. In 1972, however, a meeting of the Heads of State and Government decided that economic growth should be coupled with an improvement in the quality of life, and this necessitated environmental protection. Throughout the 1970s and 1980s the Community has set up an Environment Policy with the adoption of over 100 legislative acts relating to the environment. This was prompted by public pressure, the shock of disasters and the vigour of the European Commission.[95] Environmental protection was written into the Single European Act of 1986.[96] The achievements of the EC in the field of environmental policy have been rehearsed extensively elsewhere,[97] so we do not repeat them here. It is important to note, however, that EC agreements on large combustion plant can be seen as a beginning of regional environmental agreements.

The Non-Aligned movement has demonstrated a keen interest in environment/development affairs. While the efficacy of that group of states has been questioned, their declarations are indicative of their common ground. The closing declaration of the Ninth Conference of Heads of State or Government of Non-Aligned Countries, in September 1989, contained various paragraphs on the environment and

[95]S.Johnson and G.Corcelle, *The Environmental Policy of the European Communities*, Graham and Trotman, London, 1989, p.3.
[96]ibid, Chapter 17 for details.
[97]Johnson and Corcelle, ibid; also N.Haigh, *EEC Environmental Policy and Britain*, Longman, Essex, 1989.

development.[98] Global interdependence and the importance of cooperative multilateral efforts were stressed, as was the necessity of economic growth for the promotion of economic and environmental sustainability. New financial resources and the promotion of environmentally safe technologies were imperative. Many of the concerns outlined echo those expressed by Gorbachev and Shevardnadze. Clearly economic weakness provides a common backdrop.

Similar ideas are evident also in the discussions of the Commonwealth. In October 1989, the Heads of Government of the Commonwealth introduced their programme of action on the environment in the Langkawi Declaration.[99] The ten-point statement stressed the trans-boundary nature of the most pressing environmental concerns, the need for economic growth as a motor for sustainable development, and the importance of a coordinated, multilateral effort. Significantly, the connection between environment and development was stressed, as was equitable burden sharing of the responsibility for environmental improvement based on ability. It was emphasized too that the environment should not be used as reason to introduce new forms of conditionality in aid or to create unjustified barriers to trade, two real fears of the developing countries.

Environmental issues have won a place on the agenda of the Group of Seven (G7) industrialized western states whose leaders meet on an annual basis to discuss largely economic matters. At the 15th Annual Summit in July 1989, the leaders of Canada, France, Italy, Japan, UK, US and West Germany acknowledged that environmental threats deserve as much attention as economic threats.[100] However, while stating the potential usefulness of mechanisms such as the transfer of technology, debt-for-nature swaps and debt forgiveness, no concrete targets were set, and the fundamental connection between poverty and environmental

---

[98]'Environmental Action Needed', *Foreign Broadcast Information Service*, Daily Report, Supplement East Europe, 9th Non-Aligned Conference, 11 September 1989, p.42.

[99]'The Langkawi Declaration on the Environment', Commonwealth Heads of Government Meeting, Kuala Lumpur, Malaysia, 21 October 1989; issued by the Information Division, Commonwealth Secretariat, London, 23 October 1989.

[100]See Agence Internationale d'Information Pour La Presse, Summit of the Arch, Paris, 16 July 1989, 'Economic Declaration'. *Europe Documents*, No.1567/68, 18 July 1991, paras 33-51.

degradation in the poorer countries was not made. No radical suggestions were forthcoming. This pattern was repeated at the Houston Summit in July 1990.[101] There, the environment featured as one of three main topics for discussion (the other two being aid to the former USSR and international trade), but again tangible results were few. Major differences surfaced between the US and the Europeans, with the latter group wanting firm pledges to reduce greenhouse gas emissions.[102] At the London Summit in July 1991, interest in the environment again appeared to amount to talk and little action.[103] Moreover, environmentalists charged the summiteers with spending only 15 minutes on the subject of the environment. NGOs at The Other Economic Summit (or TOES), accused the G7 of:

> ... failure to address nine crucial issues: atmosphere and energy, species and habitats, water and oceans, transport, land-use, agriculture, waste, global relations and the public right to know.[104]

However, political developments in the USSR and eastern Europe diverted attention, and the lack of focus on the environment was hardly surprising: rather it demonstrated the continuing importance of traditional inter-state concerns.

While tangible results have been few, it is clear that the environment is an important enough topic in the minds of leaders of the G7 countries to warrant a place on the agenda for discussion. This at least is a step in the right direction.

Over the past few decades, various international groupings have come together to address specific environmental problems. Noteworthy here is the Geneva Convention of 1979 on transboundary atmospheric pollution.[105] This brought together countries of eastern and western Europe and the former USSR and USA. Also noteworthy is the 1975 Barcelona Convention on the Protection of the Mediterranean, in which both the Arab states and Israel participated as well as the other

---

[101]See Houston Economic Declaration, 11 July 1990, Houston, Texas.

[102]R.Suro, 'Ecology: Europe Faults US', *International Herald Tribune*, 11 July 1990.

[103]See 'G7 Economic Declaration: Building World Partnership', 17 July 1991, London Press Verbatim Service.

[104]*The Environment Digest*, July-August, 1991, No.49/50, p.8.

[105]See 'Geneva Convention on Long-Range Transboundary Air Pollution, 1979', in *United Nations Register of International Treaties and Other Agreements in the Field of the Environment*, UNEP, Nairobi, 1991, pp.163-168.

Mediterranean states.[106] Environmental concerns can stimulate diplomatic cooperation which in other political contexts would be unlikely.

Conclusions

Over the past two decades environmental concerns have won a place in local, national, regional and international political discourse. The huge upsurge in environmental awareness at the grassroots level has been facilitated by the intense mobilization activities of NGOs and green movements and parties, and by the dramatic impact of accidents and disasters on public opinion. At the level of intergovernmental agencies, UNEP has played a vital catalytic role in consciousness-raising throughout the UN system and beyond. As for the superpowers, the changing nature of their relationship created the political space for issues hitherto categorized as matters of 'low politics' to assume a more important role. Gorbachev, impelled by intense domestic economic difficulties, took advantage of the opportunity to promote internationally his new conception of global security in which environment, economy and disarmament were inextricably linked. Even more recently, however, the process of disintegration of the former USSR has focused political attention back on traditional security concerns.

It remains to be seen whether the momentum developed to date can be sustained in the 1990s or beyond into the next century. While the apparatus for tackling some environmental problems is in now in place, undoubtedly environmental problems themselves will pose increasingly difficult threats to traditional national security concerns. The strength of political commitment to international cooperation will certainly be tested. The fundamental environmental problem - the challenge of achieving sustainable development - has hardly begun to be addressed.

---

[106]'Barcelona Convention For the Protection of the Mediterranean Sea Against Pollution, 1975', *International Legal Materials*, Vol.XV, No.2, March 1976, pp.285-310.

The Environment on the International Economic Agenda

Over the past two decades concern has grown about the environmental implications of economic development. It has become clear that both poverty and wealth have adversely affected the environment: the former by degrading local renewable resources, and the latter by degrading global, non-renewable resources. The process of industrialization has taken place without due regard to environmental implications or sustainability. The same is true of modern agriculture, based as it is on intensive techniques. The structures of ownership and distribution have ensured the failure of such development to meet the basic needs of the world's poor and this has resulted in survival strategies that are environmentally destructive.

Concern about the environment on the international economic agenda reflects similar concern expressed on the political agenda. NGOs have played a central role in setting this agenda. Discussion has not only reached the corridors of international economic institutions such as the World Bank, but the environment is now also a factor in corporate strategy.

Among NGOs and independent analysts, there is a debate as to whether economic growth is required to pay for costly environmental protection or is a recipe for further environmental destruction.[1] At the diplomatic and policymaking level, however, the primacy of further growth is taken to be essential. This is the conventional wisdom also among academic and career economists. Their discussion concentrates on facilitating environmentally-friendly growth by the government imposition of a

---

[1]H.E.Daly, 'Free Trade, Sustainable Development and Growth: Some Serious Contradictions', *Network 92*, No.1, Centre for Our Common Future and IFC, Geneva.

price on environmentally-harmful activities. Standard-setting is the traditional regulatory mechanism; currently underway are explorations of international market-based methods of pricing the environment,[2] such as tradeable emissions permits.[3]

This chapter focuses primarily on the relationship between economic growth and development, and the environment on the post-World War II international economic agenda.[4] This is part of the larger relationship between the international economy and global environmental change. The chapter examines why the environment was ignored by the liberal international economic order. It highlights the formative role of the Brundtland Report in stimulating discussion of the relationship between economy and environment, and more particularly, promoting economic growth as a prerequisite of environmental protection and sustainable development. That report, while accepted by the majority of governments, has been criticized by some NGOs. An economic approach which attempts to translate the message of the Brundtland Report into economic policy is represented by David Pearce and his colleagues. Building on the work over the last two decades of resource economists, their emphasis is on market-oriented policies to encourage those who can most efficiently pursue an environmentally-friendly course. The chapter looks at what has been achieved at the policy level in greening multilateral aid, trade and investment. It examines the vital role of the World Bank, both as the most important multilateral development bank, and as a catalyst for policies in the regional development banks. New environmentally-orientated or relevant financial facilities such as the Global Environment Facility (GEF), and the European Bank for Reconstruction and Development (EBRD), are discussed, as is the problem of encouraging transnational corporations to act in an environmentally-benign manner. The chapter looks at the General Agreement on Tariffs and Trade (GATT), and at the immense importance

[2]See A.S.Blinder, *Hard Heads, Soft Hearts*, Chapter 5: 'Cleaning Up the Environment: Sometimes Cheaper is Better', Adison-Wesley, Reading, Mass. US, 1987; and J.Nicolaisen, A.Dean, and P.Hoeller 'Economics and the Environment: A Survey of Issues and Policy Options', *OECD Economic Studies*, No.16, Paris, spring 1991.

[3]For example, see M.Grubb, 'Global Policies for Global Problems: the Case of Climate Change', in T.Sterner (ed), *Economic Policies for Sustainable Development*, forthcoming 1992.

[4]For a brief survey, see *The Economist*, 'Costing the Earth: A Survey of the Environment', 2 September 1989.

- and immense difficulty - of reforming trade to be environmentally friendly. Throughout the chapter the crucial role of NGOs in extending the parameters of the international debate on economics and the environment is illustrated. The chapter concludes with an assessment of whether the attempts to green aid, investment and trade are adequate to meet the challenge of sustainability.

3.1 Post-World War II economic order: environmental ignorance

At the end of World War II, the slate was wiped clean for the drawing of a new international economic order. The US was the preponderant economic, political and military power amid international economic disarray, and was able to impose without too much difficulty the system of its choice.

During the war years, the US explored with the UK and other countries the shape that the forthcoming new world economic order might take. In 1944 negotiations at Bretton Woods in the US culminated in the drawing up of a new economic order which became known as the 'Bretton Woods' system.[5] This was built on neo-classical economic assumptions which marginalized environmental concerns.

This system had three fundamental pillars. Of these, two were institutional structures - the IMF[6] and the World Bank[7] - and one a regulatory mechanism for dealing with international trade, which became institutionalized by default in the GATT.[8] All three in their operations have demonstrated the environmental blindness of much post-war economic theory which assumes that the market maximizes

---

[5]For a general account of the establishment of this structure, see C.Thomas, *In Search of Security: The Third World in International Relations*, Wheatsheaf, Brighton, and Reinner, Colorado, 1987, especially Chapters 3 & 4.

[6]See *Articles of Agreement of the IMF*, IMF, Washington DC, 1978.

[7]See *Articles of Agreement of the International Bank for Reconstruction and Development*, World Bank, Washington DC, 1945; or Great Britain Treaty Series, No.21, 1946, Cmd.6885, HMSO.

[8]See *The General Agreement on Tariffs and Trade*, The UN Conference on Trade and Employment, Preparatory Committee, 2nd session, 30 October 1947, Geneva. Contracting Parties to the GATT, *Basic Instruments and Selected Documents 1955-1969*, appear in 4 volumes, Geneva, 1969. Supplements are published annually.

social welfare and generally produces socially desirable levels of consumption of natural resources.[9]

In accordance with the principles of economic liberalism, the IMF and the World Bank were seen as technical agencies which existed to facilitate the smooth functioning of the free market system. With an increasing number of former colonies as clients, the World Bank came to be viewed as a development agency making longer-term loans than the IMF. The free-market was seen as the motor of growth, and growth as synonymous with development. The GATT contribution was to liberalize trade by tariff-cutting. All this was to take on further significance as it became seen in the US as a 'key to a prosperous West and to Western security in the face of Soviet aggression'.[10] Since no value was attached to the environment, the ill-effects of exploitation were not considered. This was true both in terms of the direct use of the natural environment and finite resources by the primary commodity producers and industrialized countries; and also of the pollution of the global commons by the latter which went on unimpeded - even unnoticed by many.

The Bretton Woods system has not resulted in the enrichment of all countries. Prior to the late 1970s, the rate of industrial growth was higher in the developing world as a whole than in the developed capitalist countries taken as a group. Average per capita incomes in many developing countries were rising. Many of the poor countries exhibited an impressive economic performance. During the 1980s, however, there was a serious regression in much of the developing world, with tragic costs for hundreds of millions of people. The rich countries bear much responsibility for the severity of the crisis. Problems included indebtedness reaching crisis proportions in the 1980s and exacerbated by fluctuating interest rates; commodity price fluctuations wrecking development plans; declining terms of trade for primary commodity producers; uncertain markets for the goods of southern countries while the developed countries pursued protectionist policies; and insufficient financial and technological transfers to the developing world. In the first half of the 1980s, over half of developing countries experienced a

---

[9]G.Porter, and J.W.Brown, *Global Environmental Politics*, Westview Press, 1991, pp.26-32.
[10]J.Spero, *The Politics of International Economic Relations*, George Allen and Unwin, 1982, p.69.

declining per capita Gross Domestic Product (GDP). Over the whole decade, developing countries as a group faced a 10% decline in per capita GDP. The structural adjustment policies advocated by the IMF as a response to the grave economic circumstances in which so many developing countries found themselves put further strain directly and indirectly on the social, political and environmental fabric of those countries.[11]

In the context of rising populations, skewed land tenure and wealth distribution in the developing countries, environmental implications have been catastrophic. The same holds for the industrialized countries, which have pursued growth with little heed to pollution[12] and enjoyed massive consumption of finite resources. Slowly, an international consensus began to emerge recognizing the links between economics and the environment. In this chapter we concentrate on the relationship between environment and development.

3.2 Linking environment and development

The emerging consensus in the 1970s

The early 1970s saw a rise in the profile of environmental issues on the international economic agenda. In 1971, the UN-sponsored meeting of international development agencies and governments at Founex in Switzerland resulted in the first public statement linking environmental management and development policy.[13] Twenty-five guidelines were established aimed more at the developing countries than at the operations of donors.

Nineteen seventy-two was an important year. The Club of Rome published its report *Limits to Growth*,[14] which argued that the post war rate of global economic expansion could not be sustained otherwise natural resources would be exhausted and the environment irreparably

[11]See, for example, B.Onimade (ed), *The IMF, the World Bank and the African Debt*, Vols.1&2, Zed Press, London, 1989; and C.Thomas, 'New Directions in Strategy and Security in the Third World', in K.Booth (ed), *New Directions in Strategy and Security*, Harper Collins Academic, 1991.

[12]There had been interest in alleviating industrial pollution in industrialized countries, but this had been limited mostly to problems in specific countries or areas eg. the Clean Air Acts in the US, or regional policy on the North Sea.

[13]See 'Development and the Environment: the Founex Report', in *In Defence of the Earth: the Basic Texts on Environment* -Founex, Stockholm, Cocoyoc, UNEP, Executive Series 1, 1981, pp.1-38.

[14]D.Meadows, (Club of Rome), *Limits to Growth*, Earth Island, London, 1972.

damaged. While the conclusions of the report have been criticized, it did focus attention on a growing problem. Coupled with the Stockholm Conference,[15] the international economic community was beginning to recognize that most environmental problems in developing countries were linked with poverty and the nature of development, and that achieving development goals required the consideration of environmental concerns.

In 1974 the call for a New International Economic Order and the Charter of Rights and Duties of States at the UN General Assembly[16] raised the profile of some issues affecting the environment, such as sovereignty over natural resources and index-linking commodity prices to the price of manufactured goods.[17] The UN sponsorship of the Cocoyoc Symposium on Patterns of Resource Use, Environment and Development Strategies in 1974 acknowledged the connection between environment and development. The resulting Declaration suggested that low prices for commodities and natural resources stimulated overconsumption by the rich countries and depletion of the resources of the developing.[18] However, environment and development had still not been integrated at the operational level of multilateral institutions.

In 1979 a report[19] funded by UNEP and the Canadian International Development Agency suggested that the multilateral development agencies, particularly the World Bank as the most important and environmentally concerned, should improve their environmental analysis. The following year, the agencies singled out in the report committed themselves in the New York Declaration on Environmental Policies and Procedures Relating to Economic Development, to formulating environmental assessment procedures and to funding projects that protected the environment and the natural resource base. Also they formed the Committee of International Development Institutions on the Environment (CIDIE) as a forum for the exchange of information on environmental plans. At the UN, the General Assembly

---

[15]See back to Chapter 2, also, *In Defence of the Earth*, op.cit, pp.39-105, for deails of the Declaration emanating from the Stockholm Conference.
[16]*Yearbook of the Unites Nations 1974*,United Natons, New York, 1974.
[17]For a discussion of the demands, see C.Thomas, *New States, Sovereignty and Intervention*, Gower, Aldershot, and St. Martins Press, New York, 1985, Chapter 5.
[18]See 'The Cocoyoc Declaration' in *Defence of the Earth*, op.cit, pp.107-119.
[19]R.Stein, and B.Johnson, *Banking on the Biosphere?: Environmental Procedures and Practices of Nine Multilateral Development Agencies*, Lexington, 1979.

adopted the International Development Strategy for the Third UN Development Decade which identified the need to make development environmentally sustainable.[20]

The critical role of the NGOs in the early 1980s

Non-governmental organizations have been central in this raising of environmental consciousness. The World Bank has acknowledged their critical influence in redirecting its policies.[21] In the 1980s, the documentation of the adverse environmental impacts of development policies increased exponentially.[22] The large, capital-intensive projects of the World Bank and other multilateral development banks have caused severe problems especially in agriculture, energy, rural development and transportation,[23] but for several years there were no significant policy changes by these institutions. Rich has argued that, mindful of the limitations of ad-hoc protests to development banks, the NGOs have since 1983 developed a different approach:

> ... [which] has involved the building of a coalition that includes not only US environmental groups but European and Third World organizations as well. By winning the support of the political forces that influence the development banks, environmentalists have, in effect, let themselves in through the front door.[24]

Hence they concentrated their efforts on influencing the policies of the largest donor countries, notably the US, in the expectation that such donors would then press for changes at the banks.

---

[20]For the International Development Strategy of the 3rd UN Development Decade, which links development with environmental sustainablility, see *Yearbook of the United Nations 1980*, United Nations, New York, 1980, pp.503-519.

[21]See J.Warford, and R.Ackermann, 'Environment and Development: Implementing the World Bank's New Policies', *Development Committee*, Paper Seventeen, IMF/World Bank, Washington DC, June 1988.

[22]See for example, C.Payer, *The World Bank: A Critical Analysis*, Monthly Review Press, New York, 1982; also R.Ayres, *Banking on the Poor*, MIT Press, Cambridge, Mass, 1983.

[23]For a thorough yet succinct account of the adverse environmental impacts of multilateral development bank lending, see B.Rich, 'The Multilateral Development Banks, Environmental Policy, and the United States', *Ecology Law Quarterly*, Vol.12, December 1985, pp.681-745.

[24]P.Aufderheide, and B.Rich, 'Environmental Reform and the Multilateral Banks', *World Policy Journal*, 1989, pp.300-321, p.306.

Taking advantage of the fact that the development banks have no natural political constituency within any of the donor nations - no group, in other words, that is directly affected by the work of the banks - environmentalists, working with groups in developing and developed countries, built a constituency for greater public accountability on the part of the banks.[25]

In 1983 environmentalists testified before the US Congress (and subsequently before many subcommittees) on the links between environmental destruction and development bank funding. Rich argues that links with NGOs in developing countries have been critical to the credibility of western environmental lobby groups and hence to their success.[26] The effects on bank policy - especially the World Bank - has been pronounced.

The challenge of the Brundtland Report

Against this background, the time was ripe for an assessment of the problem of environment and development at the global level. The majority of national economies, the state of the natural environment, and the plight of the majority of the world's population had become critical. It was becoming clear that the severe recession experienced by much of the developing world in the 1980s had resulted in widespread environmental damage.

In 1983, the Secretary General of the UN called upon the former Prime Minister of Sweden, Gro Harlem Brundtland, to set up and to chair an independent commission to address the issue of environment and development. This followed two similar commissions: the Brandt Commission which had looked at North-South issues and produced a *Programme for Survival*,[27] and the Palme Commission, which had investigated security and disarmament issues and published its report on *Common Security*.[28]

The World Commission on Environment and Development produced a report, *Our Common Future*,[29] commonly referred to as the Brundtland

[25]ibid, p.308.
[26]ibid, pp.311-12.
[27]ICIDI, *North-South: A Programme for Survival*, Pan Books, London and Sydney, 1980.
[28]Independent Commission on Disarmament and Security Issues, *Common Security: A Programme for Disarmament Report*, Pan Books, London, 1982.
[29]WCED, *Our Common Future*, (henceforth Brundtland Report) OUP, Oxford and New York, 1987.

Report, which was presented to the UN General Assembly in 1987. The report is particularly significant for three reasons. Firstly, it linked environmental stresses with patterns of economic development and argued that environment and development had to be integrated in all countries. Secondly, it emphasized the centrality of continued economic growth for environmental protection. Thirdly, the report advocated the notion of sustainable development:

Sustainable development seeks to meet the needs and aspirations of the present without compromising the ability to meet those of the future. Far from requiring the cessation of economic growth, it recognizes that the problems of poverty and underdevelopment cannot be solved unless we have a new era of growth in which developing countries play a large role and reap large benefits.[30]

The concept of sustainable development,[31] popularized by the report, has become a central element in the environmental debate. As with most abstract concepts, the translation into practical policy is problematic, but certain requirements are clear from the report. Intra-generational equity, to give priority to the needs of the poor, is central, as is inter-generational equity. Both presuppose due attention to environmental protection. The level of technology and social organization limits the ability of the environment to meet present and future needs. Growth provides an essential underpinning for environmental protection and sustainable development. However, growth must become less material - and energy - intensive, more equitable in its impact, and be related realistically to the stock of capital that sustains it. Economic growth and social development should be mutually reinforcing.[32]

The report does not make specific policy recommendations. Rather, it examines the difficulties involved, argues for a more holistic approach to planning, and points out the general direction that it believes governments must take. The report emphasizes that there may be many routes to achieving sustainable development, but concludes that certain economic practices are definitely in need of reform, for example trade,

[30]ibid, p.40.

[31]The concept of sustainable development first achieved international attention with the publication of the World Conservation Strategy in 1980 by the IUCN. The emphasis of that document, however, was very much on conservation rather than economic development or a meshing of the two. See Chapter 2.

[32]Brundtland Report, op.cit, pp.52-4.

finance and aid. It makes a forceful case for multilateral cooperation on an untried scale:

> No country can develop in isolation from others. Hence the pursuit of sustainable development requires a new orientation in international relations ... The mechanics of increased international cooperation required to assure sustainable development will vary from sector to sector and in relation to particular institutions. But it is fundamental that the transition to sustainable development be managed jointly by all nations ... [the] report carries a message of hope. But it is hope conditioned upon the establishment of a new era of international cooperation based on the premiss that every human being - those here and those who are to come - has the right to life, and to a decent life.[33]

The report calls for the World Bank to play a vigorous leadership role for other funders to follow in generating policies geared towards sustainable development. There have been few critics. However, until the UNCED negotiations in 1992 there had been little real international debate about alternative ways forward. The discussions of governments and IGOs have focused not on whether to link, but how to link environmental protection with continued growth.

Some NGOs have entertained other scenarios. Notably, an alliance of Dutch environment, peace and developing country groups combined in the Alliance for Sustainable Development and produced their own report[34] in reaction to the Brundtland Report. While praising the Brundtland Report for providing much useful information and generating debate on the development/environment issue, the Alliance expressed grave doubts about the utility of the report for bringing about fundamental change. It questioned the validity of continued economic growth for tackling the core problems of poverty and inequality expressed in the distribution of power, land, resources and so forth. The Alliance rejected poverty as the cause of environmental destruction and rejects growth as its solution. It asserted that the increasing cultural homogeneity being promoted across the world will mean that sustainability cannot be achieved, for it depends on cultural diversity and

---

[33] ibid, pp.40-41.
[34] T.De La Court, *Beyond Brundtland: Green Development in the 1990s*, Zed, London, 1990.

the ability to adapt to specific local environments.[35] De La Court remarks that: 'development must come from within, and should not be imposed from outside.'[36] The Alliance argued that we must move away from the notion of growth with western standards of living as the goal. They recalled the words of Mahatma Gandhi, who, when asked whether he hoped to approximate Britain's standard of living for India, said:

It took Britain half the resources of the planet to achieve this prosperity; how many planets will a country like India require?[37]

3.3 The Pearce approach

The argument for continued growth as a prerequisite for environmental protection and sustainable development has been accepted by governments and public multilateral banking institutions. In this section we examine the economic approach to environmental issues which has generated most discussion in the UK: that of market-based instruments for the promotion of sustainable development, as popularized by David Pearce and his colleagues.[38] Drawing on the work of resource economists undertaken especially in the 1960s and 70s, but dating back even to Pigou in the 1920s,[39] Pearce suggests that economists internalize environmental costs in market-oriented economic policies. His approach is relevant to problems affecting both developed and developing countries. While Pearce's work is not entirely innovative, it has made, and continues to make, a big political impact in the UK for a number of

---

[35]ibid, p.25. Prof. Bob Rowthorn has drawn to the author's attention that the idea outlined here, that cultural homogenization undermines sustainability because the latter depends on cultural diversity in response to differing local environments, has a parallel in economics in the work of the Austrian school pioneered by von Mises and Hayek. They stress the importance of idiosyncratic (ie. personal or local) knowledge, which they use as a justification for free markets and against government intervention - on the grounds that the government cannot know what to do because it is not privy to the idiosyncratic behaviour of individuals and small groups.

[36]ibid, p.8.

[37]Cited by De La Court, ibid, p.15.

[38]For a US approach to the use of market mechanisms to draw together the requirements of economics, ecology and ethics, see H.Bormann and S.Kellert (eds), *Ecology, Economics, Ethics*, Yale University Press, New Haven and London, 1991.

[39]See A.Ulph, 'A Review of Books on Resource and Environmental Economics', *Bulletin of Economic Research*, 42, 1989; and P.Dasgupta, 'The Environment as a Commodity', *Oxford Review of Economic Policy*, Vol.6, No.1, Spring 1990; and D.Collard, D.Pearce, and D.Ulph, *Economics, Growth and Sustainable Environments*, Macmillan, London, 1987.

reasons. For example, he translates economic ideas into a form easily accessible to the interested public and policymakers; the publication of his work coincided with a resurgent interest in the environment; his suggestions were in tune with the free market philosophy of Mrs Thatcher's government. They were readily taken up for debate by a new Minister, Chris Patten, whose reputation could be enhanced by this 'new' set of ideas.

September 1989 saw the publication by Pearce et al[40] of a work, commissioned by the UK Department of the Environment, to consider whether there was a consensus to the meaning of the term 'sustainable development', and if so the implications for the measurement of economic progress and policy appraisal. The work received much publicity and stimulated debate.[41] It was followed in 1991 by *Blueprint 2*.[42]

The first book was concerned with a single economy and domestic environmental policy, but is very important to international discussion because it set out the basic ideas of the approach. It argued that:

... economics can and should come to the aid of environmental policy. Properly interpreted, economics provides a potentially powerful defence of conservation and a novel array of weapons for correcting environmental degradation. Moreover, it offers the prospect of doing it all rather more efficiently than the traditional approaches based on 'command and control'.[43]

The second book applies this theme to case studies of some global environmental problems, namely climate change, ozone depletion, tropical deforestation and natural resource depletion in the developing world.

---

[40]D.Pearce, A.Markandya, and E.Barbier, *Blueprint for a Green Economy*, Earthscan, London, 1989.
[41]See for example, J.Bowers, 'Economics of the Environment: the Conservationists Response to the Pearce Report', British Association of Nature Conservationists, 1990; and M.Jacobs, 'Sustainable Development: Greening the Economy', *Fabian Tract*, No.538, The Fabian Society, July 1990; and D.Helm and D.Pearce (eds), 'Economic Policy Towards the Environment', whole issue of *Oxford Review of Economic Policy*, Vol.6, No.1, Spring 1990.
[42]D.Pearce (ed), *Blueprint 2: Greening the World Economy*, Earthscan, London, 1991
[43]Pearce et al, op.cit, Preface.

Due to the controversy surrounding *Blueprint for a Green Economy*,[44] the central ideas of the book as explained by Pearce himself are summarized here.[45]

Sustainable development means the welfare of future generations is not damaged by current activities. This implies that future generations must be compensated for environmental damage which they inherit. Appropriate compensation is to leave the next generation an undiminished stock of capital assets - man-made and natural environmental - for it to use as it wishes. What they do with this productive potential is a matter for them. So long as the *total* of man-made and natural capital is kept *constant*, it does not matter if the balance between them varies. To ensure that we can measure and trade-off environmental assets, it is necessary to value environmental assets on a comparable basis to man-made assets. Failure to do so hitherto has resulted in environmental degradation and 'consumption' of the proceeds without suitable re-investment. Accordingly, if we take into account the high *value* of natural capital, the *uncertainty* surrounding its functions and benefits, and the *irreversible* nature of its elimination, there can be *no acceptable trade-off* of certain environmental assets termed '*critical capital*' which must be conserved by the *precautionary approach*.[46]

The economic policy *instruments* for securing sustainable development include *both the traditional 'standard-setting' regulations which Pearce et al refer to as 'command and control' and more innovative market-based instruments*. Examples of the latter include taxes on emissions and tradeable emissions permits and resource-use permits. Pearce argues that the market-based instruments are more effective guardians of the environment than the traditional regulatory controls for a number of reasons:

* they keep down the cost of compliance, in that the market determines that those who can most easily afford to act do so, and they deal with the total amount and the distribution of the problem

* they act as a continuous 'irritant' to the polluter, who therefore has a continuing incentive to avoid the cost by introducing cleaner technology

---

[44] See for example J.Adams, 'Unsustainable Economics', *International Environmental Affairs*, Vol.2, No.1, Winter 1990, pp.14-21; and Bowers, op.cit.
[45] See Pearce, 1991, op.cit, pp.1-3.
[46] ibid, p.2.

* the price of polluting products will tend to be higher than the price of clean products, and the consumer thereby encouraged to chose the latter

* environmental taxes can be used in a 'fiscally neutral' way to reduce other distorting taxes in the economy[47]

Pearce suggests changing measures of economic progress based on Gross National Product (GNP) which attributes a zero price to environmental assets. He argues for the construction of environmental and economic indicators which show the links between environment and economy in preference to costly attempts to adjust the national accounts which compute GNP. Finally, he argues that the use of 'cost-benefit' thinking would help conservation compete on equal terms with development.

Pearce argues that use of the economic approach with its market-based instruments as developed for a single economy is all the more important in the international context because of the potentially huge cost of protecting the global commons, such as the atmosphere or the oceans.[48] Moreover, this cost will have to be borne largely by the developed countries. They will also have to win the support of developing countries for tackling global problems. A transfer of new financial resources in addition to those already committed in aid will be a necessary - though not perhaps sufficient - condition for bringing those developing countries on board.

To expect developed countries to pay the vast sums required to protect the environment in conditions of no-growth is politically naive. There is a long way to go before the cost of greening will be acceptable to the average citizen. Therefore Pearce advocates:

... driving a 'wedge' between economic growth and the environment, a wedge that uncouples the economic growth process's impact on the environment. To put it another way: if we can alter the *ratio* of growth to environmental impact, we can afford to grow and generate the resources that are needed to alter the growth process in the developing world so that the same environmental mistakes are not made.[49]

---

[47] ibid, p.3.
[48] ibid, p.11.
[49] ibid, p.12.

Trade bans on certain commodities or prohibitions on exploitation of a specific natural resource may well not be observed. Pearce argues that what is required is an incentive system which serves a dual function: conservation of the natural resource and addressing the cause of the specific environmental degradation.[50]

The argument is applied to the ivory trade in Barbier et al.[51] A trade ban was recommended in 1989 by the Ivory Trade Review Group which called for an 'Appendix 1' listing by the Convention on International Trade in Endangered Species.[52] Barbier argued that a ban would not stop the trade, but push it further underground:

Like so many other international issues, the ivory trade is a 'game' in which there are many players, all with individual motives and concerns. Failure to capture those motives and concerns in an international agreement inevitably risks no agreement or its eventual breakdown.

Elsewhere, Pearce et al draw upon six developed country case studies to investigate why, despite reliable methods for economic valuation of the environment, such monetary assessments are rarely used in decisionmaking despite their centrality to a cost-benefit analysis.[53] They look at countries where such methods are being taken up, but with clear obstacles to their use, such as the UK, Italy and Norway, and others where they are used extensively, such as the US, Germany and the Netherlands. Obstacles include the higher priority assigned to non-environmental values, and the lack of governmental familiarity with environmental economics.

Elsewhere, drawing on six studies from the developing world, Pearce et al aim to 'give some structure to the concept of sustainable development and to illustrate ways in which environmental economics can be applied to the developing world.'[54]

---

[50]ibid, p.12.

[51]E.Barbier, J.Burgess, T.Swanson and D.Pearce, *Elephants, Economics and Ivory*, Earthscan, London, 1990, Preface.

[52]Discussion of the relative merits of outright bans versus limited trade has been taken up by other authors. For example, Colin Tudge has reviewed this dilemma with respect to the trade in rhino horn (C.Tudge, 'Can We End Rhino Poaching?', *New Scientist*, 5 October 1991, pp.34-9).

[53]J-P.Barde and D.Pearce (eds), *Valuing the Environment: Six Case Studies*, Earthscan, London, 1991.

[54]D.Pearce, E.Barbier and A.Markandya, *Sustainable Development: Economics and Environment in the Third World*, Earthscan, London, 1990.

Politically, the use of market instruments to meet the need for further growth, environmental protection and sustainable development is the emerging trend. Politicians are finally beginning to take on board an economics literature over twenty years old as to why such instruments might be a more effective way forward than the usual standard-setting controls.While in the UK, and to an extent in Europe, the popularizing of Pearce has been a stimulus for this, in the US a key development has been the Project 88 initiative which drew on the background of the Environmental Defence Fund in promoting tradeable permits, and culminated with the US Clean Air Act 1990 Amendments on Acid Rain. Indeed the Project 88 initiative brought market instruments more centrally to the policy debate in the US than even Pearce has done in the UK.[55]

3.4 Policy

Multilateral lending agencies

To what extent have environmental concerns entered the strategic planning and operations of multilateral lending agencies? Such organizations are extremely important in the evolving relationship between environment and economic development:

> The projects and policies of the banks have an impact on the ecological stability and environmental future of the developing world even greater than is indicated by the huge dollar amounts of their annual loan commitments. Funds lent by the banks are for the most part complemented by even greater sums provided by recipient countries, and the funding of many projects is further supplemented by cofinancing arrangements with other development agencies and with private banks. Thus, for every dollar the World Bank lends for a project, more than two additional dollars are raised from other sources; for the Inter-American bank, this cofinancing ratio approaches three to one. The influence of bank lending on

[55]This was drawn to the author's attention by Michael Grubb. See 'Project 88: Harnessing Market Forces to Protect our Environment', press coverage October 1988 - January 1991; and 'Project 88 - Round II: Designing Market-Based Environmental Strategies', Press Coverage May - September 1991. Project 88, the brainchild of Senators Tim Wirth of Colorado and John Heinz of Pennsylvania, made a case for market-based incentives as a cheaper, less intrusive alternative to traditional pollution regulation.

development policy is also magnified by the banks' funding of research, training, technology transfer, planning, and other forms of institutional support in host countries ... loan conditions and stipulations can be highly specific ... direct policy leverage is especially strong in structural adjustment and sector loans.[56]

If economic development and environmental protection are to be made compatible, not only must funding flow to specific environmental projects, but environmental considerations must be integrated into all aid projects which will require strict environmental assessment. Since the late 1980s, several multilateral and bilateral lenders have adopted such environmental criteria.

The formation of CIDIE in 1980 has already been noted. Its raison d'être was to help members establish effective environmental policies and procedures as integral parts of their development assistance procedures. Its Declaration of Principles commits members to minimize environmental damage resulting from their policies. By 1990 CIDIE, with its headquarters in Nairobi, had sixteen members. In June 1985, the European Community issued a Council Directive on the Assessment of the Effects of Certain Public and Private Projects on the Environment. In 1986, the OECD Council issued a Recommendation on Measures Required to facilitate the Environmental Assessment of Development Assistance Projects and Programmes. In October 1989, the World Bank issued an Operational Directive on Environmental Assessment, to standardize and formalize an environmental impact assessment process which it claimed was already being implemented on major projects. In June 1990, the International Finance Corporation (IFC), an arm of the World Bank, issued a Procedure for Environmental Review of projects to make sure that projects funded are consistent with the spirit and intent of World Bank guidelines.

The World Bank. The World Bank was heavily criticized by NGOs and independent analysts during the 1970s and 1980s for funding massive projects with detrimental environmental and human consequences, for example the Polonoroeste project in Brazil to open up the state of Rondonia, the Narmada Valley dam in India, and the transmigration project in Indonesia. The NGOs particularly condemned the lack of local consultation. NGOs are now looking at World Bank sectoral policies eg.

[56]Rich, 1985, op.cit, pp.635-7.

forestry[57] and energy. The critiques of Bank policy have been well rehearsed elsewhere.[58] How is the Bank responding?

The Brundtland Report admitted that the World Bank had become more sensitive to environmental concerns. In 1970 the Bank had created the post of Environmental Advisor. This was followed in 1973 by the inadequately resourced Office of Environmental Affairs, later renamed the Office of Environmental and Scientific Affairs, to review Bank projects for environmental impacts. In 1984, for the first time the Bank's Operations Manual included environmental concerns, although rendered ineffective by staff shortages. In the 1980s the Bank developed specific policies on issues such as involuntary resettlement (1980), tribal peoples (1982), and wildlands (1986). The Brundtland Report argued that even more fundamental structural and operational changes were needed to make sustainable development a core commitment,[59] as advocated for several years by the NGO community.[60] The Bank has responded.

The World Bank's role is to promote the economic development of member states by issuing loans at favourable interest rates to governments or to projects guaranteed by governments. Projects have to generate sufficient return to facilitate repayment. Given its terms of reference, it was difficult for the Bank to respond to pressure following the Stockholm Conference to take on board environmental issues.[61] Pressure continued to mount, fuelled by the serious effects of many Bank loans. By the end of the 1970s, the Bank was under pressure to introduce formal environmental assessment procedures from US groups which

---

[57]World Wide Fund for Nature, 'The World Bank's New Forestry Policy Brief', WWF International, Gland, Switzerland, 1990.

[58]Payer, op.cit; Ayres, op.cit; also P.Mosley, J.Harrigan and J.Toye, *Aid and Power: The World Bank and Policy-based Lending*, Vols.1&2, Routledge, London, 1991; and for a devastating attack on the structure and operations of the Bank and other multilateral organizations, see G.Hancock, *Lords of Poverty*, Mandarin, London, 1991.

[59]On the possibilities of incorporating the Report's recommendations into Bank policy, see J.Wettestad, 'Some Notes on the Implementation of the Brundtland Commission's Recommendations: The Case of the World Bank', *International Challenges*, Vol.7, No.3, 1987.

[60]See B.Rich, 1985, op.cit; also J.Wettestad, '"Ecological" Reform of the Multilateral Development Banks? A Summary of the Criticism Raised', *Newsletter*, The Fridtjof Nansen Institute, No.1, 1986.

[61]Institutional profile, 'The World Bank', *International Environmental Affairs*, Vol.2, No.1, Winter 1990, pp.92-4.

lobbied Congress for the US to exert its influence at the Bank.[62] In the 1980s, the crisis of development and of the environment worsened, with environmental stress aggravated by the need to earn foreign exchange for massive debt repayment from South to North. IMF lending conditions contributed to the crisis by undermining social provisions in the context of increasing need. The neo-classical economic assumptions behind structural adjustment packages meant that the environmental cost was ignored.

The breakthrough came in April 1987, when the joint Development Committee of the World Bank and the IMF, having considered a World Bank paper,[63] and aware of the Brundtland Report findings (to be published in the same month) stressed the importance of protecting the environment while pursuing economic growth and development. This became part of World Bank, though not IMF, policy.

Environment, Growth and Development was the first of three key papers setting out evolving Bank policy concerning the integration of environmental factors into economic development policy. It argued that:

Promoting growth, alleviating poverty, and protecting the environment are mutually supportive objectives in the long run. Rather than address environmental issues in isolation, decisionmakers in governments and international institutions should consider the preservation of the environment along with other issues central to the formulation of development policy. In so doing, they should take maximum advantage of the complementarities in order to help the poor, promote better resource management, and contribute to sustainable development. In the short run, however, the objectives are not always compatible, and decisionmakers often confront difficult choices in pursuing them simultaneously. It is important to consider the implications of competing claims and to determine the approaches that will help achieve the most appropriate balance.[64]

The paper acknowledges the lessons of past projects: the necessity of satisfying the multiple criteria of sustainable growth, poverty alleviation and environmental management, and of approaching projects not in

---

[62] ibid, p.94

[63] J. Warford, 'Environment, Growth and Development', *Development Committee*, Paper Fourteen, IMF/World Bank, Washington DC, 1987.

[64] ibid, p.5.

isolation but rather as part of general economic policy. Thus, the paper argues for:

... general policy instruments to influence the behaviour of natural resource users in ways that are environmentally benign and conducive to sustainable development ... Economic incentives, backed by investment programs and wide-ranging regulatory and institutional mechanisms, are indispensable for achieving major improvements in the way development activities influence the environment.[65]

The paper ends with an Agenda for Action to address environmental and economic objectives in individual countries and to achieve unprecedented levels of cooperation among development agencies. The Bank commits itself to raising policymakers' awareness of the importance of integrating natural resource management into country economic planning, to supporting studies of the economic, institutional and cultural constraints on the efficient management of natural resources, and to help design policy instruments to overcome those constraints. It pledges to expand cooperation with NGOs.

A review of the second major Bank paper, 'Environment and Development: Implementing the World Bank's New Policies',[66] which took account of the Brundtland Report, led the joint Development Committee of the World Bank and the IMF to conclude that growth, development and environment must henceforth be regarded as interrelated concepts and operational objectives, and to note a close link between environmental degradation and poverty. This paper set out organizational and operational changes designed to integrate environmental considerations into the Bank's work and identified key environmental issues which it linked to poverty and population growth.

In 1987 the Bank created a central Environment Department and four regional environmental offices to promote and monitor the environmental aspects of the Bank's activities. The regional offices, employing about thirty people, focused on the environmental impacts of projects and on identification of more general tasks. The role of the Environment Department, with around thirty staff members and consultants, was policy and research in technical, economic and social areas, the establishment and maintenance of information systems and data bases, the provision of conceptual guidance or specialized expertise

[65]ibid, p.16.
[66]Warford and Ackermann, op.cit.

for the regional offices, and training and education of Bank staff. The Bank recognized a need to involve external consultants and other institutions and bilateral agencies in making up its own shortage of skills in areas such as ecology, anthropology and sociology.

One of the most important decisions of the Bank has been to draw up general environmental issues papers on every borrowing country in line with the Brundtland recommendation that environmental management be integrated into development planning. In addition, in-depth national environmental action plans are being undertaken.[67] These will emphasize the strengthening of policies and institutions.[68] In certain instances, interrelated regional environmental issues are being analyzed, often with the involvement of other agencies. For example, the Environmental Program for the Mediterranean is being undertaken by the World Bank, the European Investment Bank (EIB), UNEP, and individual Mediterranean countries. Environmental concerns are being integrated into the Bank's lending and policy dialogue.[69] The project review process is being expanded to ensure, as requested by the Brundtland Report, consideration of ecological and behaviourial consequences of development projects. The Bank's Economic Development Institute is also developing new training material on the environment for Bank staff.

The second paper acknowledges the critical role of NGOs in the evolution of Bank environmental policy and advocates closer collaboration. This is being achieved,[70] and accords with the Brundtland argument for involving local communities in the design and

---

[67] See F.Falloux, L.Talbot and J.Larson, 'National Environmental Action Plans in Africa: Progress and Next Steps', AFTEN, World Bank, Washington DC, June 1991; and *National Environmental Action Plans in Africa*, Proceedings from a Workshop Organized by the government of Ireland, the Environmental Institute, University College, Dublin, and the World Bank, Dublin, 12-14 December, 1990.

[68] See 'Country Capacity to Conduct Environmental Assessments in Sub-Saharan Africa', *Environmental Assessment Working Paper*, No.1, Environment Division, Africa Region, World Bank, Washington DC, February 1991.

[69] For a thorough exposition of how environmental assessment has developed, see The Environment Department, *Environmental Assessment Sourcebook Vol.1: Policies, Procedures, and Cross-Sectoral Issues*, the World Bank, Washington DC, 1991; also *Vol.2: Environmental Assessment: Sectoral Guidelines*, 1991.

[70] 'Local Participation in Environmental Assessments of Projects', *Environmental Assessment Working Paper*, No.2, Environment Division, Africa Region, World Bank, Washington DC, March 1991.

implementation of projects that affect them. Resident representatives of
the Bank are asked to foster links with local NGOs (with government
agreement), and an Operations Manual statement on work with NGOs
is in hand. A Bank-NGO Committee is already operational, and links are
developing with key international NGOs such as the WWF, IUCN and
the World Resources Institute (WRI).

The Environment Department of the Bank has created
multidisciplinary task forces to assess the significance of global
environmental issues (including deforestation, conservation of
biological diversity, watershed degradation, desertification, salinity,
inappropriate pesticide use, industrial disasters, urban environmental
issues and global climate change), and their relevance to specific
countries. The Bank, in line with the Brundtland Report, accepts the need
for policy responses to these problems. The Bank has also initiated policy
work on the environmental and resource management consequences of
agricultural pricing policies. There is also a review of the extent to which
cultural and political factors, dominant institutions and the legal position
of women result in resource management problems and slower than
expected agricultural development. Work is underway in 1992 on the
integration of environmental and natural resource concerns into national
accounts.[71]

The second Bank paper foresees the necessity for harsh trade-offs
between economic and environmental objectives, particularly in
developing countries where survival rather than growth may be the
immediate problem, rendering environmental protection politically
difficult. The Bank agrees with the Brundtland Report that concessional
finance and creative financing mechanisms (eg. debt-for-nature swaps)
are imperative.

The third Bank paper was presented to the joint Development
Committee of the Bank and the IMF in September 1989.[72] It outlined
the Bank's increasing environmental concern and its efforts to heighten

---

[71] See A.Harrison, 'Environmental Issues and the SNA', *Review of Income and Wealth*,
Series 35, No.4, December 1989; see also S.El Serafy and E.Lutz, 'Environmental and
Natural Resource Accounting', in G.Schramm and J.Warford (eds), *Environmental
Management and Economic Development*, The World Bank/John Hopkins University
Press, 1989.
[72] J.Warford and Z.Partow, 'World Bank Support for the Environment: A Progress
Report', *Development Committee*, Paper Twenty-two, World Bank, Washington DC,
September 1989.

public awareness of this. The paper set out the operational procedures (such as environmental issues papers and environmental action plans) anticipated in the second paper. It maintained that over one-third of projects approved in 1989 contained significant environmental components.

The paper argued for more integration of environmental concerns into country economic and sector work. Assessment work needed to extend beyond individual projects to the environmental impacts of adjustment and other economic policy interventions. The paper argues that generalizations on the effect of structural adjustment are difficult, since 'apparently identical loan conditions may have dramatically different impacts in different countries'.[73] Nevertheless, the paper cites adjustment lending in 1989 to Gambia, Guinea-Bissau, Ghana and Laos to suggest that structural reform has great potential for achieving environmental objectives.

While acknowledging progress made by the Bank, the third paper highlights several fundamental issues not yet fully addressed: firstly, valuing the environment; secondly, the macroeconomic importance of environmental problems, and integrating the environment in national accounts; thirdly, expanding the Bank's role in identifying the causes and remedies of environmental degradation to the fundamental and politically sensitive areas of the distribution of land, wealth and power; fourth, the Bank needs to expand public awareness of its environmental role and to strengthen its links with NGOs. In short, the task of integrating environmental and economic management has only just begun.

The paper ends with an agenda for the next three years. This includes an intensification of efforts in formulating environmental guidelines, increasing lending for environmental and related projects (eg. population), integrating environmental concerns at all levels of Bank economic activity, expanding staff training, promoting environmental assessment methodology, and improving public awareness of the Bank's activities, all requiring extra resources.

A significant development since the third paper is the Bank's Operational Directive on Environmental Assessment.[74] Prepared in consultation with borrowers, it codifies an existing process for Bank

---

[73] ibid, p.24.

[74] World Bank, Operational Directive 4.00, Annex A: Environmental Assessment, October 31, 1989.

projects and aims to help borrowers build the capacity to tackle environmental policy issues, including by strengthening local institutions and coordination. However, the directive needs to be extended to the country level to permit rigorous assessment of the relationship between macroeconomic policy and the environment. This directive should provide an example for other multilateral lenders.

The Bank has developed a formal environmental policy on dams and reservoirs,[75] and updated the 1981 policy on tribal peoples.[76] Since 1990 it has published, at the request of the joint Development Committee, an annual report,[77] which covers the Bank's environmental strategy, policy and research, environmental lending operations, special funding arrangements, and relations with the international community. This provides a useful annex of all environmentally-significant projects approved in the fiscal year.

The public image of the Bank was dealt a major blow in February 1992 with the row over the leaked comments of Lawrence Summers, its Chief Economist.[78] In an internal memo, he suggested that it made economic sense to relocate polluting industries to the developing countries. While he has claimed that the memo was written tongue in cheek to provoke discussion within the organization, the leak has done the Bank much harm. Many senior economists in other international organizations have been quick to defend their profession and to critique the economic argument of Summers.[79]

Although the World Bank is attempting to address the environmental aspect of development, the changes may be slower and less fundamental than many would like, and the commitment of some of its most senior staff is questionable. Given the propensity in any bureaucracy for inertia and infighting, it is laudable that changes are occurring at all. Many major

---

[75]R.Goodland, 'The World Bank's New Policy on the Environmental Aspects of Dam and Reservoir Projects', *International Environmental Affairs*, Vol.2, No.2, Spring 1990.

[76]See J.W.Clay, 'World Bank Policy on Tribal People: Application to Africa', *AFTEN Technical Note*, No.16, World Bank, Washington DC, July 1991.

[77]*The World Bank and the Environment*, First Annual Report, Fiscal Year 1990, Washington DC, 1990.

[78]*The Economist*, 8 February 1992.

[79]For example, Jagdish Bhagwati, economic advisor to the director-general, GATT, Geneva.

NGOs now have a constructive dialogue with the Bank, which has recognized their dynamic role.[80]

The Bank's example has been taken up elsewhere.[81] The Asian Development Bank (AsDB), the African Development Bank (AfDB) and the Inter-American Development Bank (IDB) have all expressed their intention to take environmental issues on board. However, it will first be necessary for them to face the huge and expensive tasks of training staff in the environmental effects of economic development, developing institutional capacity in this respect within the banks themselves, increasing awareness within the respective regions and facilitating the development of institutional capacity for environmental assessment within member states. The AsDB is actively developing links with regional NGOs and this is something that the other development banks could benefit from.

In contrast, the European Investment Bank (EIB) has extensive resources, and operates in a region with established national and regional environmental regulations. It adopted environmental impact assessment in the mid-1980s and its technical advisers receive special environmental assessment training in order to integrate environmental concerns into the appraisal procedure.

The Global Environment Facility (GEF). The Brundtland Report recommended the establishment of a special conservation banking facility to be attached to the World Bank,[82] to provide loans and joint financing for the protection of critical habitats and ecosystems. A three-year experimental facility, the GEF[83] created in February 1991, goes some way to answer this call. It operates out of the administrative structure of the World Bank and is being managed by three sponsoring

[80]See for example M.Cernea, 'Nongovernmental organizations and Local Development', *Discussion Paper*, No.40, World Bank, 1988.

[81]See OECD/J.Wheeler, *Development Co-operation: Efforts and Policies of the Members of the Development Assistance Committee*, 1990 Report, OECD, Paris, December 1990, pp.94-7.

[82]Brundtland Report, op.cit, p.338.

[83]For a background discussion, see The World Bank, *Funding for the Global Environment*, Discussion Paper, World Bank, Washington DC, February 1990. For a thorough overview of the establishment, institutional arrangements and operations of the GEF, see GEF, *Chairman's Report to the Participants Meeting to Discuss the Global Environment Facility*, Vols.1&2, GEF, World Bank, April 1991.

agencies: the World Bank, the UNDP and UNEP.[84] It aims to provide concessionary rate funding for projects in developing countries with global benefits, thereby effecting a real transfer of resources from North to South. David Reed of WWF International comments that:

> With the creation of the GEF, the international community approaches a new threshold of collaboration in addressing the growing environmental problems that threaten the ecological balance of the planet.[85]

The GEF involves collaboration between UN agencies, public multilateral development banks, governments of developing and developed countries, and NGOs and is currently composed of two main facilities (the Ozone Layer Protection Trust Fund or OTF, established by signatories to the Montreal Protocol, and the Global Environment Trust Fund or GET, covering greenhouse emissions, waterway protection and biodiversity). Donor governments have committed US$1.5 billion and further facilities will be established as new global conventions are signed. The first project to be financed from the GEF aims to rescue and upgrade vast forest lands in eastern Europe affected by air pollution.[86]

The involvement of NGOs is interesting. Subject to host government approval, NGOs can submit project funding proposals to the GEF. Some, including the WWF, have already done so. However, notwithstanding their endorsement of the GEF, NGOs want to see it committed to sustainable development.[87] Of the NGOs, the WWF's GEF analysis has been the most thorough to date. Its recommendations covered particularly the institutional and policy framework within which the GEF will operate.

The WWF has criticized 'the failure of international financial institutions to integrate adequate environmental protection into their projects and policies'.[88] Hence, Reed suggests that fundamentally the

[84]For a breakdown of responsibilities, see World Bank Press Release, 'Global Environment Facility prepares to Launch First Projects', Bank News release No. 91/S30, World Bank, Washington DC, 2 May 1991.

[85]D.Reed, 'The Global Environment Facility: Sharing Responsibility for the Biosphere', Multilateral Development Bank Program, WWF International, Gland, Switzerland, 1991, p.1.

[86]T.Land, 'Environment Project in Poland', *Nature*, Vol.355, 13 February 1992, p.580.

[87]For example, see discussion by N.K.Dubash, 'Financial Mechanisms for Technology Transfer under a Climate Convention', *Climate Action Network Discussion Paper*, Climate Action Network, Brussels, 1991.

[88]Reed, op.cit, p.13.

WWF's concern was that the GEF, which represented only 2% of World Bank lending, should help stimulate the incorporation of environmental concerns into all lending by all multilateral development banks, and not be seen as the main facility to address environmental issues.[89]

Unless the investments of the World Bank and other development agencies strike a better balance between development of man-made capital and natural capital, they will continue to compromise the long-term economic opportunities of many countries while further aggravating the global environmental crisis.[90]

In addition, the WWF would like to see the GEF establish an evaluation function to assess the cost effectiveness in environmental terms of the financial transfers, including consideration of any conflict between Bank incentive structures and those of recipients and of the GEF's success in promoting more sustainable resource use. Reed says of this:

... the evaluation function must have a direct intersection with development operations and assumptions of the Bank's normal lending. Otherwise, the GEF risks becoming an environmental palliative that allows the World Bank to continue to apply its present methods of economic analysis and to pursue its development strategies without modification.[91]

The WWF recommended that for adequate assessment, external actors such as NGOs must be involved.

The WWF also advocated publication of all GEF information. The confidentiality between the World Bank and its clients has contributed, in Reed's opinion, to serious environmental damage, and full local participation and full accountability are required. Navroz Dubash of the Environmental Defense Fund has complained about GEF secrecy.[92] Many NGOs consider that the setting up of the Scientific and Technical Advisory Panel (STAP), while an improvement in this respect,[93] does not go far enough. Dubash argues for greater accountability to be built

---

[89]N.Dubash, 'The GEF Debate', *ECO*, 16 September 1991, p.2.

[90]Reed, op.cit, p.14.

[91]Reed, op.cit, p.15.

[92]Dubash, op.cit, p.2.

[93]On the establishment of STAP, see GEF Press Release, 'Scientific Panel for Global Environment Facility Established', World Bank, Washington DC, 1 May 1991. See also the First Report of the STAP Chairman, GEF Participants' Meeting, GEF, World Bank, Washington DC, 1-2 May, 1991.

into the Fund's governance structure. Contributors meet twice a year to discuss overall policy, but project approval is left to GEF management and then the World Bank. Some member states, such as the Netherlands speaking on behalf of the EC,[94] supported this view. Others, such as India, Malaysia and Nigeria, voiced stronger criticisms about undemocratic and secretive decisionmaking.[95] They have called for funding mechanisms to tackle problems such as climate change to be established outside of GEF.

The WWF argued for Primary Environmental Care (PEC), namely that any GEF activity affecting local communities must allow community members a role in the decisionmaking. Failing this, their cooperation is put at risk, thereby contributing to project failure.[96]

The GEF is a step forward, but there are serious problems associated with it. On the positive side, resources are transferred from the developed to the developing countries in order that the latter may avoid the mistakes of the former. However, these transfers are still only a fraction of what is required; individual projects are small and a disproportionately large amount of resources is taken up managing disbursements. A real commitment to the promotion of sustainable development and to cleaning up the global environment would need to involve an effort commensurate with the Marshall Plan after World War II. Maurice Strong, head of UNCED or Earth Summit as it is frequently called, said at the fourth prepcom in New York in February 1992 that it would cost $125 billion a year to clean up pollution and protect natural resources. A commitment by the major donors of 1% of GDP would meet this target.[97] Chatterjee has estimated from press briefings that the rich countries have suggested that $6 billion might be forthcoming.[98] Nevertheless, the GEF does suggest that the developed countries are beginning to take the environmental crisis, and their role in creating and off-setting it,

---

[94]ECO Reporter, 'GEF Guidelines Criticized', *ECO*, 18 September 1991, No.8, Vol.LXXVIII.

[95]Cited by ibid.

[96]For a list of conditions fostering success in Primary Environmental Care, see Reed, op.cit, pp.17-18.

[97]See 'UNCED: World Environmental Problems Costed', *The Environment Digest*, February 1992, No.56, p.15.

[98]P.Chatterjee, 'Who Pays for the Earth Summit?', *New Scientist*, 11 April 1992, pp.13-14.

seriously. In order to be effective, GEF must evolve in response to the environmental debate.

At the fourth UNCED prepcom, the question of additional finance and how it should be disbursed was central; the meeting achieved little.[99] The developing countries have little confidence in the GEF, which they see as being too much under the control of the World Bank and the richer countries. Assembled under the loose coalition of developing countries known as the Group of 77, they have followed the lead of China, which is not a member of their group, and called for any new funds resulting from the UNCED process to be channelled through a new facility or facilities independent of the World Bank and more democratic in its functioning,[100] and with interests in environmental issues beyond those of concern mainly to the developed countries.

There is evidence that the GEF is evolving to meet some of these criticisms. For example, it is expected to increase the number of developing country participants in its twice-yearly meetings from the current nine. (Seventeen donor states dominate proceedings to date). NGOs have been invited to meet GEF managers before these meetings, but the first such meeting in December 1991 was deemed a failure by Mohammed Al-Ashry, GEF's chairman. Nevertheless, the role of the GEF is evolving: in April 1992 it was to discuss broadening its concerns to include desertification and land-based pollution.[101]

The European Bank for Reconstruction and Development (EBRD). The EBRD is intended to help the development of the private sector in the former centrally-planned states of central and eastern Europe. In contrast to the World Bank, the EBRD can be seen as an investment bank and will be project-driven, lending mainly to the private sector to help the transition to market-oriented economies.

The Articles of Agreement were signed by 40 countries, the Commission of the European Communities and the European Investment Bank on 29 May 1990. The Bank was inaugurated on 15 April 1991, and has now begun business from its London headquarters. The Articles commit the Bank to 'promote in the full range of its activities

---

[99] ibid.

[100] See Inter Press Service Report, 'Third World Suspicious of Green Fund in World Bank', *Third World Resurgence*, No.14/15, October-November 1991, p.28.

[101] Chatterjee, op.cit, p.13.

environmentally sound and sustainable development'.[102] Yet the Chairman's Report,[103] attached to the Articles, while acknowledging the critical need to restore the natural resource base in the borrowing countries, suggests that funding for this environmental purpose must come from other bilateral and multilateral agencies such as the World Bank. However, the EBRD can finance environmental infrastructure needs which promote private sector development and the transition to a market-oriented economy. Moreover, the Articles of Agreement require the publication of an annual report on the environmental impact of the Bank's loans. The Bank's own publicity material states that:

> The European bank will devote substantial resources to developing significant expertise in environmental rehabilitation and to promoting environmentally sound and sustainable projects.[104]

It seems likely that the interests of the Bank will evolve with experience, and that in this context the central importance of the environment to economic growth will become clearer. The focus of the Bank's concerns may well change to accommodate this realization. More information on the state of the environment will feed into policy. Certainly the former Communist countries face serious environmental problems, but the idea that their environments have been severely and comprehensively degraded has been challenged recently.[105] In its statement of intent,[106] the Bank maintains that as its understanding and experience of its countries of operations develop and as circumstances change over the months ahead, so this initial document will have to be revised. In the list of challenges, the environmental challenge is noted last, even though it is maintained that:

---

[102]Article 2 (vii), EBRD, 'Agreement Establishing the EBRD', in EBRD, *Basic Documents of the European Bank for Reconstruction and Development*, London, 1991.
[103]'Chairman's Report', ibid.
[104]Press Department, 'The European Bank for Reconstruction and Development Brochure', EBRD, London, April 1991.
[105]G.A.Hughes, in *Oxford Economic Policy Review*, January 1992. Hughes claims that the extent of environmental degradation does not seem to be significantly worse than it was in western Europe 15-20 years ago. The suggestion is that the situation has been exaggerated by western journalists and by local people caught up with the past failings of their countries.
[106]EBRD, 'Operational Challenges and Priorities: Initial Orientations', EBRD, London, April, 1991.

Environmental deterioration in the countries of central and Eastern Europe has reached such alarming proportions that economic growth and the maintenance of the social fabric depend on restoring the environment. Even the most basic conditions of production - access to such fundamental resources as uncontaminated water, land and air - can no longer be taken for granted ... Major environmental policy improvements and direct restorative investments are prerequisites for the successful transition to a market-oriented economy.[107]

The statement of intent specifies environmental rehabilitation as one of seven areas to which the Bank will give initial emphasis in its support. Environmental management is claimed to be at the forefront of the Bank's operations to promote sustainable economic growth,[108] and this will be pursued largely through infrastructure projects, assistance in environmental policy formulation and help in the development of an environmental goods and services industry. The Bank is also committed to regional programmes addressing transboundary pollution in Europe. It is already involved in the Baltic Sea Task Force.

The EBRD is only just in 1992 beginning to take shape. Thus much of the debate surrounding it relates to how it should function rather than how it is functioning. In this context the NGOs again are playing an important role, documenting environmental pros and cons associated with other lenders to the private sector, such as the IFC and the EDB, and making suggestions as to how the EBRD can learn from their experiences and play a formative role in addressing the environmental degradation which is seen as a major obstacle to growth.

The WWF International published an informative document on the potential shape the EBRD might take as it evolves.[109] Some of its main recommendations are outlined here. As an investment bank operating in countries with severely degraded environments, the EBRD, WWF International argued, has a special responsibility for using its lending operations to restore the region's natural resource base. First, the Bank must ensure that efforts to broaden the private sector do not aggravate the environmental degradation begun under centrally-planned

[107]ibid, p.11.
[108]ibid, p.15-16.
[109]D.Reed, 'The European Bank for Reconstruction and Development: An Environmental Opportunity', WWF International, Gland, Switzerland, October 1990.

economies.[110] Thus, rigorous assessment and monitoring of all loans is paramount, and should include funds lent on through intermediary lenders (the latter is very difficult to achieve). Secondly, the Bank should actively encourage economic activities aimed at restoring the natural environment.[111] This should include the development of environmental goods and services industries in countries receiving financial support, and financial support - even concessional funding - for environmental infrastructure projects and other environmental purposes. A Special Fund should be set up providing grants and concessional loans.

To facilitate the achievement of the above goals, the WWF made certain managerial recommendations. Firstly, the EBRD needs to support multilateral efforts to help the governments of recipient countries set up environmental regulatory and monitoring mechanisms for their respective countries and transborder projects. Secondly, the Bank must employ sufficient staff qualified to undertake all necessary environmental reviews, planning, monitoring and assessment. Third, the Bank should adopt a proactive environmental stance, from which would emanate such policies as concessional funding through a Special Fund, strengthening the environmental services and products in recipient countries, promoting environmental restoration strategies, and environmental training activities.[112] It remains to be seen how much of WWF International's analysis is taken on board.

It is far too early to judge the performance of the Bank, but it is certainly the case that if it is to meet the challenge of promoting economic growth via the private sector, then, given the environmental degradation in the region, environmental concerns will have to figure high on its list of priorities. It does not yet appear to be central to the Bank's thinking that economic growth itself is predicated upon environmental improvement. However, the announcement in February 1992, of a series of guidelines to ensure that environmental priorities are incorporated into every project which the Bank supports, indicates that it is taking the environment seriously and its policies are evolving.[113]

---

[110]ibid, p.1.

[111]ibid, p.1.

[112]ibid, pp.1-2; 19-21.

Transnational corporations

The Brundtland Report recognized the importance of ensuring that transnational investment is undertaken in an environmentally sensitive manner.[114] TNCs are an important motor of growth in the developed and developing economies, and they supply foreign exchange, technology and managerial skills. In the context of developing countries, TNCs play a key role particularly in the mining and manufacturing sectors, and they dominate the world trade in primary commodities. If, as the Brundtland Report suggests, further growth is a necessary condition of environmental protection, then it is imperative that the activities of TNCs are regulated in an appropriate manner. The report calls for international measures to regulate their behaviour:

> Transnationals can have a substantial impact on the environment and resources of other countries and on the global commons. Both the home and host countries of TNCs share responsibilities and should work together to strengthen policies in this sphere. For example, information on policies and standards applied to and followed by corporations when investing in their own home country, especially concerning hazardous technologies, should be provided to host countries. Moreover, the policies of some industrialized countries that major investments are subject to prior environmental assessment should be considered for application to investments made elsewhere and should be broadened to include sustainability criteria. The information and recommendations thus arrived at should be shared with the host countries, which of course would retain the final responsibility.[115]

The role of TNCs in spreading technology has far reaching environmental implications. To develop sustainably, it is imperative that all parts of the world have access to clean, efficient technology. If the cost is prohibitive, developing countries will not adopt it, and their industrialization will pollute the atmosphere just as that of the developed countries has done. Brundtland argued that we must fight against the situation where patents and proprietary rights make the cost of sustainable development prohibitive.

---

[113]*The Environment Digest*, February 1992, No.56, p.7.

[114]Brundtland Report, op.cit, p.85-7.

[115]ibid, p.86.

Brundtland called for the drawing up of codes of conduct internationally between industry, governments and NGOs.[116] Various documents have appeared in response to this, and here we consider two: that drawn up by the United Nations Centre on Transnational Corporations (UNCTC), entitled 'Criteria for Sustainable Development Management'[117] and the International Chamber of Commerce's (ICC) 'Business Charter for Sustainable Development: Principles for Environmental Management'.[118]

UNCTC initiative. The UNCTC was requested by the ECOSOC at its July 1989 session to draw up criteria aimed at enhancing the involvement of large industrial enterprises in environmental protection. The UNCTC presented these criteria to ECOSOC at its July 1990 session. Peter Hansen, the Executive Director of UNCTC, believes that the criteria are essential, given the central role played by TNCs in global production and the development of new products, technologies and markets:

> The importance of transnational corporations is seen in that they affect one quarter of the world's productive assets; 70% of the products of international trade; 80% of the world's land cultivated for export crops, and the major share of the world's technological innovations.[119]

Hansen also argued that a balanced relationship between business and the natural environment must be developed, a relationship that contributes to sustainable development by maintaining economic growth whilst simultaneously reducing environmental risk and over-exploitation of resources. Industry must accept responsibility for environmental protection.

The aim of the criteria was to shift management perspectives from the traditional, short-term, profit-oriented business-as-usual approach to an attitude in line with the long-term requirements of sustainable development. In order for this to be so, management decisions and strategy must be informed by a valuation of the costs of resource depletion and environmental destruction, so that nature's capital is not

---

[116]ibid, p.329.
[117]UNCTC, 'Criteria for Sustainable Development Management', New York, 1991.
[118]ICC, 'The Business Charter for Sustainable Development: Principles for Environmental Management', International Chamber of Commerce, Paris, April 1991.
[119]UNCTC, op.cit, Preface.

eroded. Corporate executives must extend their vision not only over time but also over space, and concern themselves with the effects of their activities beyond the factory gates locally, nationally and internationally. Uncertainty about the environmental effects of products should not be taken as an excuse to do nothing; the precautionary principle should be adopted. Natural resources must be used in an environmentally efficient manner, with waste reduced to the bare minimum. Appropriate technology that is nature-sparing or nature-enhancing must be transferred. Diversification of productive activities around the world must be encouraged to coax countries away from excessive reliance on, for example, monoculture or over-exploitation of non-renewable resources. Corporate practices must not threaten species diversity or indigenous cultures; rather they should promote bio-diversity and socio-diversity. There should be more corporate investment in poorer parts of the world to generate employment and training opportunities. Sustainable development management requires environmental auditing and performance assessment on a continuous basis. Environmental advantages and disadvantages of a TNC's operations should be made public, and managers must follow the path of participatory learning, meeting with members of the government, community groups and environmental groups frequently.

Having outlined these general principles, the UNCTC document then suggested ten simple steps which corporations might take to begin the process of moving their activities into line with environmentally-sustainable development. First, they should devise and publish a transnational corporate sustainable development policy statement incorporating sustainable growth, environmental protection, resource use, worker safety and accident prevention. Second, they should review strategic planning, resource acquisition plans, and operating procedures to align them with the sustainable development policy. Third, they should review and modify corporate structure, lines of responsibility and internal reporting mechanisms to reflect sustainable development policy. Fourth, staff should be educated on how the goal of sustainable development affects their firm, and use rewards as incentives for employee interest in environmental aspects of operations. Fifth, sustainable development assessments should be prepared on all investments under consideration. Sixth, environmental audits should be undertaken of all activities in progress. Seventh, public reports should be issued on hazardous products, processes and toxic emissions. Eighth, research and development of environmentally-friendly technologies should be undertaken to reduce emissions of greenhouse gases. Ninth, joint venture partners and subcontractors should be made aware of the corporate sustainable development policy, and business with firms which choose to disregard the policy should be curtailed. Tenth, these criteria should be disseminated as widely as possible to other firms or affiliated companies. With all the above criteria, special care should be taken to ensure their application to overseas affiliates, and to make available guidelines in the language of the country concerned.

ICC initiative. The Business Charter for Sustainable Development drawn up by the ICC reflects many concerns similar to those outlined in the UNCTC document. Its aim was to provide a voluntary set of guidelines to 'assist enterprises in fulfilling their commitment to environmental stewardship in a comprehensive fashion'.[120] As such it provides a framework for action by individual companies. The Charter was formally launched at the Second World Industry Conference on Environmental Management, April 1991 in Rotterdam. (The first World Industry Conference on Environmental Management - WICEM - took place in 1984). It is based on the belief that there is a common goal between economic development and environmental protection, and that business provides the driving force for sustainable economic development and for the provision of managerial, technical and financial resources to help address environmental challenges. It is therefore seen to be imperative that as many businesses as possible commit themselves to bringing their management practices and operational procedures into line with the requirement of improved environmental performance in an atmosphere of openness and accountability.

Sixteen principles are outlined, and they all mirror the corporate steps of the UNCTC document. First, environmental management must be recognized as one of the highest corporate priorities, and second, in recognition of this, policies for sound environmental management must be incorporated into all management functions. The rest of the criteria are supportive of these goals. For example, the development and operation of activities and facilities at home and abroad should be consistent with efficient use of energy and raw materials, and safe disposal of waste, undertaken in the spirit of the precautionary principle.

---

[120]ICC, op.cit, Foreword.

Also the Charter calls for the promotion of employee and customer environmental and safety education, and the undertaking of environmental impact assessments before beginning new projects and prior to winding up old ones. Environmental audits are called for, along with public reporting and technology transfer. Contractors should be required to adopt the practices set out by the corporation.

The ICC publishes a list of companies and national business organizations which have expressed support for the Charter. At the end of May 1991, this stood at 242 companies from a wide variety of countries, mostly, though not exclusively, from the industrialized west. By the middle of August 1991, there were a further 107 additions to the list.[121] While there may be a world of difference between publicly lending support to the Charter and acting on its principles, public acknowledgment is an important first step to implementation. For it becomes harder for companies to ignore the Charter when they have made a public commitment to it and are likely to come under the critical scrutiny of NGOs and the media.

Some businesses have been taking environmental concerns seriously for decades. For example, environmental technology and protection became big business, especially in the US and Japan, in the 1960s and 1970s. The difference now is that some businesses are beginning to take sustainability concerns seriously.[122] In March 1992, the ICC agreed with UNEP to set up a panel to review progress of the 16-point voluntary code.[123] This is a sign that greater scrutiny of business is on the way.

The NGO response. The NGO response to these initiatives has been supportive yet cautious. They await a detailed programme for global implementation of the directives of the two documents. The IUCN, the WWF and the WRI have all applauded the principles of the Business Charter, and look forward to seeing compliance by companies.[124] In the

---

[121] See ICC, 'The Business Charter for Sustainable Development: Supporting Companies and National Business Organizations', Special Update for the Environment Nordic Seas Conference, Stavanger, Norway, August 1991, International Chamber of Commerce, Paris.

[122] For example, see M.Brown, 'Clean, But Not Quite Green', *The Times*, 5 November 1991, p.30; and J.Hill, 'Industry Inches Towards Green Goals', in a special report on the environment, *The Independent*, 10 September 1991.

[123] Chatterjee, 11 April, op.cit, p.14.

[124] See ICC, 'The Business Charter for Sustainable Development: Messages from International Organizations', Publication 210/356C, ICC, Paris, 1991.

meantime, they continue to campaign for a more open dialogue with industry and to encourage companies to adopt the best environmental practices available. They direct their efforts on a practical basis to bringing about specific changes. To illustrate this we look briefly here at the issue of eco-labelling.

NGOs believe that consumers should be given the full information about product history from cradle to grave so that they can make informed choices about which goods to buy. Recent years have seen the rise of the 'green consumer',[125] with many people in the richer countries choosing to purchase goods which they believe have been developed and marketed in the least environmentally-harmful manner. This has resulted in some manufacturers introducing labelling, whose sole purpose is to promote sales, which suggests a degree of environmental sensitivity which their product may not enjoy. Such misleading labelling has led to calls for eco-labelling by consumer groups, the European Commission and several national parliaments. The NGO community has been at the forefront of trying to shape legislation before it is enacted. Noteworthy here are the efforts of the WWF to influence the European Parliament in September 1991.[126] While the WWF welcomes the proposal to introduce eco-labelling, it advocates far more stringent standards than those suggested by the Commission. For example, the WWF calls for a mandatory four-step system to assess the environmental impact of all products before they are awarded a label. This should include standard-setting, monitoring to check that the standards are met, tracing products from cradle to grave, and certifying products by an independent panel or commission. Until companies act in an environmentally-friendly manner out of choice or because of legislative standards, this type of NGO input into the policy debate is crucial. We have already seen how effective NGOs have been in influencing policy in other fora such as the World Bank.

Trade: the challenge ahead
While the relationship between trade and the environment has barely been addressed multilaterally in GATT, its significance has not escaped

[125]See for example J.Elkington, and J.Hailes, *The Green Consumer Guide*, Victor Gollancz Ltd, London 1988.
[126]WWF, 'Eco-labelling', Memorandum of Evidence to the European Parliament, September 1991.

the attention of independent commentators, NGOs, and governments.[127] It has been remarked that:

> ... for most of the world, trade practices determine the scale and character of resource exploitation. This in turn greatly affects the environmental crises facing the planet, including global warming, ozone depletion, acid rain, deforestation and desertification.[128]

The Brundtland Report recognized that trade practices would have to be harmonized with environmental concerns if sustainable development is to stand any chance of being implemented. Since GATT is the most important trading arrangement, covering 90% of world trade between around 100 countries, it is logical that attempts to put trade on a more sustainable footing start with reform of GATT.[129] The Brundtland Report suggested that GATT would have to change to:

> ... reflect concern for the impacts of trading patterns on the environment, and the need for more effective instruments to integrate environment and development concerns into international trading arrangements.[130]

This was reiterated by many countries at the Bergen Conference on the Brundtland Report in May 1990,[131] where it was concluded that international bodies such as GATT should ensure the right of all countries to protect the environment and conserve natural resources within GATT rules.[132] Thirty-four developed countries signed the Bergen Declaration on sustainable development, and agreed to:

> ... accelerate in ... GATT ... the dialogue on the interlinkages between environmental and trade policies. The dialogue should focus on, inter alia, the role of international trade in promoting sustainable

---

[127] For a useful study of trade, the environment and public policy, see K.Anderson and R.Blackhurst (eds), *The Greening of World Trade Issues*, Harvester Wheatsheaf, 1992
[128] C.Hines, 'Green Protectionism: Halting the Four Horsemen of the Free Trade Apocalypse', Earth Resources Research, London, December 1990, p.6.
[129] See S.Shrybman, 'International Trade and the Environment: An Environmental Assessment of the GATT', *The Ecologist*, Vol.20, No.1, Jan/Feb 1990, p.30.
[130] Brundtland Report, op.cit, p.84.
[131] L.Starke, *Signs of Hope*, OUP, Oxford and New York, 1990, Chapter 8.
[132] Cited in NGO's release, 'General Accord', 15 September 1990.

development and how to ensure that trade does not bring about harmful environmental consequences.[133]

The commitment of the developed countries as expressed at Bergen has not been translated into positive action in the Uruguay Round[134] of trade negotiations in progress in early 1992. Environmental protection as a goal has not been on the Uruguay agenda.[135] Raghavan has pointed out that in these negotiations,which are to set the rules of trade for many years to come, the competing nature of the claims of environment and trade liberalization are all too clear.[136] On the one hand, for developing countries, environmental protection implies sustainable development, which means that the demand for resources has to be managed and there must be restrictions on trade. On the other hand, the Uruguay Round has been aimed specifically at removing restrictions. Over the spring of 1992, the position moved very quickly to a recognition that, once past the Uruguay Round, the next round will need to be more environmentally oriented. Indeed in early March 1992, in response to environmental critiques, the GATT secretariat published a study on trade and the environment as part of the International Trade Report.[137]

If environment and trade are to be harmonized, then the structure and rules governing trade must be re-examined with a view to fundamental reform.

NGO proposals for the reform of GATT. One of the most important challenges facing the international community is the reform of the GATT to take into account the effects of trade on the environment.[138] The raison

---

[133]See *Action for a Common Future*, Report on the Regional Conference at Ministerial Level on the follow-up to the report of the World Commission on Environment and Development in the ECE region, (Bergen Declaration), 8-16 May 1990, Bergen, Norway, pp.12-14.

[134]On the Uruguay Round, see C.Raghavan, *Recolonisation: GATT, the Uruguay Round and the Third World*, Third World Network, Penang, and Earthscan, London, 1990. See also M.Khor Kok Peng, 'The Uruguay Round and the Third World', *The Ecologist*, Vol.20, No.6, Nov/Dec 1990, pp.208-213; and in the same edition of *The Ecologist*, C.Raghavan, 'Recolonisation: GATT in its Historical Context', pp.205-207.

[135]See W.Bown, 'Trade Deals a Blow to the Environment', *New Scientist*, 10 November 1990.

[136]Raghavan, quoted in Bown, ibid, p.21.

[137]GATT, 'Trade and the Environment', in *International Trade 1990-91*, GATT, Geneva, March 1992.

[138]For a thorough critique, see C.Arden-Clarke, 'The GATT, Environmental Protection and Sustainable Development', *WWF Discussion Paper*, Gland, Switzerland, June 1991.

d'être of GATT is to work towards the greatest possible liberalization of trade, and this is to be achieved by working towards the removal of barriers to trade between countries. If the natural environment is not costed, then the environmental effects of different methods of production of goods for trade are not taken into account. This means that a government which allows, for example, the unsustainable production of timber, is in fact providing a form of subsidy compared with a government which insists on more expensive but sustainable forms of production. The idea of subsidy runs counter to the GATT ethos. However, until the environment figures as a cost in GATT methods of accounting, then countries will continue to be penalized for protecting the environment rather than rewarded for it. Their goods suffer a disadvantage in the market place because their production has been more expensive.

GATT has never received the public attention and criticism that the World Bank and the IMF have been exposed to. However, environmental and developmental NGOs became aware of the adverse implications of the Uruguay negotiations only once they were underway,[139] and indeed of the general structure of trading relationships as regulated by GATT.

The delay in finalizing the Uruguay Round, scheduled for December 1990 but still in progress in early 1992, presented the NGOs with an opportunity to canvass governments, publics and the GATT Director-General, and to raise general awareness of the failure of GATT to take environmental considerations into account. They argued that this failure demonstrated that GATT is out of touch with the popular sentiments that built up during the 1980s in support of extraordinary measures to protect the environment. It has failed to take note of the Brundtland Report's advocacy that trade relations cannot be separated from environmental concerns, and that sustainability is the yardstick by which these relations should be judged. International environmental law has been developing at a rapid pace, and international institutions like the World Bank have taken environmental factors on board. NGOs argued that GATT should follow suit.

---

[139]For example, see *The Ecologist*, Special edition on GATT, Vol.20, No.6, November/December 1990. See also M.Ritchie, 'The Environmental Implications of the GATT Negotiations', Institute for Agriculture and Trade Policy, Minneapolis, USA, June 1990.

In July 1991, a group of NGOs representing environmental, development and consumer health groups, sent a letter to Mr Arthur Dunkel, Director-General of the GATT, expressing their concern at the direction of the Uruguay Round negotiations, the general structure of trading relationships as advocated by GATT and the adverse environmental effects of specific policies. They made four specific environmental recommendations, plus others indirectly related to the environment.[140]

Firstly, they urged him to begin the process of integrating environmental concerns into the GATT through discussions at the 1992 UNCED.[141] This would at least make GATT more in tune with the recommendations of Brundtland, the goal of sustainable development and trends in other international institutions like the World Bank.

Secondly, they proposed an amendment of the GATT so that the treaty does not infringe either on existing or future international environmental agreements, or on national efforts to raise environmental standards. One of the main problems with GATT from an environmental viewpoint is that it can be seen to lower standards in the name of free trade rather than raise them. Article I rules out discrimination between trading partners. Articles III and XVI, by forbidding the use of trade subsidies or restrictions for environmental purposes, mean that GATT fails to acknowledge the legitimacy of trade restrictions in the pursuit of sustainable development.

There has been a debate as to whether, under Article XX of the GATT agreement, trade measures can legitimately be taken for environmental protection purposes. This Article allows contracting parties to place health, safety or domestic resource conservation goals above non-discrimination in certain specific circumstances. However, when Indonesia on the basis of such criteria banned the export, though not the felling, of raw logs and rattan from its rainforests in 1985, the EC tried to prohibit its action through recourse to GATT rules. The EC attempted to overturn the Indonesian ban by arguing that the real motive behind the ban was to restrict the supply of raw materials to third parties so that Indonesia could develop the manufacture of more value-added products

---

[140]I.Linden, 'Letter to Mr Dunkel', *Catholic Institute for International Relations*, London, July 1991.
[141]For a damning critique of how trade issues have been presented at the UNCED prepcoms, see Daly, op.cit.

for export eg. furniture. The EC argued that the action contravened Article 1 of GATT which says that foreign and domestic industry must be treated equally. Hines argues that even if the real motives of the Indonesian government were commercial, the effect of the ban has been to slow down the destruction of the Indonesian rainforest. In contrast, Hines argues that GATT is already being used in ways which destroy the rainforest rather than protect it.[142] In another example, Japan has objected to a ban on the export of logs from the ancient forests of the northwest US, complaining that this unfairly reduces the supply of wood to Japan. GATT is already being used to take authority away from national governments for setting environmental standards.

While the GATT allows some scope for domestic protection of exhaustible national natural resources,[143] it does not allow for extra-territorial protection by embargoes or other means which go against the free trade ethos. A report of the GATT dispute panel, convened to investigate Mexico's complaint that the US embargo on the import of 'dolphin safe' tuna was illegal under GATT rules, caused a furore internationally and also within the US, where the interests of environmentalists were seen to be in direct conflict with the advocates of unfettered free trade. The Bush Administration appeared divided.[144] After a three-week hearing behind closed doors, the panel ruled that a US law banning the import of yellow-fish tuna from Mexico was contrary to the rules of international trade. Originally the ban had been imposed to prevent the deaths of dolphins who swim above the tuna and get caught in the Mexican drift nets. The ruling confirmed that if there is no visible difference in the product, countries cannot dictate via trade restrictions preferences concerning how the product is produced. The reason is that this would open up a huge can of definitional worms, and create opportunities for the abuse of environmental criteria as a facade for discriminating to protect domestic industry. In other words, GATT allows countries to impose *product standards*, but not *process standards*. The March 1992 GATT study on trade and the environment, referred to above, states specifically that a country may not restrict imports of a

---

[142]Hines, op.cit, p.7.

[143]Arden-Clarke, June 1991, op.cit, p.22, for past examples such as the dispute in 1987 between the US and Canada over the latter's prohibition of the export of unprocessed herring and pink and sockeye salmon.

[144]For initial coverage of the dispute panel's decision, see J.Vidal, 'Global Conservation threatened as GATT Declares War', *The Guardian*, 6 September 1991.

product just because it originates in a country whose environmental policies are different.

Charles Arden-Clarke of WWF International suggested that the panel ruling could have potentially catastrophic consequences for the environment.[145] This is because it set two legal precedents. Firstly, it decided that a signatory to the GATT could not take trade measures to protect wildlife or natural resources outside its legal jurisdiction ie. outside of the territory of the state itself. Moreover, he argued that the ruling appears to open the way for non-signatories or misbehaving signatories to use the GATT against trade restrictions designed to have extraterritorial conservation effects. Secondly, the panel ruled that no country could restrict imports on account of their method of production. Yet as he argued, 'the ability to do this is of crucial importance if sustainable, environmentally-friendly methods of production are to gain ground around the world'.[146] The implication is that a trade measure designed to discriminate between, for example, tropical timber that is sustainably or unsustainably produced can be challenged under GATT rules. In other words, environmental costs remain externalized. The central problem according to Arden-Clarke, is that 'the GATT rules are interpreted as if trade liberalization is the only objective that matters'.[147]

He suggests that even the process of dispute settlement within GATT is essentially flawed, since environmental impacts of policies are ignored, as are the effects on legislation which is designed to protect the environment. NGOs fear that GATT can now be used to challenge and overturn much existing domestic and international environmental legislation.

The panel decision prompted US Senator Max Baucus, Chairman of the Senate's international trade sub-committee, to call for the creation of an Environmental Code in GATT.[148] He proposed that this code should be in force until such a time as an international agreement setting environmental standards is negotiated - which, he admitted, could be decades away. He said that the code would correct 'an obvious deficiency' in GATT which puts trade law above environmental

---

[145]C.Arden-Clarke, 'The Cruel Trade-Off', *The Guardian*, 13 September 1991, p.29.
[146]ibid.
[147]ibid.
[148]N.Dunne, 'US call for a GATT Code on the Environment', *Financial Times*, 18 September 1991.

considerations. Referring to the dispute panel's decision, he commented that while this:

> ... may accurately reflect the current provisions of the GATT ... this is an argument for changing the GATT, not for ending our efforts to protect dolphins.[149]

Under the proposed code, each country should be allowed to set its own environmental protection standards, and failure of imports to meet these standards could result in the imposition of punitive duties. For this to operate, three conditions must be fulfilled: the environmental standards must have a solid scientific basis; they should be applied to all competitive domestic production; the imported products must be causing economic injury to competitive domestic production.[150] Baucus argued that such a code would encourage US competitors to adopt higher environmental standards so as to avoid punitive duties as their goods entered the US market. He also recommended that each country be allowed to impose trade sanctions to enforce international environmental agreements, and called for the establishment of GATT panels to settle environmental code disputes.[151]

Attitudes in the US diverge sharply over the issue of trade sanctions as a conservation weapon. For many their efficacy is apparent from the recent Japanese decision, taken in the wake of trade sanction threats under the US Pelly amendment,[152] to stop importing the shell of the endangered hawksbill turtle.[153] For the environmentalists, such trade

---

[149]Cited in ibid.

[150]Cited in ibid.

[151]Baucus statement, 'Baucus wants GATT Environmental Talks', and B.Odessey, (USIA Staff Writer), 'Senator Proposes GATT Environment Code, Sanctions: Baucus Seeks Commitment to Negotiations', United States Information Service, first week of November, 1991.

[152]The Fishermen's Protective Act of 1967 was amended (The Pelly Amendment), 22 U.S.C. 1978 (a) (2) thus:

> When the Secretary of Commerce or the Secretary of the Interior finds that nationals of a foreign country, directly or indirectly, are engaging in trade or taking which diminishes the effectiveness of any international program for endangered species, the Secretary making such finding shall certify such fact to the President.

The President, on receiving such certification, may direct the Secretary of the Treasury to prohibit the importation of fish or wildlife products from the offending country.

[153]In March, 1991, Secretary of the Interior Manuel Lujan and Secretary of Commerce Robert Mosbacher certified to the President under the Pelly Amendment that Japanese trade in sea turtles severely diminishes the effectiveness of CITES. Therefore the US Government had negotiations with its Japanese counterpart, and allowed a 30 day period

sanctions are a legitimate policy option, while for the free-traders they are illegitimate. Opinion within the Bush Administration is divided. While the US put up a defence against the Mexican complaint over tuna, some people felt that the US did not fight the case hard enough due to a vested interest in having a negative outcome which it could itself use against many other trading partners in different circumstances. Yet on other issues the Administration is lending its support to the environmentalists. For example, on 1 August 1991, the US Senate passed the 'Drift Net Moratorium Enforcement Act' as part of an effort to implement UNGA Resolution 44-225, approved 22 December 1989.[154] That Resolution had called for an immediate cessation to further expansion of large-scale driftnet fishing, and for a June 30, 1992, moratorium on the use of large-scale driftnets beyond the exclusive economic zone of any country. The US Act required a prohibition on imports of fish from countries ignoring the UN ban. Along similar lines, the US has warned Canada that the latter could face trade sanctions if Inuit Indians are allowed to resume bowhead whaling in the Arctic without the permission of the International Whaling Commission.[155] Clearly the recent GATT ruling, if upheld by the GATT General Council, could make such trade policies illegal.

The third NGO environmental proposal to GATT's Director-General was that international treaties on environmental resource management should take precedence over the GATT. If this were to occur then many of the problems outlined above would be avoided. Gatt could not be invoked to undermine international environmental agreements such as the Montreal Protocol (see Chapter 6).

In addition, the NGOs urged the Director-General to ensure that a final agreement on liberalization measures in the Uruguay Round is not implemented in advance of a comprehensive assessment of its possible

---

to assess whether Japan had taken measures to stop the trade before the US would take measures to ban imports of wildlife from Japan. Japan agreed that there would be no further imports after 1992, and the threat of US trade sanctions was lifted. See USIS, 'Message to Congress from President Bush: Actions Regarding Japan's Trade in Certain Sea Turtles', EPF303, 22 May 1991; and J.Stilkind, (USIA Staff Writer), USIS, 'Japan to Reduce Turtle Imports, Avoids US Sanctions', ECO303, 19 June 1991.

[154]I.Guest, 'Drifting To War', *The Guardian*, 13 September 1991, p. 29. See USIS for Bill Text, S.884, 102d Congress, 1st Session, S.884, 'An Act to Require the President to Impose Economic Sanctions Against Countries that Fail to Eliminate Large-Scale Driftnet Fishing, or the Driftnet Moratorium Enforcement Act of 1991'.

[155]ibid.

impact on environmental and natural resources. Indeed, Arden-Clarke calls for an immediate audit of GATT's environmental impact and says that this should be used as the basis for reform of GATT.[156]

In their letter the NGOs also made recommendations on consumer health, and some of these have a direct bearing on environmental concerns. Noteworthy here is the criticism voiced at the intention in the Uruguay Round to introduce global harmonization of pesticide laws.[157] The proposal, put forward by the US, would 'harmonize' international standards for food safety by using international standards such as the FAO-derived Codex Alimentarius (Food Code) for determining if a pesticide residue standard is really a trade barrier in disguise. This issue gets to the heart of the question of what level of authority should set environmental, health and safety standards: local or national government, international institutions, chemical companies or citizen's groups. The agency Codex is composed of government officials, and executives from chemical and food companies often participate. NGOs do not have a voice there. Under the harmonization proposal, Codex would have the final say in judging scientific evidence concerning food safety worldwide. Many NGOs complain that this would be undemocratic.

The harmonization proposal has caused alarm amongst health and environmental NGOs in the US in particular. In their national context, if implemented, harmonization could result in a lowering of standards.[158] This is because the Codex is in many cases weaker than the standards set by the US Food and Drug Administration (FDA) or Environmental Protection Agency (EPA). Also, if a state within the US tried to impose a stricter standard than that laid down in Codex, GATT might judge it guilty of protectionism. Thus there would be pressure from the US Federal government to make states such as California, renowned for their high standards, conform to the international standards so as to avoid retaliation from US trading partners.

The problem is not merely academic. Some chemicals banned in the US are not banned under Codex. Anne Lindsay, Director of Pesticides

---

[156]Arden-Clarke, June 1991 and September 1991, op.cit.
[157]M.Ritchie, 'Trading Away Our Environment', The Institute for Agriculture and Trade Policy, and National Toxics Campaign Fund, Minneapolis, May 1990.
[158]Friends of the Earth Release, 'GATT Threatens to Trade Away US Standards in the Name of "Harmonization"', FOE, Washington DC, 24 May, 1990.

Registration at the EPA estimates that 16% of the pesticide tolerances set by Codex are weaker than current US tolerances.[159] One example is DDT. The Codex standard exceeds the FDA standard by 50 times for bananas.[160] The US allows foods imports with only extremely low DDT residues - much lower than the Maximum Residue Levels (MRLs) set by Codex. If harmonization becomes the rule at GATT, then any state whose goods have been denied entry on account of higher US standards could complain to the GATT dispute panel. The higher US standards could be ruled illegitimate, and retaliation, such as tariffs against US exports or the demand for compensation, might be authorized.[161]

If Codex standards become a ceiling rather than a floor for imported goods, then US farmers will find themselves severely disadvantaged, as their products will be competing with imported products produced under far less harsh environmental and health and safety standards. Taken to extreme, countries with higher standards than Codex could find themselves subject to 'greenmail' by states with lower standards. For example, the latter could demand compensation in return for not exporting goods with higher pesticide residues than those allowed by the national standards of the importer.[162] Ultimately if the US economy is badly affected, then Congress may well lower national standards so that US producers can compete on more equal terms with their competitors abroad.

Within the US the debate in 1992 was particularly heated. Agriculture Secretary Yeutter was keen to establish the precedence of federal over state laws, since he saw the high standards set by some states as running counter to his aims at GATT of liberalizing trade as much as possible.[163] The health and safety lobby remains ranged directly against the trade and commerce lobby. Yeutter's enthusiasm for harmonization was undoubtedly fuelled by the sight of an opportunity for US exports to enter the markets of countries with even higher standards than those of the US, primarily Europe. Also, he wanted to contain the efforts of consumer groups at home and abroad who were pushing for a 'fourth criterion' for evaluating new food chemicals: they wanted social and economic values

---

[159]Cited in Ritchie, op.cit, May 1990, p.3.

[160]FOE Release, 24 May 1990, op.cit.

[161]Ritchie, May 1990, op.cit, p.3.

[162]A.Hittle, 29 May 1990, *Washington Post*, cited by Ritchie, May 1990, op.cit, p.4.

[163]Ritchie, May 1990, op.cit.

to stand as the fourth, alongside safety, quality and efficacy. Many food and chemical companies were worried that the fourth criterion might result in tougher regulations.[164] Ritchie cites as recent examples of the fourth criterion in practice, bans by various states in the US on the commercial use of the genetically-engineered growth hormone, BST, because it would bankrupt thousands of small dairy farmers, and the 1989 European ban on BST as a response not to scientific evidence but rather to consumer demand. Official US negotiators at GATT saw this fourth criterion as political and therefore unacceptable.[165]

Tackling structures.

GATT is the one place where policies can be coordinated at the global level, based on mutually agreed upon rules and a transparent dispute settlement process. Unfortunately, it totally fails to integrate ecological concerns into its economic function.[166]

This statement masks the fact that trade issues are notoriously difficult to resolve, with conflicts of interest between the parties being acute. When environment comes into the picture, the tensions are exacerbated. Take for example the argument that international standards should be a floor, and not a ceiling, for national action. Many developing countries perceive this as a form of Northern protectionism. This is symptomatic of their more general fear that environmental measures are another discriminatory barrier impeding the flow of goods from South to North. Another example concerns proposals for the general reform of GATT. Given the centrality of GATT to the relationship between environment and economy, reform must come about within the GATT context; yet most of the arguments for change voiced up till now have been made by Northern NGOs. However, developing country governments are extremely wary of Northern environmental NGOs, and are suspicious of Northern environmental initiatives more generally. The road ahead is fraught with difficulty. The GATT decision on 8 October 1991 to revive a working group on trade and the environment that has not met since it

---

[164]M.Ritchie, 'GATT, Agriculture and the Environment', *The Ecologist*, Vol.20, No.6, Nov/Dec 1990, p.218.
[165]C.Kramer, 'Implications of the Hormone Controversy for International Food Safety Standards', *Resources*, Fall 1991, No.105. pp.12-14.
[166]Ritchie, Nov/Dec 1990, op.cit, p.220.

was established twenty years ago was a hopeful sign.[167] The central debate as to whether more trade liberalization helps or hinders environmental protection and sustainable development has only just begun in the GATT framework, and the opposing forces are already ranged against one another.

The task ahead is formidable. Changes are needed not simply in the day-to-day processes and rules of trade relations, but in the underlying structures governing these transactions. The linkages between trade, finance and aid need to be addressed. Without a satisfactory solution to the problem of debt repayment, then changes in the rules of trade to accommodate environmental concerns will amount to little more than tinkering at the edges. The debt burden increases the pressure on developing countries to export more so that they can earn the foreign exchange they require to meet the burden of interest payments. This often drives production of cash crops onto land which could otherwise be used to meet the basic food requirements of the expanding population. Production from finite natural resources is increased. Yet both these measures can contribute to a lowering of the world market price of commodities. At the same time, structural adjustment policies undermine the very limited welfare provisions in these countries, increase poverty and therefore drive more people into forests and onto marginal land which cannot sustain them. The relationship between trade and the environment, therefore, cannot be tackled in a vacuum. Solutions must be worked out within the larger structure of the underlying international economic system.

3.5 Conclusions

Efforts to integrate environmental concerns into the economic policies of governments and international organizations are developing at a rapid pace. NGOs must take much of the credit for this, but so too must a range of international institutions and the governments and bureaucrats who pushed to shape their agenda. The recent proliferation of environmental funds and facilities and the adoption of environmental concerns by multilateral lenders are all testimony to the importance attributed to this integration of concerns at the highest levels of international policymaking. The idea that growth is necessary for environmental

---

[167]W.Dullforce, 'GATT Revives Working Group on Environment', *Financial Times*, 9 October 1991.

protection and sustainable economic development has been accepted by governments, and the outstanding issues concern how best to achieve this. Market-based instruments are fast winning the day over the more traditional standard-setting controls. With the passing of the command economies of eastern Europe and the former USSR, it seems all the more likely that the agenda for the next decade has been set in terms of the market.

What we see to date is the rapid growth of a 'patchwork quilt' of ad hoc environmental regulations, standards, guidelines, conditions and instruments. Where issues are global (and not all environmental issues are), what is needed is a set of global goals, but with in-built flexibility to allow for special regional, national or sectoral problems which will influence the national response. There is a tension between the globalization of the international economy and the environmental crisis, and the real need for local circumstances and peculiarities to be taken into account. The priority allotted to specific global environmental problems and goals, the methods for achieving those goals, and the pace of fulfilment, will vary in different national settings. After all, the costs of protecting the environment relative to other priorities vary across countries. A balance must be struck between long-term environmental protection and the immediate requirement of survival facing the majority of the world's inhabitants.

While most of the developments so far have concerned government policy and the functioning of IGOs, there is no doubt that the activities of business must come under further scrutiny if sustainability is to be achieved.

Ultimately, revisions to the underlying global economic structures of production, finance and trade are in order to deal with global environmental change. This requires a level of political consensus that until now the international community has not achieved. In the meantime, however, problems must be tackled at the most appropriate pragmatic level. The path ahead will be fraught with difficulty, as the integration of economic and environmental concerns challenges entrenched political and economic interests at all levels. To stand any chance of success, such efforts will have to promote understanding and empowerment at the grassroots level in Northern and Southern countries. Lifestyle issues - and lives - are at stake. While ultimate solutions must be framed in a global context, they will stand little chance of success if they are perceived as being imposed on unwilling communities.

Democratization is necessary from the level of the village up to the running of international institutions if the concerns of environment and economy are to be successfully integrated and the cause of sustainable development thus furthered.

Whereas environmental concerns have been pushed onto the international political and economic agendas primarily because of the efforts of NGOs, their place in the security debate has until recently been confined largely to the domain of academic discussion. The environmental devastation resulting from the Iraqi invasion of Kuwait in 1991 and Operation Desert Storm prompted more widespread interest in the relationship between environment and security, to include NGOs and governments.[1]

This chapter elaborates a political context in which to locate environmental issues and to assess their impact on security. The utility of traditional conceptions of security are assessed for understanding the dominant contemporary forms of political conflict and new environmental challenges. An understanding of the legitimacy crisis experienced by numerous states is crucial to an elucidation of the security implications of environmental problems. Strategic analysis must transcend the established concept of sovereign states as the centrepiece

[1]For the current discussion, see T.F.Homer-Dixon, 'Environmental Change and Violent Conflict', *Emerging Issues Occasional Paper No.4*, International Security Studies Program, American Academy of Arts and Sciences, Cambridge, Mass., June 1990; N.Brown, 'Climate, Ecology and Security', *Survival*, Vol.XXXI, No.6, Nov/Dec 1989, pp.519-532; C.Thomas, 'New Dimensions in Strategy and Security in the Third World', in K.Booth, *New Directions in Strategy and Security*, Harper Collins Academic, London, 1991; P.Gleick, 'Environment, Resources, and International Security and Politics', in E.Arnett (ed), *Science and International Security: Responding to a Changing World*, American Association for the Advancement of Science, Washington DC, 1990; the discussion between Gleick and Deudney in *Bulletin of the Atomic Scientist*, April 1991, pp.15-28; and J.Kakonen (ed), *Perspectives on Environmental Conflict and International Relations*, Pinter, London and New York, 1992.

of international relations if our understanding of new threats and our readiness to meet them are to be advanced. The security implications of environmental problems are explored by focusing on two examples: the potential effect of rising sea levels, and the competition for scarce freshwater resources. The critical effect of other factors, such as population growth, on the evolution of the environment-security relationship is illustrated. The reverse relationship - that of military security on the environment - is also addressed, as is environmental warfare. The conclusion returns to the problem of political instability and analyzes the likely effects of environmental problems on violent conflict both within and between states. It is argued that only through an integrated approach to development, the environment and security can we hope to alleviate the crisis of the state and avert more violent conflict at the local, national, regional or global levels. The challenge will be to cooperate without resorting to the use of weapons which degrade the environment and intensify the competition for scarce resources.

4.1 Environment and security: acknowledging the links

The current realization that some of the most pressing security issues of our time are environmental, and that the traditional notion of the sovereignty of states fails to acknowledge and address these issues, is not new. Two decades ago Richard Falk outlined the security threat posed by environmental degradation and the inability of the system of sovereign states to deal with global issues which cut across sovereign territorial boundaries.[2] His efforts were largely ignored by the academic and policymaking communities. More recently he has been joined by scholars such as Arthur Westing, who advocates an expanded concept of security to take into account the increasing demand being made on natural resources both by growing human numbers and by rising expectations.[3] Westing develops what he calls comprehensive approach to security, linking environmental and political aspects.[4] Over the last few years, these analysts have been joined by many others who for a

---

[2]R.A.Falk, *This Endangered Planet*, Random House, New York, 1970.
[3]A.Westing (ed), *Global Resources and International Conflict*, SIPRI/ Oxford University Press, Oxford and New York, 1986.
[4]A.Westing (ed), *Comprehensive Security for the Baltic: An Environmental Approach*, Sage, London, for PRIO/UNEP, 1989.

variety of reasons feel that the traditional 'realist' approach[5] to analyzing international relations is inadequate. For some, the build-up of national military power is regarded as an inappropriate response to a security challenge that is more rooted in a domestic legitimacy crisis and the failure of economic development.[6] Thus a group has emerged whose members for a variety of reasons have expressed dissatisfaction with security studies to date. A common thread uniting disparate authors is the belief that the nation-state as a political unit cannot, acting alone, address successfully the problems which beset it, and that development and international cooperation are vital components in any strategy aimed at greater security nationally, regionally and globally. Thus the very nature of security has come under scrutiny.[7]

The linkages between environmental change and violent conflict have only recently become a focus for the attention of researchers, and the few findings available are generally the result of efforts by lone individuals.[8] Within the next few years, however, we can expect greater activity in this area. The American Academy of Arts and Sciences has joined with Toronto University to sponsor a major two-year project to investigate the linkages between environmental change and potentially violent conflict in the developing world, and to present a case for environmentally-sound policies likely to reduce the potential for international and domestic

[5]For an exposition of this approach, see H.Morgenthau, *Politics Among Nations*, Alfred Knopf, New York, 1955.

[6]See for example A.M.Al-Mashat, *National Security in the Third World*, Westview Press, Boulder, Colorado, 1985; M.Ayoob, 'Security in the Third World: the Worm about to Turn?', *International Affairs*, Vol.60, No.1, pp.41-51; E.Azar, and Chung-in Moon (eds), *National Security in the Third World: the Management of Internal and External Threats*, Edward Elgar, Aldershot, 1988; B.Buzan, *People, States and Fear*, Wheatsheaf, Sussex, 1983; C.Thomas, *In Search of Security: the Third World in International Relations*, Wheatsheaf, Brighton, 1987; C.Thomas and P.Saravanamuttu (eds), *The State and Instability in the South*, Macmillan, Basingstoke and London, 1989; and C.Thomas and P.Saravanamuttu (eds), *Conflict and Consensus in South/North Security*, CUP, 1989.

[7]For example, see R.Ullman, 'Redefining Security', *International Security*, No.8, 1983; and J.Mathews, 'Redefining Security', *Foreign Affairs*, Vol.68, No.2, 1989; N.Brown, 'New Paradigms for Strategy', *The World Today*, June 1990; T.Sorensen, 'Rethinking National Security', *Foreign Affairs*, Vol.69, No.3, 1990.

[8]For example, Westing, op.cit, and 'The Environmental Component of Comprehensive Security', *Bulletin of Peace Proposals*, Vol.20, No.2, 1989; N.Myers, who has published several articles indicating the link eg, 'The Environmental Dimensions to Security Issues', *The Environmentalist*, Vol.6, No.4, 1986.

conflict.[9] The Scandinavian Institute for African Studies has sponsored work on the environment and security in Africa.[10]

The reduction in east/west tension provided a timely opportunity for attention to be turned toward global problems which required simultaneous local, national, regional and global efforts for their resolution. Given the grave proportions of the current environmental crises, and their equally serious security implications, it is to be hoped that current interest represents more than a fad. The enormity of the problems presents opportunities for creative political thinking which can spill over into other areas of global concern, such as debt and development; indeed, these areas are intimately interconnected, and one cannot be tackled in isolation from the others. The interdependence of sectors, issues and possibilities must be the foundation stone of any attempt to build a less violent and less environmentally-destructive world.

4.2 Security, the crisis of legitimacy and violent conflict

The popular view that there has been peace in the world since 1945 is, of course, incorrect. While the superpowers achieved peace with each other through nuclear deterrence, the majority of states in the southern hemisphere and even some in the north have not been as fortunate. Research has shown that of the 216 wars occurring in the period 1945-86, 168 represented domestic conflicts, while 48 involved border conflicts between states.[11] Moreover, these statistics do not include many internal conflicts which have not reached the proportion of a war, but where anti-regime activity (real or perceived) prompts the government to pursue organized and systematic repression of civilians such as has happened in Chile, Argentina, Cambodia, Uganda and Guatemala. The majority of wars that have been fought since 1945 have taken place *within states, not between states.*[12]

---

[9] See *Emerging Issues*, (Newsletter of the Committee on International Security Studies, American Academy of Arts and Sciences), Vol.11, No.1, Summer 1990, p.1.
[10] A.H.Ornas and M.A.Mohamed Salih (eds), *Ecology and Politics: Environmental Stress and Security in Africa*, Scandinavian Institute of African Studies, Uppsala, 1989.
[11] See I.Kende, 'Twenty Five Years of Local Wars', *Journal of Peace Research*, No.8, 1971, pp.1-31; and 'Wars of Ten Years', *Journal of Peace Research*, No.3, Vol.XV, 1978, pp.227-41; also M.Kidron and R.Segal, *The New State of the World Atlas*, Pan Books, London and Sydney, 1987.
[12] Thomas, in Booth, op.cit.

Internal challenges to political authority reflect the lack of domestic legitimacy experienced by the majority of states in the developing world. These states exist as legal entities, but not as social facts.[13] A state is said to enjoy legitimacy when there is a consensus among its citizens to accept the authority of its institutions to make decisions on their collective behalf. Where the consensus is weak, or easily fragmented, the state has to employ either persuasive or coercive measures to ensure compliance with its decisions. The greater the legitimacy, the less coercive force is needed. This lack of legitimacy has had, and continues to have, profound implications for security not only domestically but regionally and globally. Given that environmental problems will be played out generally on the stage of this system of insecure states, their potential for exacerbating instability and conflict is magnified. This point cannot be overstressed; it is only through understanding the nature of instability and violent conflict in the present international system that we can hope to guess at the effects of environmental problems on security.

Why do the majority of states suffer a crisis of legitimacy? A comparison with the states of western Europe is helpful here, for they are often taken as a model for the development of the nation-state, being characterized by a high level of domestic legitimacy and stability compared to the rest of the world. They enjoy bounded territories, social homogeneity and a monopoly of violence by a single centre - the government. Western Europe has not always been like this; for centuries borders shifted with the changing relative abilities of rulers to hang on to or extend their territory. In such a hostile and competitive international environment, rulers encouraged domestic development so that they could tax their populations to finance war. Thus development was vital to their survival. In the process, the majority of states disappeared.[14] Rulers of the surviving states were strong both despotically (ie. power over life and death) and infrastructurally (through the bureaucratic development of the state). By this gradual process of integration and

---

[13] R.H.Jackson, and C.G.Rosberg, 'Why Africa's Weak States Persist: the Empirical and the Juridical in Statehood', *World Politics*, Vol.35, No.1, pp.1-24; and by the same authors, 'Sovereignty and Underdevelopment: Juridical Statehood in the African Crisis', *The Journal Of Modern African Studies*, Vol.24, No.1, pp.1-31.

[14] See M.Mann, 'The Autonomous Power of the State: its Origins, Mechanisms and Results', *Archives Europeennes de Sociologie*, Vol.25, No.2; and J.Hall, *Powers and Liberties: the Causes and Consequences of the Rise of the West*, Blackwell, Oxford, and Penguin, Harmondsworth, 1985.

disintegration, which was often bloody, the nation-states of western Europe were forged. Today, multiparty politics and a shared internal consensus pushes internal conflict to the margins of political activity.

The development of the majority of states stands in contrast to the experience of western Europe. Many states in Africa, Asia and the Middle East achieved independent statehood either through armed struggle against colonial powers or peacefully when international law established former colonial boundaries as the legitimate boundaries of new states. Especially on the African continent, these arbitrary boundaries cut through ethnic, religious and other social groups. In the case of Latin and Central America, while boundaries may not be the key issue, many states have experienced - and continue to experience - extreme crises as the governments swing between authoritarianism and democracy.[15] The benign international political environment of today offers the legal protection of sovereignty, and thus in the post-colonial era there has been a separation between the struggle for the existence of the state, which is now taken for granted, and the imperative of development for survival.[16] Leaders in these countries are often strong despotically, but not infrastructurally.[17] While a wave of democracy has swept over the countries of eastern Europe, they nevertheless display many of the characteristics of the insecure developing countries, and their legitimacy crises are far from resolved. The problems of ethnicity and borders are as real for them as for many of the developing countries, and are also apparent in the newly independent republics following the disintegration of the USSR. The developing world provides us with many examples of ethnicity becoming the focus of violent conflict within and between states either in the competition for scarce resources or in the need for a scapegoat.

This crisis of legitimacy has been exacerbated by the eagerness of the superpowers to arm client states. The superpower competition which dominated postwar politics until recently was played out in other areas of the globe, and vast arsenals of weaponry found their way to proxy regimes. Thus a very poor country like Somalia acquired a huge arsenal.

---

[15] N.P.Mouzelis, *Politics in the Semi-Periphery: Early Parliamentarism and Late Industrialisation in the Balkans and Latin America*, Macmillan, London, 1986.

[16] A.F.Mullins, *Born Arming: Development and Military Power in New States*, Stanford University Press, 1987.

[17] J.S.Migdal, *Strong Societies and Weak States: State-Society Relations and State Capabilities in the Third World*, Princeton University Press, New Jersey, 1988.

The contrast with the developmental experience of the states of western Europe is striking: there were no such external patrons to provide arms for rulers who could not provide them for themselves either through production or purchase via taxation.

Security studies, as they have developed over the last thirty years, have been founded on the integrity of the nation-state and on identifying physical threats emanating from outside the territorial boundary of the state. The build-up of military power has been seen as the most appropriate response to this perceived external challenge. If states are sovereign, their internal affairs must be immune from external scrutiny and comment; this principle of non-intervention has been a cornerstone of international law. In turn, the concept of national security has been used by governments to legitimize all actions taken in apparent defence of the nation-state. The flaw in the argument is that the majority of states do not contain homogeneous nations within them, and in many cases what has been pursued is the interest of the regime in power dressed up in the language of national security to lend it an air of legitimacy internationally. All too often the sacred cow of national security has been used to justify domestic persecution of groups which oppose the government in power, and the concept of national security itself removes such actions from public international discussion.

Clearly the failure to acknowledge the importance of internal conflict and its indigenous roots represents a major analytical shortcoming of security studies. Moreover, even where interstate conflict has occurred, it has not necessarily challenged state boundaries. Time after time we have seen occupying armies withdraw as in the case of Vietnam in Cambodia, Tanzania in Uganda, and the Soviet Union in Afghanistan. Despite the evidence, effort has remained concentrated on monitoring relations between states. This is a direct result of the political realism informing security studies, which sees states as homogeneous units in perpetual competition. What goes on inside these political units has not fallen within the realm of concern of security analysts, except as it has directly affected inter-state relationships.

The lack of attention paid to the significance of internal conflict must be highlighted and overcome if the security ramifications of environmental developments are to be addressed. For environmental change is likely to lead to political stress within states as often as between them. Violent domestic conflict will doubtless ensue as groups fight over diminishing natural resources and populations migrate internally in search of a livelihood. Since in the majority of states a domestic consensus is lacking, and the states themselves are in fact in crisis, the potential for pre-existing tensions - be they rooted in ethnicity, religion or anything else - to be exacerbated by environmental problems is vast. Already we can see the distribution of resources such as food and water playing a crucial role, as in the civil war in Sudan.[18] Current environmental problems, especially soil degradation and climatic change, have a huge impact on subsistence, and popular perceptions of related government policy can be a factor for grave political instability. For example, in Sri Lanka popular perceptions of government discrimination of a positive or negative kind has already fuelled civil war. In assessing the likely impact of environmental problems then, the basic instability of the state, and the potential for internal violent conflict, must be taken as given. If this is overlooked, then any planning or predictions will be inadequate at best, and misplaced at worst. There can be little doubt that environmental problems will exacerbate the current instability which plagues developing countries. Moreover, with the momentous changes that have taken place in eastern Europe and the dissolution of the Soviet Union, the group of sovereign states characterized by domestic instability has been further swelled. Most of these states are characterized by internal ethnic differentiation, economic collapse and environmental degradation.

Having stressed the importance of moving beyond the traditional approach to security to make sense of current threats to political stability within states, the traditional approach will nevertheless have a central role to play in analyzing likely inter-state conflicts resulting from a competition for scarce resources. Undoubtedly violent conflict over access to water sources shared between two or more states is likely in the next few decades. The Middle East is a case in point (see p.140). Yet we must remember that much competition over scarce resources takes place within states rather than between them, as in the competition for fuelwood and land. What is needed, therefore, is an approach to security which can look at intra-state as well as inter-state dimensions, where appropriate.

---

[18]For examples, see several contributions in Ornas and Salih, op.cit.

4.3 Security implications of environmental problems

The range of environmental problems with actual or potential security implications is huge. They may result from natural causes or human activity, and in scope they may be confined to localities or extend across the globe. They may be intermittent or ongoing. What is clear with virtually all such problems, however, is that no single state or even small group of states can curb them. Problems such as water shortages, desertification, global warming, ozone depletion, deforestation, transboundary air pollution, toxic waste, loss of biodiversity, and so forth are transnational in character. They are part of a global political, economic and strategic canvas. These problems must be viewed in a holistic manner; strategies to overcome them must extend beyond dealing with the immediate environmental hazard.

The security implications are as diverse as the environmental problems which give rise to them. Their significance will vary geographically and over time in terms of adaptive responses. Generalization can therefore take place only at a very broad level. The range of possible topics for discussion in the environment-security debate is very wide. Here, we examine the potential security implications of rising sea levels which may well result from global warming. This issue has been chosen both because of its global strategic significance and because it offers an excellent example of the interconnected nature of environmental and other problems with human causes, and the wide range of ramifications. Moreover, in raising issues both of an intra-state and inter-state kind, it highlights the necessity of taking what is relevant from the traditional approach to security while moving beyond it. We also examine the competition for scarce resources, as illustrated by freshwater shortages. While the traditional approach to analyzing security may lend itself to analysis of this problem, again we need to go beyond that approach for suitable answers.

Uncertain scientific understanding of both cause and effect exacerbates the task of predicting how the whole spectrum of environmental problems may manifest themselves in terms of political stability. Nevertheless, it is imperative that we familiarize ourselves with possible strategic and political implications at least of certain aspects of such problems.

Rising sea levels

While the debate continues as to the nature, extent and speed of global warming, the Intergovernmental Panel on Climate Change (IPCC) science suggests that a one metre sea level rise by the year 2100 is possible assuming current trends, and a 30-50cm rise by 2050.[19] We cannot assume from political commitments to date that a diminution of current trends is imminent. The extent of the rise, coupled with other factors such as subsidence, and government response, will determine the effects at different locations.[20] These may range from the complete disappearance of low-lying islands, to the flooding of deltas and other low-lying coastal areas. The effect on the human population in such circumstances would be dramatic. Hekstra has argued that:

> The map of the world would effectively be redrawn; many densely populated areas (with a total population of one billion people) could be flooded; coastal erosion would be severe; salt water intrusion inland would salinize many potable groundwaters; and one-third of the world's croplands could be lost to production.[21]

For several small islands in the Indian and Pacific Oceans, survival is the issue as they will disappear with increased sea level rises. The Maldives, the Line Islands, the Marshall islands, Tokelau, Tuvalu, Kiribati and Tonga head the list of those whose very existence is threatened; others in the Caribbean are at risk too.[22]

The insecure position of the Maldives prompted that government to play a leading role in pushing for international studies of the rise of the sea level, especially as it affects poor, low-lying countries. The Maldives is a chain of approximately 1,190 islands, none of which are more than two metres high. In 1987 a cyclone hit the country and resulted in the swamping of the international airport at Hulele. This prompted President Maumoon Abdul Gayoom to raise the issues of environment and

---

[19] J.T.Houghton, G.J.Jenkins and J.J.Ephraims (eds), *Climate Change: The IPCC Scientific Assessment*, CUP, 1990.

[20] For a general discussion of the problem, see J.Ince, *The Rising Seas*, Earthscan, London, 1990.

[21] G.P.Hekstra, 'Global Warming and Rising Sea Levels: the Policy Implications', *The Ecologist*, Vol.19, No.1, 1989, p.4. For a more detailed discussion by the same author, see, 'Sea-Level Rise: Regional Consequences and Responses', in N.Rosenberg, W.Easterling, P.Crosson and J.Darmstadter (eds), *Greenhouse Warming: Abatement and Adaptation*, Resources for the Future, Washington DC, 1989, pp.53-68.

[22] Ince, op.cit, Chapter 5.

development, particularly the effects of rising sea levels on coastal and island states, at the Commonwealth Heads of Government meeting in Vancouver and then again at the United Nations General Assembly on 19 October 1987. His plea resulted in a call for a Commonwealth study on the impact of the greenhouse effect on Commonwealth countries. Since twenty-one of the Commonwealth's fifty members are small island developing countries, the forum was appropriate.[23]

It is not simply the rising sea level which threatens such states, but in the short term the threat is greater from a combination of this feature and cyclones. Adamson has reported that the storm surge drawn into the vortex of a cyclone can result in sea level rises of one or two metres, or even much more.[24] The result of such temporary flooding is to gradually make the islands uninhabitable as freshwater supplies are destroyed and previously fertile land becomes salinated and unproductive. Lewis in his study undertaken for the Commonwealth Secretariat noted in 1988 that damage from saline intrusion into freshwater wells was already apparent in southern Kiribati and Tuvalu.[25]

It is an irony of course that these poor island states have contributed nothing to the global warming that is taking place, yet they will suffer its harshest consequences as their vulnerability to natural phenomena is the greatest. They are the least able to cope financially and technologically, and they have very little influence in international community. The cost of precautionary local measures such as dyke-building, estimated at $1,800 per metre, renders them out of the question, particularly while there is no guarantee that they would work. These states are completely powerless in the face of imminent national disaster. Even the Small States Conference on Sea-Level Rise, convened in the Maldives in November 1989 and attended by the representatives of fifteen threatened states, received virtually no coverage in the media of the developed world. The call of the Maldivian Director of Environmental Affairs, Hussein Shihab, that 'We, the low-lying nations of the world, are the most vulnerable, and indeed the least responsible

---

[23]J.Lewis, *The Implications of Sea Level Rise for Island and Low-Lying Countries*, Report for the Commonwealth Secretariat, London, 1988.

[24]D.Adamson, 'Greenhouse Effect Threatens Tiny Islands', *The Guardian*, 15 July 1988.

[25]J.Lewis, *Sea Level Rise: Tonga and Tuvalu*, Report for the Commonwealth Secretariat, London, 1988, cited in Report by a Commonwealth Group of Experts, *Climate Change: Meeting the Challenge*, Commonwealth Secretariat, London, 1989; p.39.

for this state of affairs', went unheeded in developed countries.[26] These states have to rely on external agencies even for information. Thus the office of the Prime Minister of Tuvalu has to ask UNEP to keep the country informed 'for planning purposes'.[27]

If these states become uninhabitable (which is simply a matter of time if present predictions on global warming are proved correct) we can expect to see their populations looking for sanctuary in other countries where of course they will be competing with local populations for a livelihood. The populations of the disappearing islands are relatively small, even if growing at a high per cent. The population of the Maldives for instance, stands at around 180,000, but its growth rate is 3.1%, and this has implications for states that might be willing/persuaded to take Maldivian refugees. However, globally the problem of environmental refugees[28] resulting from sea level rises will sharpen if present global warming trends continue to the point where low-lying delta areas housing vast populations and producing significant amounts of food become inundated with sea water. It is to this problem that we now turn.

In 1989 UNEP published a detailed inventory of high risk areas with regard to sea level rises.[29] This represented the first systematic attempt on a global basis to plot vulnerability, and not surprisingly, the survey was hampered by a lack of data. The importance of the exercise cannot be overstated, however, when we consider that over half of humanity inhabit coastal regions and that population growth is most acute there.[30] Nevertheless, the UNEP project was a step in the right direction, and a

---

[26]*Earthwatch*, No.38, 2nd quarter, 1990, p.7.

[27]'Vanishing Islands', in *Earthwatch*, ibid, p.7.

[28]Little has been published on the problem of environmental refugees. Myers has suggested that governments often fail to apply such a categorization even where it is clearly the cause of the population movement. The term 'economic' refugee is becoming fashionable, and it is surely often the case that such refugees have no means of economic livelihood due to environmental degradation in their homeland. For a useful discussion of the problem of environmental refugees, with several short case studies, see Earthscan, 'Environment and Conflict: Links Between Ecological Decay, Environmental Bankruptcy and Political and Military Instability', *Earthscan Briefing Document 40*, Earthscan, London, 1984. For a specific study, see O.Nnoli, 'Desertification, Refugees and Regional Conflicts in West Africa', in Ornas and Salih, op.cit, pp.169-180.

[29]United Nations Environment Programme, *Criteria for Assessing Vulnerability to Sea-Level Rise: A Global Inventory for High Risk Areas*, Delft Hydraulics Laboratory, Delft, Netherlands, 1989.

[30]Report of a Commonwealth Group of Experts, op.cit, p.39.

foundation on which others can build.[31] The project used four main criteria to assess vulnerability. For each country, it looked firstly at the share of total land area between 0-5 metres above mean sea level. Secondly, it assessed the density of coastal populations, marking out areas where the population density exceeded 100 people per square kilometre as the most vulnerable. Thirdly, it monitored the extent of agricultural productivity, highlighting countries where lowland agricultural productivity grew on average more than 2% a year in the period 1980-85. Finally, it noted the degree of biological productivity within low-lying areas, noting the regions with the largest inventories of coastal wetlands and tidal mangrove forests.

Using the four criteria outlined above, UNEP identified the ten countries most at risk: Bangladesh, Egypt, the Gambia, Indonesia, the Maldives, Mozambique, Pakistan, Senegal, Surinam and Thailand. These are all poor states, and all except the Gambia, the Maldives, Surinam and Senegal are also very populous. The UNEP project distinguished between primary and secondary impact areas, the former being land areas below 1.5 meters elevation which would be submerged with a 1.5 meter sea level rise, and the latter land lying at 1.5 to 3 meters above today's mean which would have the burden of influx of refugees and greater pressure on resources. It is important to remember that the adverse effects of the rising sea-level will be felt before the primary areas are submerged, as dramatic weather conditions result in temporary sporadic flooding with all that that means for the productivity of the land and the utility of freshwater resources. Moreover, the effects will not be felt in isolation but will interact with other processes such as subsidence to create combined havoc.

Bangladesh. Bangladesh is likely to be the worst hit. Eighty per cent of the country is made up of the delta of three great rivers: the Ganges, the Brahmaputra and the Meghna, and much of this area is only one or two metres above sea level now. Indeed, over half the country lies at below five metres elevation.[32] It is here that most of the population of 114.7 million people live. We can already see the kind of devastation that it will undergo with rising sea levels, as for the past few years it has already

---

[31]For a summary of the UNEP project, see J.Jacobson, 'Holding Back the Sea', in L.R.Brown (ed), *The State of the World: 1990*, Unwin, London, 1990, pp. 79-97.
[32]J.D.Milliman, et al, 'Environmental and Economic Implications of Rising Sea Level and Subsiding Deltas: the Nile and Bengal Examples', *Ambio*, Vol.18, No.6, 1989.

experienced drastic flooding, but this resulting from deforestation of the Himalaya combined with the impact of cyclonic flooding (itself arguably the product of the greenhouse effect). Moreover, this must be seen against the background of a population growing at an annual rate of 2.6%, and projected to reach 165 million by the year 2005. The age structure and location of the population is politically very significant: in 1987, 50.6% were under sixteen, and the average life expectancy was 52. Only 13% of the population was urbanized.

The study prepared for the 1989 Commonwealth Prime Ministers' Conference estimated that a sea level rise of one metre would mean a loss of 16% of Bangladesh's land area equivalent to 14% of its cropped area, currently producing annually two million tonnes of rice, 400,000 tonnes of vegetables, 200,000 of sugar, and 100,000 of pulses and supporting 3.7 million cattle, goats and sheep.[33] It would displace 10% of its population, result in output loss in the order of 13% of GDP, and destroy 10,300 bridges, 1,470kms of railway and 20,000kms of roads. This must be seen in the context of current per capita incomes of $160 per annum, but with the bottom 40% of the population having an average income of $64 per capita.[34]

Studies conducted by John Milliman and his team at the Woods Hole Oceanographic Institute in the US make even more alarming reading.[35] They suggest that by 2050, greenhouse-related rising sea levels and local subsidence will forge a lethal combination, resulting in sea level rises of over two metres in the Bengal Delta and leading to the dislocation of over 40 million people. Indeed, they place greatest emphasis on the degree to which the land is already sinking, partly due to the effects of the presence of over 120,000 wells which have been drilled for drinking water. Over the period 1978-85, there was a sixfold increase in the number of wells drilled, and the rate of subsidence has thereby been raised to twice the natural level. They estimate that 18% of the land will be under water by 2050, and by 2100 a third of the land housing 35% of the population may well have disappeared. Moreover, the physical consequences will not be confined to the delta areas: rivers will rise with

---

[33]Reported in *Earthwatch*, op.cit, p.4-5.
[34]UNICEF, *The State of the World's Children, 1989*, OUP, 1989, p.74, for a discussion of the significance of looking at per capita income of the bottom 40% of a country's population as opposed to an average per capita.
[35]Milliman et al, op.cit.

the sea level rise, with all the implications for river course, flooding, salination and so forth. Thus a city like Chittagong may be affected catastrophically.

The security implications of this are all too clear. Moreover, our knowledge of them is not merely theoretical or conjecture, but gained from practical experience. With nowhere else to go within Bangladesh, millions of Bangladeshis will be forced to flee as the only alternative to death. This will not be the first time that large-scale population movements have taken place from here into India. During the civil war in Pakistan in 1971/72, millions of refugees fled from East Pakistan across the border into India to escape the ravages of the Pakistan army which was composed primarily of people from the western side of the spatially divided country. Out of this civil disturbance, and with crucial Indian involvement, the state of Bangladesh was eventually created. However in the run up to this, India housed millions of refugees in camps near the border and conditions were appalling. Knee-deep in mud with the onset of the monsoon rains, the refugees suffered enormously from ill health. Moreover, suffering was not confined to them. The local Indian population found the labour market disrupted as the refugees were willing to work for even less than they themselves were paid, and this resulted in political unrest among the indigenous population who saw their labour being undercut. Tensions rose significantly.

As well as the experience outlined above, the more recent natural history of Bangladesh, marked by severe flooding, is informative. In August and September 1988 Bangladesh was hit by the worst monsoon floods on record. At the height of the flooding, over 75% of the country was submerged and 25 million people (a quarter of the population) had been made homeless.[36] Ten million were stranded on trees, rooftops and other areas of higher ground. Large-scale damage to the infrastructure meant that it was tremendously difficult to reach the millions who needed help. There was widespread suffering due to venomous snake bites and diseases such as cholera which spread as people ate contaminated food and drank impure water. The international airport at Dhaka was inaccessible, and even when it was reopened the collapse of the domestic transport system meant that aid could not be distributed efficiently. President Ershad set up a Disaster Prevention Council under his own chairmanship in order to minimize the impact of future floods. He

---

[36] *Keesings Record of World Events*, Vol XXXIV, Bristol, November 1988, p.36288.

believed that only a coordinated regional effort could tackle the problem. While the exact cause of the flooding remains a matter of debate, there is a school of thought which blames deforestation in the Himalaya of Nepal and India.[37] Tree loss is thought to have to have resulted in decreased water retention and increased silting and soil erosion. Coupled with the effects of melting Himalayan snow, this resulted in the subcontinent's river systems being swollen even before the monsoon arrived. (For expansion of this argument, and an alternative view, see Chapter 7).

The floods of 1988 were river floods, which in recent history have occurred only once every 150 years or so. Their greatest adverse impact was on property and infrastructure. Deposition of rich sediment and water ensured a bumper harvest. Numbers of people killed ran into hundreds rather than thousands, though indirectly the toll was greater due to health problems mentioned above. However in May 1991, flooding caused by cyclones in the Bay of Bengal (a regular occurrence), killed over 100,000 people. (In 1970, similar cyclonic flooding killed between 150,000-500,000 people - the precise figure is unknown because the inhabitants of the islands at the mouth of the coastal delta are the poorest, landless peasants). The Flood Action Plan launched in late 1989 by the Bangladesh government and the World Bank aims at reducing the effects of river floods rather than cyclone-induced flooding. While this may protect agricultural production, which is considered a national priority, it will do nothing to save lives.[38]

If we magnify the 1971, 1988 and 1991 scenarios several fold to take into account the huge increase in the numbers we could be considering (ie upwards of thirty million), and the fact that there will be no land for them to return to, then the picture is very grim. This is a very important consideration, since standard practice is to plan for the ultimate return of refugees to their homeland. Added to this also are the problems that India itself will be facing due to the various facets of climate change and other environmental problems such as deforestation.

Clearly, some mechanism must be instituted well in advance to plan for such huge population movements. Moreover, it must be remembered

---

[37]ibid; also, for a discussion of the role of politics rather than deforestation, see 'Drowned by Politics: Bangladesh Floods', *The Economist*, 17 September 1988, p.74.
[38]F.Pearce, 'Human Lives Shrugged off in Flood Plan', *New Scientist*, 11 May 1991, p.11.

that other environmental problems will also result in similar huge population movements, thus the overall problem will be even greater. This will need international cooperation for strategic advance planning if we are to avoid the worst excesses of intra- and inter-state conflict. We need to look into the potential role for regional organizations such as the South Asia Association for Regional Cooperation in this case. Indeed, SAARC has already begun to develop an interest in environmental issues, though to date this has been confined mostly to the commissioning of studies on natural disasters and discussion of a food reserve to operate in time of such natural disasters.[39] The UN High Commission for Refugees will certainly have a role to play, as it has experience in these matters albeit on a vastly reduced scale. There needs to be urgent international discussion about the possible relationship between the UNHCR and regional bodies, and contingency planning needs to be undertaken immediately. The experience of large-scale flooding in Bangladesh over the past few years has already given health and infrastructure workers some idea of the nature of the problems that will be faced, and this experience could be shared with other threatened regions if a suitable forum were to be provided. There is an argument for the UNHCR to become the central coordinator for information and action by all involved parties. These would range from public international bodies such as the WHO, UNDP and the FAO which could provide information and help on likely developments in food, health and infrastructure, to individual governments and regional organizations that will play a crucial role relocating people.

To date the disaster emergency operations launched internationally to deal with specific crises such as famine in the Horn of Africa have met many problems, yet there is a learning curve. While the disasters resulting from rising sea levels will probably be intermittent but rising in severity, and involve millions more people, there is still much that can be gleaned from the smaller-scale operations that have taken place. These need to be built on. For example, the logistical problem of providing basic needs for these refugees is only the beginning; next will come the task of integrating them into local communities and finding employment for millions of youths, since the age structure of the refugees will mean that most of them may be very young, as in the case of Bangladesh. The magnitude of the task will doubtless result in many governments wanting

---

[39]*Keesings Record of World Events*, Vol XXXIII, Bristol, December 1987, p.35614

to ignore the problem; yet its urgency makes immediate national and regional planning and international cooperation vital. Without this, the ominous scenario of national armies holding back incoming environmental refugees may become a reality.[40] Even with planning and cooperation, local, regional and global security will be severely strained.

Solutions must be multilateral, but the evidence suggests that political cooperation is not easy when states have conflicting priorities. President Ershad, for whom flooding in Bangladesh is a 'man-made curse',[41] has worked at a regional response to the problems of his country, but he has encountered many difficulties. Immediately following the floods of September 1988, he visited Delhi for talks with the then Indian Prime Minister, Rajiv Gandhi, and they decided to set up a joint task force on flood control. The honeymoon was over, however, when Ershad then visited Kathmandu to seek King Birendra's support for a regional approach. India wanted a bilateral effort, not a multilateral approach. Relations between India and Bangladesh soured further when Ershad visited China in November 1988 to enlist Chinese involvement in flood control measures. India opposed this since one of its river development projects was located in the Arunachal Pradesh border region which China claimed.[42]

Egypt. While the example of Bangladesh is the most serious in terms of human numbers and the extent of land inundation, it is unfortunately only one among several crisis points. The case of Egypt is frequently cited, and like Bangladesh it has been the subject of a special study by the Woods Hole Group which has been used by UNEP in its own study of vulnerability to sea level rises. The Egyptian population is currently estimated at 54.8 million people, with a growth rate of 2.7%.[43] Since more than 96% of the country is desert, the majority of Egyptians live

---

[40]The idea of fencing foreigners out was considered by Delhi in 1983 following violence in Assam between Indian Hindus and recently arrived Bengali Muslims. The situation was complicated by the fact that while many of the Bengalis came from Bangladesh, some were from Bengal in India. While the violence took place along religious lines, roots in resource scarcities in Bangladesh acted as a push factor for the refugees. When in Assam, they found themselves in direct competition for land and resources with the local Assamese. For further details, see *Earthscan, Briefing Document 40*, op.cit, p.26.

[41]*Keesings Record of World Events*, Vol.XXXIII, Bristol, Dec 1987, p.35614.

[42]*Keesings Record of World Events*, Vol.XXXV, No.3, 1989, p.36559; and for details of river talks in the region to date, see The Economist, op.cit, p.74-76.

[43]UNICEF, op.cit, p.102.

and work in the long, thin, fertile Nile Valley and the Nile Delta at a population density of 1,800 per square kilometre - twice that of Bangladesh. Agriculture is Egypt's main source of revenue and an important foreign exchange earner. It employs over half the population and contributes about a quarter of gross national product.[44] Currently, the average per capita income is $680 per annum, but more importantly, the average income of the bottom 40% of the population is only $281. This bottom 40% consumes only 16.5% of total GNP (similar to Bangladesh, where the bottom 40% consumes 17.3% of total GNP). In 1987, 21.4% of the population was under 16, life expectancy stood at 62 years, and 48% of the population was urbanized. These population statistics have great political significance especially in the context of growing societal stress.

Coastal retreat of up to 200 metres per year has been noted in certain parts of Egypt.[45] This is a result of subsidence, erosion and high sea levels. Vital to the fertility, extent and level of the Nile Delta is the transport of sediment downstream by the river. This was adversely affected as far back as the 1880s when the first barrages constructed on the Nile led to a reduction in the amount of sediment reaching the delta. It was exacerbated by the construction of the Aswan Dam in 1902, but only reached serious proportions after the opening of the Aswan High Dam in 1962. Since then a negligible amount of silt has been transported to the delta, as it gets trapped in the dam's reservoir. The amount of sediment reaching the delta plays a major role in determining the impact of rising sea levels, as it can affect if and when the delta is converted into estuary. A rising sea level then further erodes deltaic deposits and a new equilibrium must be found between the width of the estuary mouth and the rate of sedimentation and erosion.[46] The volume of flow reaching the delta has also been affected by the diversion of water for irrigation. Milliman's team has estimated that a likely local sea level rise of 1-1.5 metres by 2050 will result in the loss of 19% of Egypt's habitable land which is already in extremely scarce supply. By 2100, a possible rise of 2.5-3.3 metres would result in a loss of 26% of the habitable land which

[44]M.A.Kishk, 'Land Degradation in the Nile Valley', *Ambio*, Vol.15, 1986, pp.226-30.
[45]J.Broadus et al, 'Rising Sea Level and Damming of Rivers: Possible Effects in Egypt and Bangladesh', in J.G.Titus (ed), *Effects of Changes in Stratospheric Ozone and Global Climate, Vol.IV: Sea Level Rise*, Environmental Protection Agency, Washington DC, 1986.
[46]Hekstra, op.cit, p.7.

houses a quarter of the population and provides the productive environment for a quarter of the country's GDP.[47]

Unfortunately government policies aimed at development in one context can result in problems in another context. Thus just as the High Dam, seen as crucial for power generation, has resulted in delta subsidence, so the demarcation of development areas around Port Said will threaten the dunes and lakes which until now have played a major role in natural defence against encroachment by the sea. Moreover, Broadus has also shown that Lakes Maryut, Burullos, Idku and Manzalah are the source of 80% of the country's annual fish catch of 100,000 tons. In any event, he claims that the area will be flooded some time during the 21st Century.[48]

Many other areas of the world will suffer from rising sea levels. Chinese experts have estimated that a half metre rise would flood the city of Canton, while a metre rise would flood most of the country's rich low-lying plains: the southern half of the Lower Liao river plain, the eastern part of the Yangtze Delta and the North China Coastal Plain, and all the Pearl River delta.[49] Thirty million people would be homeless, and food production would be devastated. In the case of Guyana, a half-metre rise will inundate the area where half of the country's 900,000 inhabitants live. Clearly in such cases government response will be crucial, but as Hekstra has argued:

> Many other problems compete for the attention of decision-makers. Major factors influencing policy decisions are: the vested interests that are threatened, the availability of finance, the employment opportunities, political responsibilities and national prestige. Sadly, experience dictates that only disasters trigger counter-measures, even if there is prior warning and awareness of a problem.[50]

While individual developing countries can do little to affect greenhouse gas emissions into the atmosphere, their governments can try to protect vulnerable national areas by better land-use practices, protecting and extending natural defences such as mangroves and curbing population growth. Unfortunately, given intense pressure on limited resources, it is unlikely that major steps will be taken by most governments until disaster

---

[47]Milliman et al, op.cit.
[48]Broadus, op.cit.
[49]*Earthwatch*, op.cit, p.5.
[50]Hekstra, op.cit, p.9.

strikes; but by then it will be too late. Social, economic and political chaos will result. Defence against sea encroachment remains a financial and technological luxury which only a few countries, such as the Netherlands, are able to undertake. Even in that particular case, there was a time lag after the 1953 flood disaster of nearly a decade before the flood protection plan began.[51]

The migration problem. The discussion has considered the problem of environmental refugees resulting directly from a sea level rise. However, it is important to note that such migration, while serious in its own right, will probably be a relatively small part of a much larger picture. On the wider canvas, we can expect population growth and associated environmental and economic problems in the developing world to prompt very large scale migration. The example of Egypt is instructive. Professor Rowthorn argues that with a hypothetical sea level rise of 2.5 to 3 meters by 2100, the loss of habitable land is estimated to be 26%, housing one-quarter of the population. The effect on per capita land availability is equivalent to less than 20 years population growth in Egypt. If, by some miracle, Egypt could halt population growth for twenty years, this would compensate for the total loss of habitable land resulting from global warming.[52] Sea level rises will have a highly localized effect, creating extreme difficulties for specific populations; the strain of growing numbers on environment and economy is a much bigger problem of a more general nature. The security implications are enormous.

Competition for scarce resources: the case of water

The availability of essential resources is likely to diminish in the future as a result of global climatic change[53] and rising populations.[54] It is probable that the distribution of loss will be uneven, with some heavily populated regions suffering a decline which may be offset by increases in more sparsely populated regions such as northern Canada. The likely regional effects of global warming remain uncertain. However, on

---

[51] ibid, p.9.

[52] Personal communication, 23 March 1992.

[53] See P.Gleick, 'The Implications of Global Climatic Changes for International Security', *Climate Change*, No.15, 1989, pp.309-325.

[54] See N.Myers, 'Population, Environment and Conflict', *Environmental Conservation*, Vol.14, No.1, Spring 1987, pp.15-22; also M.Leroy, 'Human Population as a Factor in Strategic Policy and Action', in Westing, 1986, op.cit, pp.159-181.

balance, competition for scarce resources is likely to increase as a source of violent conflict. Fuelwood and water spring to mind as two resources for which the competition is already intense within certain states as well as between them. Both are essential to life in the developing countries, and in both cases millions of peasants - usually women[55] - walk for miles every day in search of supplies for the household. At another level, both are needed for agricultural and industrial activities. In this section we concentrate on water.[56] (For details on fuelwood, see Chapter 7).

Water is essential to life. The United Nations Drinking Water Supply and Sanitation Decade (1981-90) set a target of safe water for everyone by 1990. While this target has not been achieved, great steps forward have been taken in providing clean water to 700 million people since 1980, and sanitation for 480 million.[57] In rural areas, 60% of families are still without safe water, but people in cities fare better with provision at around 75%. Of course, these figures are averages and there will be important differences between and within developing countries. Many areas of the developing world face acute water shortages already, often not due to a shortfall in annual precipitation but to seasonal variability. As populations grow, so the availability of water per capita will diminish.[58] Global warming can be expected to exacerbate the water problem for the majority of the world's inhabitants and countries. Frederick and Gleick have commented that:

> ... greenhouse warming is certain to have major impacts on both water availability and water quality. Temperature, precipitation patterns, evapotranspiration rates, the timing and magnitude of runoff, and the frequency and intensity of storms will be affected by increasing concentrations of carbon dioxide and other trace gases. A rise in sea levels ... could threaten the freshwater supplies of coastal

[55]On the issues of women, water and fuelwood, see V.Shiva, *Staying Alive: Women, Ecology and Development*, Zed Press, London, 1988, and I.Dankelman, and J.Davidson, *Women and Environment in the Third World: Alliance for the Future*, Earthscan, London, 1988.
[56]For a clear statement of the problem and possibilities, see M.Falkenmark, 'New Ecological Approach to the Water Cycle: Ticket to the Future', *Ambio*, Vol.13, No.3, 1984, pp.152-160. Also, R.Clarke, *Water: the International Crisis*, Earthscan, London, 1991.
[57]UNICEF, op.cit, p.47.
[58]For a useful general discussion of the freshwater issue, see P.P.Rogers, 'Fresh Water', in R.Repetto, *The Global Possible*, Yale University Press, 1985, pp.255-298.

communities. And changes in temperature and rainfall levels will affect the demand for water, especially for irrigation.[59]

A consensus exists amongst climate modellers that global warming will increase global precipitation, although this may be offset by evaporation. However, the models tell us very little about regional changes. Given that water problems to date have been regional rather than global in nature, and that we can expect climate change to have differential regional results, this is an extremely important gap in our knowledge. What seems likely is that the majority of developing countries will fare worst. For the developed, the problem is likely to be one of devising efficient responses to variability in supply of water and ordering priority usages. For the developing world the problem of dealing with vulnerability to variability and shortage of supply will be much greater. The lack of certainty in our hydrological knowledge must not be taken as reason for complacency and inaction. For again as Frederick and Gleick argue:

> The quantity and quality of freshwater resources is of critical importance for both natural ecosystems and human development. Pressures on water resources are already rising due to population growth and industrial and commercial development. Any new threats to existing water resources must, therefore, be viewed with concern, especially where water is already limited in availability.[60]

Sub-Sahara Africa. The African continent stands on the brink of environmental disaster.[61] Sub-Sahara Africa is the driest region of the developing tropics, and the net effect of global warming may well be to make it drier still.[62] Repeated droughts have already plagued the Sahel zone and the Horn and East Africa, and resulted in millions of environmental refugees.[63] The situation is compounded firstly by the fact

---

[59]K.D.Frederick and P.H.Gleick, 'Water Resources and Climate Change', in Rosenberg, Easterling, Crosson, and Darmstadter, op.cit, p.133.
[60]ibid, p.141.
[61]For an excellent general overview, see L.Timberlake, *Africa in Crisis: the Causes, the Cures of Environmental Bankruptcy*, Earthscan, London, 1988.
[62]N.Myers, 'Population Growth, Environmental Decline and Security Issues in Sub-Saharan Africa', in Ornas and Salih, op.cit, p.213.
[63]For an important micro-study see A.De Waal, *Famine that Kills: Darfur, the Sudan, 1984-85*, Clarendon Paperbacks, Oxford, 1989; and for an interesting collection on the problem in Africa, see M.Glantz, (ed), *Drought and Hunger in Africa*, CUP, 1987.

that population is still growing rapidly,[64] thus making the outlook for the future even more bleak, and secondly by the general state of economic decline that characterizes the majority of states in the region.[65] The current population of 508 million is projected to rise to 678 million by the end of the century, and the political implications of this are staggering. The structural adjustment packages which the IMF and major western donors expect these governments to implement exacerbate social problems and fuel political tensions.[66] Myers has written of the linkage between excess numbers and environmental decline, and has illustrated this by reference to the natural resource base which supports food production. He argues convincingly that 'the linkages connect up with economic viability, political stability and ultimately with security concerns'.[67] In these already highly weak and fragmented states, unless adjustment takes on a more human face then political violence will surely occur on a wide scale.[68] It may take the form of the already common food riots or anti-IMF riots, or it may take on religious overtones, or may gel along ethnic lines. The signs of all of these are already apparent in parts of the continent.

Many of Africa's rivers are overused already. The security implications are enormous, especially when we consider that several of the continent's major rivers run through numerous countries. Thus the Nile is shared by nine countries, the Zambezi by eight and the Niger by ten states. Even smaller rivers flowing through fewer countries, such as the River Senegal through Senegal and Mauritania,[69] are a potential source of violent conflict. Falkenmark has indicated that by the year 2000, around 350 million people, or half of Africa's sub-Saharan population, are projected to be living in water-stressed states, and another 150 million in countries suffering from absolute scarcity of water. By 2025, Nigeria, Ethiopia,

---

[64]For a detailed breakdown see World Bank, *Population Growth and Policies in Sub-Saharan Africa*, World Bank, Washington DC, 1986. For a discussion, see N.Myers, *Population, Resources and the Environment: The Critical Challenges*, UNFPA, 1991.
[65]See the World Bank, *Sub-Saharan Africa: From Crisis to Sustainable Growth*, The World Bank, Washington DC, 1989.
[66]On the impact of these policies see B.Onimode, (ed), *The IMF, the World Bank and the African Debt: Vol 1, The Economic Impact*, Zed Books, London, 1989.
[67]Myers, in Ornas and Mohamed, op.cit, p.211.
[68]On the idea of adjustment with a human face, see G.Cornia, R.Jolly and F.Stewart, *Adjustment with a Human Face*, OUP, 1987.
[69]M.Doyle, 'Troubled Waters', *West Africa*, 19-25 June, 1990, pp.1007-1009.

Somalia, Tanzania, Malawi, Lesotho and Zimbabwe are projected to suffer from absolute water scarcity.[70]

Control of water will grow in significance as a potent weapon in the relations between states. As Falkenmark has argued:

... a secured supply of water and control of river flow must be cornerstones in national planning and development, particularly in regions where water is scarce or where increases in population reduce the degree of freedom by decreasing the amount of water available on a per capita basis.[71]

Already Egypt is well aware of its vulnerability; it is 99% dependent on water from the Nile, yet the source of that water lies outside - in Ethiopia particularly, but also in Tanzania, Uganda, Kenya, Rwanda, Burundi and Zaire. Sudan is in the same predicament. In the context of rising populations and greenhouse warming, the level of cooperation achieved in sharing water resources will become increasingly important and difficult. Historically water issues have been settled amicably, but the future outlook is not encouraging. The Egyptian government fears that the development of dams upstream will deprive Egypt of vital water supplies, and the former Foreign Minister Dr Butros Ghali has commented that future wars in the region will be fought over water, not oil. The failure of the Ethiopian government to recognize the agreements, negotiated by the colonial powers, stipulating that no hydrological project could be developed along any part of the Nile sources or tributaries without Egypt's consent has been a cause for considerable concern within Egypt.[72] From the Ethiopian standpoint, the distribution of water is iniquitous; it suffers from drought, yet contributes 86% of Nile waters while using less than 1%. Given its vulnerability, Egypt has played a leading diplomatic role in regional water negotiations, offering the carrot of cheap electricity to Nile-using countries in return for secure water agreements. Since 1983 UNDUGU has been in operation, an unofficial ministerial level meeting in which seven of the nine users discuss obstacles to water cooperation. Yet only in 1990 did Ethiopia agree to discuss the possibility of cooperation.[73]

---

[70]Falkenmark, cited by Myers in Ornas and Mohamed, op.cit, p.216.
[71]M.Falkenmark, 'Fresh Waters as a Factor in Strategic Policy and Action' in Westing, 1986, op.cit, p.85.
[72]D.Pugh, *Environment Guardian*, 12 October 1990, p.33.
[73]ibid, p.33.

Clearly the nine riparian states need to find a mechanism for water sharing if inter-state conflict is to be avoided. Many of their governments are already under pressure domestically as their power is challenged, and the ongoing civil wars have certainly made long-term water planning more difficult. For example, the development of the Jonglei Canal in southern Sudan, a project financed jointly by Egypt and Sudan for the benefit of both states, was brought to a halt in 1983 because of attacks on the construction workers by southern Sudanese guerillas. Their grudge was that water from their part of the Sudan was to be channelled to the north of the country.[74] Thus the cooperative effort foundered at the altar of internal strife within Sudan. While this example relates directly to water, there are many others that have an indirect bearing on the issue. Several governments distrust their neighbouring counterparts who they see as providing sanctuary for rebels or encouraging internal dissent. This problem exists throughout sub-Sahara and is a major impediment to cooperation for resource sharing.

The Middle East. The African experience is common to the countries of the Middle East, where the waters of the Jordan, Litani, Orontes and Yarmuk rivers are shared. The potential for inter-state conflict over water has received more attention in relation to the Middle East than to any other region. The literature is growing fast so the remarks here will be brief.[75]

The region has already experienced water as a major contributory factor in the outbreak of war. Cooley sees the 1967 Arab-Israeli conflict having roots in the unsuccessful attempt of the Arab states to divert Jordan River headwaters into Arab rivers, and argues that:

> The constant struggle for the waters of the Jordan, Litani, Orontes, Yarmuk, and other life-giving Middle East rivers, little understood outside the region, was a principal cause of the 1967 Arab-Israeli War and could help spark a new all-out conflict.[76]

[74]Falkenmark, 1986, op.cit, p.95.

[75]See J.K.Cooley, 'The War over Water', *Foreign Policy*, Vol.54, 1984, pp.3-26; J.R.Starr, and D.C.Stoll, *US Foreign Policy on Water Resources in the Middle East*, The Center for Strategic and International Studies, Washington DC, 1987; and edited by the same authors, *The Politics of Scarcity: Water in the Middle East*, Westview Press, London and Boulder, 1988; *The Environment Guardian*, 12 October 1990; and T.Walker, 'Mideast Faces Yet Another Issue of Life and Death', *Financial Times*, 7 October 1991.

[76]Cooley, op.cit, p.3.

The outlook is not good, as the region is characterized by a mass of conflicting water claims and desires which will intensify with population growth and the need to produce more food in a region which is climatically suited only to irrigated agriculture. Coupled with domestic instabilities and deep-seated inter-state rivalries and suspicions, successful mediation and cooperation are unlikely. Cooley has remarked that:

> While the need for a rational, overall water-sharing scheme steadily grows more apparent, it seems less attainable, as water issues are aggravated by political tensions and by the fact that, while its neighbours consumptions are rapidly rising, Israel still consumes roughly five times as much water per capita as each of its less industrialized and less intensively farmed neighbours.[77]

Israel has been accused of stealing Palestinian water from the West Bank,[78] and of occupying southern Lebanon partly to gain access to the waters of the Litani. Israeli and Ethiopian denials have not allayed the fear harboured by the Egyptians that Israel will provide the technology for the Ethiopians to harness more of the resources of the Nile and take some for itself as part of the bargain. Syria has stated that it will not depart from the Lebanon without a water agreement ensuring that the headwaters of the Orontes, which rises in the Bekaa valley, stay in friendly hands. Syria is dependent on that water for irrigation and drinking water for the populous western part of the country. Clearly what is needed is a regional water sharing and development plan. At present, however, what seems more likely is unilateral action by Israel, and perhaps also Syria, to control the water that they, particularly Israel, need desperately. Cooley maintains that a Middle Eastern war over water will only be averted if the US government[79] puts pressure on regional participants, particularly Israel, to join in old water plans[80] such as damming the Yarmuk which has been approved for funding by the World Bank. There is little to make us question Cooley's assessment that:

---

[77]ibid, p.3.

[78]See Cooley, ibid, p.16; E.Anderson, 'Water: the Next Strategic Resource', in Starr and Stoll, 1988, op.cit, and R.Irani, 'Water Wars', *New Statesman and Society*, 3 May 1991, p.24.

[79]On the position of the US government, see Starr and Stoll, 1987, op.cit, pp.25-38.

[80]For details of these old plans, see S.Taubenblatt, 'Jordan River Basin Water: A Challenge in the 1990s', in Starr and Stoll, 1988, op.cit, pp.43-49.

... long after oil runs out, water is likely to cause wars, cement peace, and make and break empires and alliances in the region, as it has done for thousands of years.[81]

South Asia. In South Asia, sharing of water has long presented challenges to the cooperative capacities of the governments.[82] Even before partition in 1947, the provinces of Sind and Punjab had water disputes. Partition drew the border between India and Pakistan right across the Indus River system, thus making inter-state conflict over water almost inevitable. In 1960 the two states, with the help of the World Bank, signed the Indus River Treaty.[83] This provided for exclusive Indian use of the eastern rivers of Beas, Sutlej and Ravi, while Pakistan was given exclusive rights to the waters of the western rivers Indus, Jhelum and Chenab. Simultaneously an agreement was signed between India, Pakistan, the World Bank, Canada, New Zealand, Australia, West Germany and the UK for the financing of the Indus River Basin Development Fund of $900 million. The agreements were in the mutual interest of India and Pakistan, for both needed a steady supply of water for irrigation for land that would otherwise be desert. At the time of the signing of the agreements, the extent of irrigation planned would support 40% of the population of Pakistan, and 10% of the Indian population.

India and Bangladesh have also disagreed strongly over the sharing of the water of the River Ganges, with the Farraka Barrage giving India direct control over the dry season flow of the Ganges into Bangladesh.[84]

Myers states that water-based conflicts can be expected to increase as the total population of the region grows from 1.1 billion at present to a projected 1.8 billion by the year 2020. Moreover, the greenhouse effect will probably disrupt the monsoon system.[85] Pakistan is dependent on irrigation for 80% of its food production, and has one of the largest irrigation networks in the world. Intra-province conflicts in Pakistan over water sharing may be the forerunner of an inter-state conflict with India. Like Pakistan, India has already experienced domestic disagreement over water sharing, with Sikh nationalists in the Punjab claiming that too much of their water is being diverted into water-short Haryana and

---

[81]Cooley, op.cit, p.3.
[82]N.Myers, 'Environmental Security: The Case of South Asia', *International Environmental Affairs*, Vol.1, No. 2, Spring 1989, pp.138-154.
[83]For the full text, see *Keesings Contemporary Archives*, Vol.XII, 1959-60, pp.17655-8.
[84]Myers, 1989, op.cit, p.148.
[85]ibid, p.139.

Rajasthan.[86] Domestic strife in the region will be exacerbated by rising population and insufficient resources. It can only be a matter of time before the already tense political relationship between India and Pakistan is fuelled by the issue of water sharing.

The water issue will undoubtedly fall upon ground that is ripe for violent conflict both intra-state and inter-state. Myers poses the question:

... how can we realistically suppose that environmental problems will not exert substantial and adverse influence over the prospects for the regions security within the foreseeable future?[87]

Population. It must be recognized that growing numbers pose a threat to security at all levels: from the local, to the national, the regional and ultimately to the stability of the international system. Any mechanism designed for water sharing, whether it is in Africa, South Asia, the Middle East or elsewhere, will be placed under increasing strain if population continues to rise. At some point the strain will be intolerable and the water sharing mechanism is bound to break down, with grave security implications. Population increases can place a huge burden on the environment and natural resources, and must therefore be taken into account by individuals, states and regions as they search for security.[88]

4.4 Environmental impacts of military security

Our discussion of the relationship between environment and security would be incomplete if at least brief mention were not made of the environmental impacts of preparation for war[89] and of warfare itself,[90] and also of environmental warfare whereby the environment is manipulated for hostile military purposes.[91] Historically destruction of

---

[86]ibid, p.146.

[87]ibid, p.150.

[88]See Myers/UNFPA, op.cit, Chapter Two: 'Population Impacts on Environment, Natural Resources and Quality of Life'.

[89]For a general discussion of this, see M.Renner, 'Assessing the Military's War on the Environment', in L.Brown, (ed), *State of the World, 1991*, Norton & Co for the Worldwatch Institute, London and New York, 1991, pp.132-52.

[90]For an up-to-date examination of the environmental impacts of warfare in the industrialized age, see A.Westing, (ed), *Environmental Hazards of War*, Sage, London, 1990.

[91]For a very interesting discussion of the influence of culture on the relationship between environment and warfare, see A.Westing, (ed), *Cultural Norms, War and the Environment*, OUP for SIPRI/UNEP, 1988.

forests and the release of waters have been standard procedures in this area. In 1938 the Chinese released waters of the Yellow River by dynamiting the Huayuankow dike to hold back the advancing Japanese. The US made extensive use of herbicides in the Second Indochina War, 1961-75.[92] In 1986, South Korea regarded the North Korean proposal to construct the Kumgangsan hydroelectric dam on a northern tributary of the Han River as an aggressive act. It was seen as a potential military threat because of its capacity to store up to 20,000m tonnes of water, which, if released, could submerge much of central Korea.[93] At minimum, if the dam were to collapse, whether accidentally or by intention, the Soeul metropolitan area would be flooded, and the ensuing chaos would facilitate the progress of an invading army.[94] Similarly, Syria has accused Turkey of using its control over the headwaters of the Euphrates for political ends.[95] With the burning of the Kuwaiti oilfields by the retreating Iraqi army and bombardment of Iraqi chemical, biological and possibly even nuclear facilities by the multinational force in the 1991 gulf conflict, a new phase of environmental warfare was entered, for the ramifications extended throughout the region and beyond. We do not know what the precise effects of these actions have been on Kuwait or Iraq, let alone on wider climatic conditions or on the South Asian monsoon.[96] The scope for environmental warfare today is vast, being commensurate with technological advances. Certain international legal instruments exist to regulate this form of warfare, but the exercise is fraught with difficulty not only because of perceived conflicting national interests but also because some of the areas for which regulation is sought are undeveloped. Even the peaceful destruction of

---

[92]For a comprehensive study of the use and effects of herbicides in this war, refer to A.Westing, *Herbicides in War: the Long-term Ecological and Human Consequences*, Taylor and Francis for SIPRI, London and Philadelphia, 1984.

[93]*Keesings Record of World Events*, Bristol, February 1987, p.34924.

[94]S.Chira, 'North Korea Dam Worries the South', *New York Times*, 30 November 1986, p.3.

[95]A.Cowell, 'Now, A Little Steam. Later, Maybe, a Water War', *New York Times International*, 7 February 1990, p.A4.

[96]See R.Small, 'Environmental Impact of Fires in Kuwait', *Nature*, Vol.350, 7 March 1991, pp.11-12; J.Porritt, in *Environment Guardian*, 8 February 1991, p.29, and F.Pearce, on the same page; S.Pain, 'Is Kuwait's Foul Air Fit to Breathe?', *New Scientist*, 26 October 1991, p.13.

lethal weapons, such as the nuclear weapons of the former Soviet Union, can pose enormous environmental problems.[97]

Holdgate, Kassas and White suggest that the best way to make sense of the areas covered is to categorize issues under three headings. Their schema is repeated in full here as it is the clearest available.[98]

1. The environmental consequences of current and past wars
* hazards from unexploded weapons
* physical and biological effects of damage to soil and landscape
* human suffering resulting from the disruption of social systems

2. The environmental impacts of preparations for war
* indirectly, through diversion of resources from environmental development
* through the impact of the armaments industry
* directly, through weapons testing and military operations
* through the proliferation of nuclear technology

3. The hazards of possible future warfare
* the possible impacts of conventional warfare
* the possible impacts of nuclear war
* the possible impacts of chemical and biological warfare
* the possible impacts of environmental modification

We can address the list outlined above to the five contexts identified by Westing where environmental manipulation can actually or potentially take place.[99]

1. Celestial bodies or space

2. The atmosphere

3. The land

4. The oceans

5. The biota, either terrestrial or marine

---

[97]P.Pringle, and P.Felgenhauer, 'CIS Faces Danger of Toxic Rocket Fuel Leaks', *The Independent*, 25 March 1992.
[98]M.Holdgate, M.Kassas and G.White (eds), *The World Environment, 1972-82*, Tycooly International Publishing Ltd, Dublin, for the United Nations Environment Programme, p.594.
[99]A.H.Westing, 'Environmental Warfare: an Overview', in A.H.Westing (ed), *Environmental Warfare: a Technical, Legal and Policy Appraisal*, Taylor and Francis, London and Philadelphia, 1984, p.3-12.

The consequences of nuclear accidents or warfare on all five of the above areas would be enormous.[100] Relatively unconsidered, the current potential for destruction through climatic manipulation, redirection of asteroids, herbicides, tsunamis (seismic sea-waves), and the creation of ozone windows to name but a few possibilities is extensive. While some analysts might regard such a suggestion as fanciful, since the major powers have shown little public interest in such tools, we have only to recall earlier perceptions of the Star Wars or SDI concept. The field of environmental warfare is potentially huge.

Interest in this area grew in the 1970s alongside the growing general international interest in environmental issues and particular concern over large-scale use of herbicides by the US in the Second Indochina War. It is noteworthy that the effects of military activities on the environment were specifically excluded from the 1972 UN Conference on the Human Environment in Stockholm because of US sensitivity to potential criticism of its actions in SE Asia. (The official Declaration emanating from the UN conference in Stockholm did however make the point in Principle XXVI that 'Man and his environment must be spared the effects of nuclear weapons and all other means of mass destruction.'[101] This was supported by the US). An unofficial counter-conference was held simultaneously in Stockholm drawing attention to the issue.[102] Interest developed further in the 1980s as the anti-nuclear lobby paid more attention to the potential environmental devastation that would result from a nuclear war and as the general public become more aware of the meaning of a nuclear winter. For those born after the bombing of Hiroshima and Nagasaki, the adverse consequences of nuclear disasters on the environment are just beginning to become apparent from the

---

[100] We need only consider the consequences of nuclear testing. See, for example, 'Testimonies from the Atoll', *Environment Guardian*, 7 September 1990.

[101] See United Nations General Assembly, *Report of the UN Conference on the Human Environment, Stockholm 5-16 June 1972*, UNGA Document No.A/CONF.48/14/Rev.1, New York, 1973.

[102] R.A.Falk, 'Environmental Disruption by Military Means and International Law', in Westing, 1984, ibid, pp.33-51.

Chernobyl disaster.[103] Of course, the long term health effects of Chernobyl will take generations to unfold.[104]

Legal and diplomatic attempts to meet the challenges posed by the possibility of environmental warfare have not proceeded very far. Environmental vandalism is legally constrained by Protocol 1 of 1977 on the Protection of Victims of International Conflict.[105] Articles XXXV.1 and LV.1 prohibit means of warfare intended or expected to cause widespread, long term or severe damage to the environment which would thereby prejudice the health of the population. Article LV1.1 prohibits attacks on installations if such attacks may cause the release of dangerous forces which would harm the civilian population.[106] Protocol 11 of 1977 on the Protection of Victims of Non-International Armed Conflicts makes similar prohibitions.[107] Obtaining compliance with such international agreements is notoriously difficult.

The example of the Environmental Modification (ENMOD) Convention of 1977 is instructive, and we shall consider it here in more detail.[108] The purpose of the Convention is to prohibit military or other hostile uses of environmental modification techniques. It resulted from lengthy bilateral talks between the two superpowers, and multilateral discussions convened by the Geneva Conference of the Committee on Disarmament. It received much popular support at the time due to public concern at the recent experience of US environmental warfare in SE Asia. While in principle this convention represents a major step forward, in practice its achievements are limited.[109] For example, it is severely circumscribed by dealing specifically with deliberate human

---

[103]See for example P.R.Ehrlich, 'Nuclear Winter: a Forecast of the Climatic and Biological Effects of Nuclear War', *Bulletin of the Atomic Scientists*, Chicago, Vol.40, No.4, pp.1S-15S; and by the same author 'Nuclear Winter: Discovering the Ecology of Nuclear War', *Amicus Journal*, New York, Vol.5, No.3, pp.20-30.

[104]On the effects of Chernobyl, see M.Bojcun, and V.Haines, *The Chernobyl Disaster*, Hogarth Press, 1988; D.R.Marples, *The Social Impact of the Chernobyl Disaster*, Macmillan, London, 1988; and I.Shcherbak, *Chernobyl: A Documentary History*; Macmillan, London, 1989.

[105]Westing, 1988, op.cit, p.166.

[106]ibid.

[107]ibid.

[108]For the text of the Convention, see Westing, 1984, op.cit, pp.93-8.

[109]L.Juda, 'Negotiating a Treaty on Environmental Modification Warfare: the Convention on Environmental Warfare and its Impact Upon Arms Control Negotiations', *International Organization*, Vol.32, No.4, Autumn 1978, pp.975-991.

manipulation of natural processes, and excluding conventional warfare which might have as a repercussion harmful effects on the environment. Moreover, it fails to prohibit all hostile acts which affect the environment; instead it covers only those having widespread, long-lasting or severe effects. Goldblat has argued that:

> ... to be effective, the constraints must be unambiguous, as nearly all-inclusive as possible and without any loopholes. The Enmod Convention is far from meeting these requirements. It is not clear what is actually banned by the Convention, nor is it clear how hostile intent can be adequately established ... The Convention thus appears to condone hostile manipulation of the environment with some unspecified 'benign' means. It is also deficient in that it bans only hostile use, but not the development or possession of modification techniques for such use. No wonder that five years after its entry into force, the Enmod Convention could claim no more than 43 parties, including only three of the five permanent members of the United Nations Security Council.[110]

He is not alone in his criticism of the Convention. Krass has been even more scathing:

> No agreement to prevent certain kinds of destructive activity should be ignored, yet there should also be no illusion that marginal treaties such as the Enmod Convention represent significant progress towards disarmament. They can in fact serve as a public relations cover designed to hide the lack of any real progress in this area.[111]

Both Krass and Goldblat detect the need for greater US commitment to the Convention if it is to attract the support of more states. Unfortunately many small states have seen the US commitment to a partial ban, rather than a comprehensive one which would forbid any environmental modification techniques, as potentially sinister and threatening. (The former USSR supported a comprehensive ban as opposed to one restricted to widespread, long-lasting and severe techniques). The ineffectual impact of the Convention reflects the wider weaknesses of enforcement in international law.

---

[110]J.Goldblat, 'The Environmental Modification Convention of 1977: an Analysis', in Westing, 1984, op.cit, p.62.
[111]A.S.Krass, 'The Environmental Modification Convention of 1977: the Question of Verification', in Westing, 1984, op.cit, p.75.

In 1982 the UN General Assembly adopted the World Charter for Nature, an initiative by the developing countries to protect the environment. The vote stood at 112 for and 1 (the USA) against, with 18 abstentions.[112] The 36-nation draft was brought forward by Zaire.[113] The US had attempted unsuccessfully to get the discussion postponed, on the grounds that the language in places was imprecise and the obligations placed on individuals for upholding the Charter under Article XXIV were inappropriate. Importantly, the Charter states in Article V that: 'Nature shall be secured against degradation caused by warfare or other hostile activities'.[114] Falk has remarked that:

> ... the one negative vote ... was by the USA, the state that has relied on large-scale, systematic environmental warfare in a recent conflict.[115]

He maintains that while the general direction of international normative thought is clear, it lacks authority given the position of the US and the provisos of all nuclear states relating to testing etc.

The difficulties pertaining to regulation of environmental war and environmentally hostile acts are clear. Even where agreement has been achieved, such as in the ENMOD Convention, membership is often limited, verification[116] is almost impossible, and key areas are not covered. Moreover, new areas requiring regulation are constantly opening up. One environmental problem which has escaped diplomatic discussion let alone legal regulation, and where a code of practice is needed urgently, is that of rubbish in space. Wood-Kaczmar has commented that:

---

[112]Westing, 1988, op.cit, p.169.

[113]See H.W.Wood, 'The UN World Charter for Nature: The Developing Nations Initiative to Establish Protections for the Environment', *Ecology Law Quarterly*, No.12, 1985, pp.977-996.

[114]For the text of the World Charter for Nature, (UN General Assembly Resolution No.37/7, 28 November 1982) see *UN Yearbook, 1982*, Vol.36, United Nations, New York, pp.1023-26.

[115]Falk, 1984, op.cit, p.38.

[116]Verification of arms control agreements is notoriously difficult, for political and technical reasons. Politically, it conflicts directly with the concept of sovereign statehood; technically, there can be real difficulties in establishing whether, for example, a chemical facility caters for peaceful or military purposes. Moreover, the aims of states regarding verification are different: some take a minimalist approach, others, a maximalist approach. See J.B.Poole (ed), *Verification Report, 1991: Yearbook on Arms Control and Environmental Agreements*, Vertic Press, London, and Apex Press, New York, 1991.

Indiscriminate pollution, and in some instances wilful degradation of the space environment by both the US and the Soviet Union, have resulted in an estimated 3.5 million pieces of rubbish in orbit around the Earth.[117]

Tiny fragments of rubbish travelling at a high velocity could cause fatal damage to spaceships and astronauts, as well as to space stations. Moreover, that damage will itself result in many more dangerous fragments in space. Most space rubbish is related directly or indirectly to security. Half the rubbish is the product of explosions - accidental or deliberate - and both superpowers are responsible. Wood-Kaczmar reports that in the period 1973-81, seven American Delta rockets exploded in space before the manufacturers, McDonnell Douglas, realized their fate. Over the period 1964-86, the Soviets destroyed over thirty satellites for security reasons.[118] Another formidable problem is posed by the fact that many satellites are nuclear powered. In April 1990, the superpowers broke a ten-year deadlock and managed to establish international guidelines on the safe operation of nuclear power sources in space. By the early 1990s, there should be a complete set of international legal principles governing nuclear safety in space. This is long overdue.

Whereas up to now the main culprits have been the superpowers, the planned extensive proliferation of space reconnaissance by other states will make the negotiation of a code of practice all the more urgent.[119]

4.5 Conclusions

The relationship between environment and security is complex. Clearly it does not exist in a vacuum. Environmental problems are played out on the stage of world politics, and their effect on security will largely be determined by pre-existing social tensions, legitimacy crises, and political instability. Moreover, factors such as population growth have a crucial input into the equation. Nevertheless, environmental problems will themselves make the world a far more insecure place in which to live both at the local and state level. The challenges presented for international leadership and cooperation are enormous. We live in an

[117] Wood-Kaczmar, 'The Junkyard in the Sky', *New Scientist*, 13 October 1990.
[118] ibid, p.37.
[119] J.Richelson, 'The Future of Space Reconnaissance', *Scientific American*, Vol.264, No.1, January 1991, pp.18-24.

interdependent world, and environmental issues are inextricably bound up with local economic policies and the world capitalist economy. The idea that issues such as debt, development, disarmament and the environment may be disentangled is essentially flawed, as ultimately solutions cannot be separate. Holdgate et al have argued that:

Development cannot proceed at the required pace, or a healthy environment be guaranteed, if scarce human and material resources are absorbed by a widening and constantly escalating arms race. Moreover, development and environment are threatened by the armaments, and especially the nuclear weapons, already stockpiled; and the use of these, whether through error, intent or sheer madness, would severely jeopardize mankind's very existence and bring ecological disruption to vast areas of the globe.[120]

There is no doubt that a holistic conception of security is imperative. The traditional approach based on military preparedness to meet an external military threat to a sovereign state is inadequate. The challenges today come from two main sources: domestic instability fuelled by economic stagnation, and global problems such as debt and the environment. These factors exacerbate one another. Inter-state hostilities will be aggravated by environmental pressures. This fundamental problem must be addressed by a developmental approach to security.

---

[120]Holdgate et al, op.cit, p.614.

PART II: CASE STUDIES

Since 1988 in particular, it has been increasingly perceived by the international community that the problem of global warming warrants a serious international response. Because of the truly global nature of the problem, and the fact that responding is likely to affect large sectors of all economies, global warming arguably presents a great challenge to the international system as it currently functions. A successful response may depend upon unprecedented levels of international cooperation. This chapter outlines the nature of the challenge, the response of countries in the international arena to date, and some of the political issues involved.

5.1 The science of global warming

The scientific theory of the greenhouse effect was first described by Baron Jean Baptiste Fourier in 1827, when he calculated that the temperature of the earth's surface is affected by the chemical composition of the atmosphere, in an analogous manner to how the glass in a greenhouse traps and heats the air.[1] In 1896, it was argued by the Swedish scientist Svante Arrhenius that it was possible that human activities such as burning fossil fuels could, in theory, lead to an increase in the earth's surface temperature. According to him, a doubling of carbon dioxide (CO_2) concentrations in the atmosphere, which might occur over a period of centuries, would increase average surface

---

[1]S.Boyle and J.Ardill, *The Greenhouse Effect - A Practical Guide to the World's Changing Climate*, Hodder and Stoughton, London, 1989, p.12.

temperature by 5°C, and by greater amounts at higher latitudes.[2] For a long time this remained purely a theory. It was not until 1938 that a British scientist, G.S.Callendar, suggested that humans were emitting greenhouse gases in sufficient quantities to alter climate significantly.[3] However this view remained uninfluential until 1957, when Roger Revelle, a leading US oceanographer, coined the phrase 'a large-scale geophysical experiment'.[4] By that year, which was International Geophysical Year,[5] interest in the issue had become sufficient that a permanent CO_2 monitoring station was set up on Mauna Loa in Hawaii.[6] Gradually during the post-war period, monitoring of climatic conditions increased in scale and complexity, much because of national efforts.

The warming theory was by no means widely accepted; indeed during the early 1970s the fear that the earth might be moving into a natural cooling cycle was widespread. By the 1980s, however, fears among much of the scientific community of the possibility of a significant global warming had grown considerably, and scientific cooperation on the issue grew to develop knowledge on the subject. By 1990, the Intergovernmental Panel on Climate Change (IPCC), a body set up by the United Nations Environment Programme and the World Meteorological Organization to consider the state of scientific knowledge on the subject, had considered the available scientific evidence and produced a report which was widely perceived as reflecting the consensus among most of the world's climate scientists.[7]

---

[2] ibid. Also F.Pearce, *Turning up the Heat - Our Perilous Future in the Global Greenhouse*, Paladin, London, 1989, p.97.

[3] Pearce, op.cit.

[4] ibid; S.H.Schneider, 'The Greenhouse Effect: Science and Policy', *Science*, Vol.243, 1989, pp.771-781; R.Revell and H.Suess, *Tellus*, Vol.9, No.18, 1957.

[5] M.S.Soroos, 'The Atmosphere as an International Common Property Resource', in S.S.Nagel (ed.), *Global Policy Studies: International Interaction Toward Improving Public Policy*, MacMillan, London, 1991, p.201. The International Geophysical Year actually ran for 18 months during 1957-8.

[6] M.L.Cain, 'Carbon dioxide and the climate: monitoring and the search for understanding', in D.Kay and H.Jacobson, *Environmental Protection: The International Dimension*, Allanheld, Osmun, 1983, pp.75-98.

[7] J.T.Houghton, G.J.Jenkins and J.J.Ephraims (eds), *Climate Change: The IPCC Scientific Assessment*, Cambridge University Press, Cambridge, 1990; for a discussion of the nature of the IPCC scientific consensus, see L.Lunde, 'Science and Politics in the Greenhouse. How Robust is the IPCC Consensus?' *International Challenges*, Vol.11, No.1, 1991, pp.48-57. For more on the IPCC, see below, section 5.

The greenhouse effect is a natural phenomenon, whereby certain gases in the atmosphere keep the earth's temperature significantly higher than it would otherwise be; they produce conditions at the earth's surface which are suitable for life. These gases allow radiation to pass through from the sun, but absorb the lower frequency, longer wavelength radiation from the earth's surface, thereby trapping heat in the atmosphere. It is estimated that without these gases, the earth's surface temperature would be 33°C lower than at present.[8]

The main anthropogenic gases involved in the greenhouse effect, are carbon dioxide (CO_2), chlorofluorocarbons (CFCs), methane (CH_4), and nitrous oxide (N_2O). All of these are being emitted by various human activities at steadily increasing rates (for details of these activities, see below, section 4). These increases in greenhouse gas emissions are predicted to produce increases in the earth's average surface temperature. Figure 5.1 shows the relative contribution of each of these gases to global warming during the 1980s.[9] The precise responsibility varies for each gas depending upon the timescale chosen since each gas remains in the atmosphere for a different period of time; if a 100-year timescale is chosen, then the importance of CO_2 increases to 61%, while that of CFCs declines to 11.5%.[10]

The gases involved have all increased significantly during the 20th Century, both in terms of emissions and atmospheric concentrations. Figure 5.2 (pp.160-161) shows the increases in concentrations of some of the major gases. These increases can be compared to the increase in global average surface temperature during a similar period, estimated at between 0.3°C and 0.6°C.[11] While correlation does not in itself prove cause,[12] the view of the IPCC was that the likelihood of a link is increasingly convincing; they were certain that 'these increases [in

[8]J.Leggett, 'The Nature of the Greenhouse Threat', in J.Leggett (ed.), *Global Warming: The Greenpeace Report*, OUP, Oxford, 1990, pp.14-43; W.A.Nierenberg, R.Jastrow and F.Seitz, *Scientific Perspectives on the Greenhouse Problem*, Marshall Institute, Washington DC, 1989.
[9]Intergovernmental Panel on Climate Change, *Policymakers Summary of the Scientific Assessment of Climate Change*, World Meteorological Organization/United Nations Environment Programme, 1990 (hereafter referred to as 'Working Group I Policymakers Summary'), p.11.
[10]ibid, p.12.
[11]ibid, p.2.
[12]ibid, p.22.

Figure 5.1 Relative contribution of greenhouse gases to radiative change in the 1980s

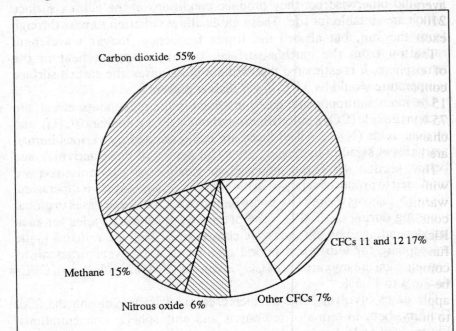

Carbon dioxide 55%

CFCs 11 and 12 17%

Methane 15%

Nitrous oxide 6%

Other CFCs 7%

The contribution from tropospheric ozone may also be significant, but cannot be quantified at present.

Source: Intergovernmental Panel on Climate Change, *Policymakers Summary of the Scientific Assessment of Climate Change*, World Meteorological Organization/United Nations Environment Programme, 1990.

greenhouse gas atmospheric concentrations] will enhance the greenhouse effect, resulting on average in additional warming of the Earth's surface'.[13]

The IPCC produced projections of the sort of warming they anticipated, given both a 'business-as-usual' scenario of how the world would evolve, and considering various possible responses. A business-as-usual scenario (ie. one where the assumption is that no policies are implemented to

[13]ibid, p.1.

affect greenhouse gas emissions and that therefore emissions will follow their current trends) would, in their view, involve an increase in global average surface temperature of approximately 1°C by 2030 and 3°C by 2100.[14] It has been widely noted, that such a magnitude of change would exceed any experience in human history.

The IPCC also estimated the magnitude of reductions in the emissions of each gas which would be necessary to stabilize atmospheric concentrations at current levels. These were estimated at >60% for CO_2, 15-20% for methane, 70-80% for nitrous oxide, 70-75% for CFC-11, 75-85% for CFC-12, and 40-50% for HCFC-22.[15] Thus significant changes in existing strategies for those sectors which produce these gases are likely to be necessary.

The projections and estimates that the IPCC made are of course beset with considerable uncertainties and problems. Not least is that the warming experienced to date is still within the bounds of what is considered 'natural variability'. This has enabled sceptics such as Richard Lindzen to voice their doubts more forcefully.[16] The other fundamental problem in this regard is that since the climate system is so complex, and since the traditional scientific control experiments cannot be undertaken on it, the 'normal' tests of scientific certainty cannot be applied. No individual climatic event can ever be definitively attributed to human-induced global warming. There will always be an element of uncertainty.

Two other types of uncertainty exist. One relates to the relative contributions of different gases. Estimates of the responsibility of each gas have changed repeatedly in the research undertaken by scientists, and uncertainties persist in assessments of each gas's radiative capacity, its lifetime in the atmosphere, and its sources. Secondly, there are significant uncertainties about how the climate system responds to

---

[14]ibid. The uncertainty is of a factor of two, so that the projection of a 3°C rise gives a range of 2-4°C.

[15]ibid, p.8.

[16]Other prominent sceptics have been scientists from the George Marshall Institute. See Nierenberg et al, op.cit. The main objection to conclusions such as those of the IPCC has been based around assumptions about the role of water vapour changes in the atmosphere in response to warming. Lindzen and others argue that water vapour increases will offset any warming. See R.S.Lindzen, 'Some Coolness Concerning Global Warming', *Bulletin of the American Meteorological Society*, Vol.71, No.3, March 1990, pp.288-299; R.S.Lindzen, 'Review of IPCC Report', *Times Higher Education Supplement*, 21 October 1990.

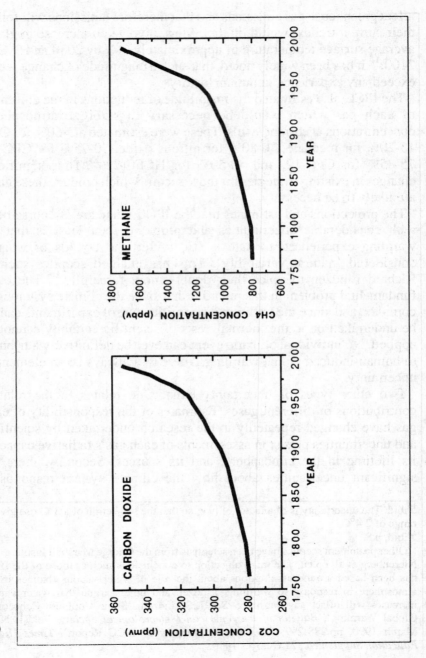

Figure 5.2 Increases in atmospheric concentrations of major greenhouse gases

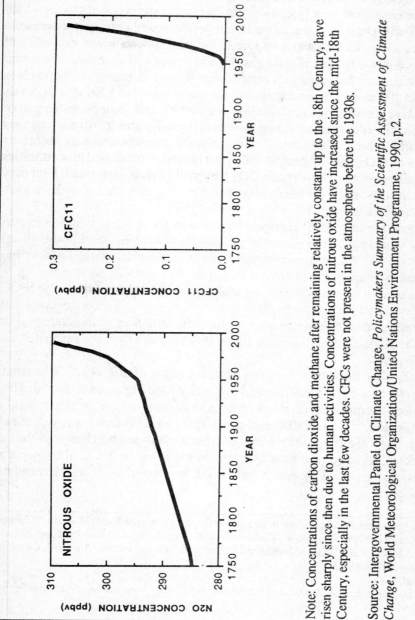

Note: Concentrations of carbon dioxide and methane after remaining relatively constant up to the 18th Century, have risen sharply since then due to human activities. Concentrations of nitrous oxide have increased since the mid-18th Century, especially in the last few decades. CFCs were not present in the atmosphere before the 1930s.

Source: Intergovernmental Panel on Climate Change, *Policymakers Summary of the Scientific Assessment of Climate Change*, World Meteorological Organization/United Nations Environment Programme, 1990, p.2.

increases in greenhouse gas concentrations. Several feedback mechanisms are widely known. It is likely that the types of clouds which form will change, since a rise in temperature will cause an increase in the concentration of water vapour in the atmosphere, water vapour itself being a powerful greenhouse gas. This increase will also affect the extent and location of snow and ice cover. Both of these changes will themselves affect the rate of warming, but since some types of clouds will act as positive feedbacks (enhancing warming) and others as negative feedbacks (dampening down warming), predictions of likely changes become more problematic.[17] Similarly, the role of oceans as absorbers both of CO_2 and of heat is still poorly understood, and uncertainties remain relating to how much CO_2 they will absorb, how much heat they will absorb, and over what timescale it will release stored-up heat back into the atmosphere.

There are also feedbacks not included in the models which relate to how warming might generate greater emissions of greenhouse gases themselves. An example of this type of feedback would be possible methane releases from tundra as permafrost recedes with warming.[18] While these feedbacks were not included in formal modelling, the IPCC believed that 'it appears likely that these feedbacks will lead to an overall increase, rather than decrease, in natural greenhouse gas abundances. For this reason, climate change is likely to be greater than the estimates we have given'.[19]

A further uncertainty relates to the nature of the IPCC scenarios. Energy-economic scenarios and projections are highly uncertain and the subject themselves of much debate, a debate which is often highly politicized.[20] Hugely different projections about future energy demand have been given by various analysts, each assuming no change in future policies, and as a result the assumption made by the IPCC about what a 'business-as-usual' scenario is should be treated with an element of caution.

---

[17]For a discussion of problems in estimating the effects of clouds, see M.Allen, 'Climate Research Review: The Clouds Controversy', *Energy Policy*, October 1990, pp.793-4.
[18]G.J.MacDonald, 'Role of Methane Clathrates in Past and Future Climates', *Climatic Change*, June 1990.
[19]ibid, p.19.
[20]T.Baumgartner and A.Middtun, *The Politics of Energy Forecasting*, Clarendon Press, Oxford, 1987.

A final point when considering these uncertainties and the rate of any warming, is that the nature of the climate system means that temperature changes may be rapid and disruptive rather than smooth and gradual. Analogies drawn from the end of the last ice age suggest that major temperature changes are possible in very short timescales, possibly as short as fifty years.[21] Thus many of the impacts may be made more severe because the changes occur in rapid bursts.

5.2 The physical impacts

The uncertainties about the timing and extent of temperature changes are reflected and amplified when the likely impacts of global warming are examined. The IPCC's Working Group II found it very difficult to make clear predictions about what impacts would occur, given the uncertainties relating to the temperature and other changes. However, the following changes, to sea levels, to rainfall and water run-off, and to forests and other natural terrestrial ecosystems, were anticipated.

Generally it has been argued that the temperature changes are likely to be uneven, being greater towards the poles than at the equator. Earlier estimates suggested that it could be the case that warming would be as little as 0.1°C in the tropics and as much as 8°C at the poles.[22] The IPCC stated that, generally speaking, 'high latitudes warm more than the global mean in winter'.[23] They then refined this by looking at particular regions. They suggested for example that while central North America would experience a warming of 2-4°C in the winter and 2-3°C in the summer under the business-as-usual scenario by 2030, the warming in the Sahel region of Africa would be 1-3°C.[24]

Sea level rise is expected, due predominantly to the melting of glaciers and to the fact that water expands when it is heated.[25] The combination of possible melting, but also accumulation of snow at the poles adds considerable uncertainties. Working Group I noted that 'Although, over the next 100 years, the effect of the Antarctic and Greenland ice sheets is expected to be small, they make a major contribution to the uncertainty

[21]S.Schneider, 'The Science of Climate-Modelling and a Perspective on the Global Warming Debate', in Leggett (ed.) op.cit, p.58.
[22]Cited in Boyle and Ardill, op.cit, p.52.
[23]Working Group I Policymakers Summary, op.cit, p.1.
[24]J.T.Houghton, et al (eds), op.cit.
[25]Working Group I Policymakers Summary, op.cit, p.22.

of predictions'.[26] The final IPCC judgement was again hedged round with considerable uncertainties, predicting a rise of about 6cm per decade under the business-as-usual scenario (but with an uncertainty range of 3-10cm) and an overall rise of approximately 20cm by 2030 and 65cm by 2100.[27] These projections were lower than those made by previous assessments.

Uncertainty increases in relation to other impacts. Changes in precipitation and water surface run-off are widely anticipated but the precise regional breakdown of this is very difficult to predict. The IPCC suggested that precipitation would, for its sample regions, increase by about 10-15% (except for southern Europe), but changes in soil moisture would vary greatly; while the moisture in central North America could decline by 15-20% in summer, it could increase by 15-25% in southern Europe.[28] Working Group II suggested that those areas already most vulnerable to shortages of available water (eg. the Sahel), or most susceptible to marked changes in the level of water supplies (eg. South East Asia), could be hardest hit. This would result in increased desertification in some areas; 'in the semi-arid, arid, and hyper-arid ecoclimatic zones of the Mediterranean, greenhouse-gas-induced climate change will reduce plant productivity and result in desertification of the North African and Near Eastern steppes owing to increased evapotranspiration'.[29] They suggested that a decline in the available water of as much as 40-70% was possible in some limited areas.[30] The most vulnerable areas were argued to be the Maghreb, the Sahel, the north of Africa, Southern Africa, western Arabia, South East Asia, the Indian subcontinent, Mexico, Central America, southwest US, eastern Brazil and the Mediterranean zone.[31] In contrast, the problem in other areas could be from too much water causing extensive flooding, as has been suggested could occur in the northern CIS.[32] Biodiversity could be

[26]ibid.
[27]ibid.
[28]ibid, p.18.
[29]Intergovernmental Panel on Climate Change, *Policymakers Summary of the Potential Impact of Climate Change*, World Meteorological Organization/United Nations Environment Programme, 1990 (hereafter referred to as 'Working Group II Policymakers Summary'), p.21.
[30]ibid, p.4.
[31]ibid, p.24.
[32]G.M.Woodwell, 'The Effects of Global Warming', in Leggett (ed.) op.cit, pp.116-132.

adversely affected in many areas whether precipitation rose or fell, since in many ecosystems, it is already at an optimal level.[33] Conversely, however, it is known that increasing CO_2 (in laboratory studies) enhances plant growth, and thus is likely to offset at least some of the potential losses in productivity, depending in part on the rate and absolute degree of change.

In relation to forests, Working Group II of the IPCC noted several ways in which they were likely to be harmed: through increases in the numbers of insects and diseases; through shifts in climatic zones towards the poles which could well be considerably faster than the ability of tree species, as well as than that of many other species of flora, to migrate; through increases in the number of forest fires; and through flooding in some areas which experienced much greater rainfall and water run-off.[34] The areas already closest to the biological limits in terms of temperatures and moisture would be hardest hit.[35]

5.3 Human impacts and adaptation

One of the most immediately obvious possible impacts on human societies is through effects on agriculture. Much of the early speculation on who would be 'winners' and who would be 'losers' under global warming took the form of trying to estimate how agriculture would shift in response to changing climatic zones. Thus it was suggested that the United States would cease to be the 'grain basket' of the world, and that this function would be taken over by the countries of the former Soviet Union and by Canada. The IPCC stated that 'studies have not yet conclusively determined whether, on average, global agricultural potential will increase or decrease'.[36] However, it is evident that, taken on a regional basis, potential yields may be significantly altered. They suggested that the regions most likely to experience significant reductions in their agricultural potential would include 'Brazil, Peru, the Sahel Region of Africa, Southeast Asia, the Asian region of the USSR and China'.[37] Overall, they stated that the impact would be negative

---

[33]D.Western, 'Climatic Change and Biodiversity', in S.H.Ominde and C.Juma (eds), *A Change in the Weather: African Perspectives on Climate Change*, African Centre for Technology Studies, Nairobi, Kenya, 1991, pp.87-96.
[34]Working Group II Policymakers Summary, pp.15-17.
[35]ibid, p.3.
[36]ibid, p.12.
[37]ibid, p.2.

unless the impacts of the temperature and other climatic changes (including increases in pests) were offset by the possible benefits of increased CO_2 on photosynthesis.[38]

Detrimental impacts on agriculture would be for the following reasons. Firstly, as climatic zones migrate, some crops would no longer be able to grow where they previously had been cultivated, since the temperature would be outside the range which they could cope with. Secondly, pests, both insects and diseases, are likely to be some of the first organisms to be able to adapt to a warming because of their short breeding time, and may flourish in the new conditions. This may affect crop yields. Lastly, the amount of water available to plants may change significantly, and the number of days in which some crops have less water than they can cope with may increase to above critical levels.[39]

Other impacts on human societies are evident however. While the implications of sea level rise has been dealt with in detail in Chapter 4, here it is worth noting that its impacts are likely to include the possible disappearance of several island states, the inundation of low-lying areas by salt-water, making agriculture impossible and contaminating freshwater supplies, and will force the migration of large numbers of people (Chapter 4 suggested 30 million for Bangladesh alone, p.130).

Many societies will also be vulnerable to the possible increase in frequency and intensity of freak weather conditions, such as tropical storms, which had been predicted by some.[40] However, the IPCC stated that it was impossible to conclude firmly that tropical storms would increase or decrease. While the area of ocean which was warm enough (26°C) for a tropical storm to occur over it would expand as temperature increased, the critical temperature might itself also rise.[41] And while the theoretical maximum intensity of a tropical storm might also increase, computer models failed to show consistently any indication of whether the intensity would actually increase.

The ability of human societies to adapt to these impacts clearly depends on the economic capabilities of countries. Industrialized countries will obviously be more easily able to adapt to sea level rise, or to changes in agricultural potential, than will developing countries, a fact which has

---

[38]ibid, p.12.
[39]ibid, p.13.
[40]D.A.Wirth, 'Climate Chaos', *Foreign Policy*, Spring 1989, pp.3-22.
[41]Working Group I Policymakers Summary, pp.17-18.

influenced countries' positions in the negotiations (see below, section 5.6). The difference in the abilities to respond and adapt to sea-level rise between The Netherlands and Bangladesh, for example, is obvious. While The Netherlands already has both the technological and economic ability to strengthen existing techniques for keeping the sea out, Bangladesh may be left with large numbers of environmental refugees.[42] In relation to agriculture, industrialized countries have a much greater ability to control not only their environments, through their ability to supply water artificially from elsewhere if it is being lost from the soil, but also by having the technological and financial ability to manipulate crop strains genetically to adapt to new climatic conditions.

The costs of adapting to global warming, because of the uncertainties about the timing and rate of warming, and about its impacts themselves, remain very uncertain. Some economists have attempted to quantify the overall costs of adapting to global warming,[43] but as Grubb argues, 'all that can be usefully said is that the less the rate of atmospheric change, the less the risks and costs are likely to be'.[44] Even many economists formally committed to cost-benefit analysis accept that for most of the likely outcomes of global warming, the range of uncertainty about the costs of the impacts on which to base an analysis is too great.[45] What remains certain, however, is that some countries will be significantly more able to bear the costs of adapting than others, a fact that becomes relevant when equity issues are discussed later on. Other impacts which will be of particular international relevance will be the increase in environmental refugees, those from low-lying island states or otherwise affected by sea level rise, and those affected by desertification, and also the possible disputes which may arise or be exacerbated over shared water resources such as the Nile or the Jordan rivers (see Chapter 4).

---

[42] Wirth notes that a 1 metre rise, at the upper end of the IPCC projections for 2100, would displace 9 percent of Bangladesh's population, which currently stands at about 112 million. Wirth, op.cit, p.9. See also A.C.Ibe and L.F.Awosika, 'Sea level rise impact on African coastal zones', in Ominde and Juma (eds), op.cit, pp.105-111, for some of the problems facing developing countries in adapting.

[43] See for example W.Nordhaus, 'Greenhouse Economics: Count Before You Leap', *The Economist*, 7 July 1990, p.21.

[44] M.Grubb, *Energy Policies and the Greenhouse Effect, Volume One: Policy Appraisal*, Dartmouth, Aldershot, 1990, p.12.

[45] See, for example, D.Pearce, 'The Global Commons', in D.Pearce (ed.), *Blueprint 2 - Greening the World Economy*, Earthscan, London, 1991, pp.11-30.

Table 5.1 Greenhouse gases and their main anthropogenic sources

Carbon dioxide (CO_2)	Fossil fuel burning
	Deforestation and land use changes
	Cement manufacture
Methane (CH_4)	Rice paddy cultivation
	Ruminants (eg. cows and sheep)
	Biomass (wood, wastes etc) burning and decay
	Releases from fossil fuel production
Chlorofluorocarbons (CFCs)	Manufactured for solvents, refrigerants,
	aerosol spray propellants, foam packaging, etc
Nitrous oxide (N_2O)	Fertilizers
	Fossil fuel burning
	Land conversion for agriculture

Precursor gases (involved in ozone and methane chemistry):

Nitrogen oxides (NO_x)	Fossil fuel burning
Non-methane hydrocarbons	Evaporation of liquid fuels and solvents
Carbon monoxide (CO)	Fossil fuel and biomass burning

5.4 Sources of the gases

Where then do the greenhouse gases come from? To be able to consider the political responses, it is necessary to look at the sources of greenhouse gas emissions, both at which economic sectors are primarily responsible, and at which countries they predominantly originate in. These underpin the political negotiations on the issue, and uncertainties over emissions and their sources are significant in the struggles to identify who is to be mainly responsible for responding.

Table 5.1 shows the main anthropogenic sources of these gases.[46] This indicates that while the sources are varied, encompassing energy

---

[46]M.Grubb, *The Greenhouse Effect: Negotiating Targets*, Royal Institute of International Affairs, London, 2nd edition 1992, p.6.

production, agriculture, forestry, industrial chemical production (of CFCs), the burning of fossil fuels (coal, oil, natural gas) is the predominant activity involved. This accounts for approximately 80% of the CO_2,[47] and is also involved in CH_4, N_2O, and the ozone precursors. The IPCC estimated that the relative contribution of different economic sectors to global warming during the 1980s is as outlined in Figure 5.3,[48] indicating energy (including transport) to be the single most important sector, accounting for 46% of all greenhouse gas emissions. When we consider that CFCs are currently being regulated under the Montreal Protocol and its 'London Revisions' of 1990 (see Chapter 6) and that the uncertainties surrounding emissions of methane and nitrous oxide, the gases which are largely represented by the forestry and agriculture sectors, are much greater than those for CO_2, the unavoidability of focusing on energy in response measures becomes clear.

The overall contribution of each country to global warming depends on which gases are to be counted and on what basis. This has become the subject of considerable political controversy, as discussed below (section 5.6). The responsibility changes depending on which gases are regarded as the most important, on what assumptions are made in relation to those gases (primarily methane, nitrous oxide and the part of CO_2 emissions which come from deforestation) around which much uncertainty persists, and on whether emissions are counted simply by each state, or by each state on a per capita or per GNP basis. The figures below will look mainly at fossil CO_2 emissions (because of the argument above).

The countries or regions which are primarily responsible for fossil CO_2 emissions are shown in Figure 5.4.[49] This shows clearly that the major

---

[47] The precise contribution of the fossil fuel industry to overall CO_2 emissions depends on estimates of CO_2 emissions from deforestation, around which there is still considerable uncertainty. Estimates for emissions from deforestation range from 0.4-1.6GtC/yr, to 0.9-2.5GtC/yr. CO_2 emissions from fossil fuel burning are about 6GtC/yr. See D.O.Hall, 'Carbon flow in the biosphere: present and future', *Journal of the Geological Society*, London, Vol.146, 1989, pp.175-81, and R.A.Houghton and G.M.Woodwell, 'Global climate change', *Scientific American*, No.260, 1989, pp.36-44, for differing estimates of emissions from deforestation. Grubb, op.cit (1990), pp.18-19.
[48] Intergovernmental Panel on Climate Change, *Policymakers Summary of the Formulation of Response Strategies*, World Meteorological Organization/United Nations Environment Programme, 1990 (hereafter referred to as 'Working Group III Policymakers Summary'), p.2.
[49] *BP Statistical Review of World Energy*, London, June 1991.

Figure 5.3 Contribution to radiative forcing by sector, 1980s

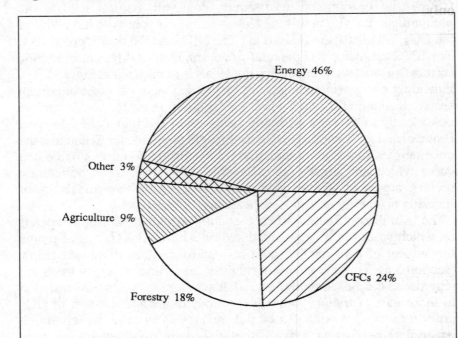

Energy 46%

Other 3%

Agriculture 9%

CFCs 24%

Forestry 18%

Source: Intergovernmental Panel on Climate Change, *Policymakers Summary of the Formulation of Response Strategies*, World Meteorological Organization/United Nations Environment Programme, 1990.

emitters are the industrialized countries. Developing countries contribute only about 26% to global fossil CO_2 emissions,[50] while they have about 75% of the world's population. Per capita emissions from for example China are about one-tenth of the OECD average, and most developing countries are still lower in per capita terms.

If we look at changes in emissions over time, then it becomes clear that the relative contribution of countries and groups of countries is likely to change significantly, a factor which further complicates the political

---

[50]*Greenhouse Gas Emissions: The Energy Dimension*, International Energy Agency/Organization for Economic Cooperation and Development, Paris, 1991, p.15; World Resources Institute, *World Resources 1990-91*, WRI, Washington DC, 1990.

Figure 5.4 Fossil carbon emissions (commercial energy consumption only) Units: MtC

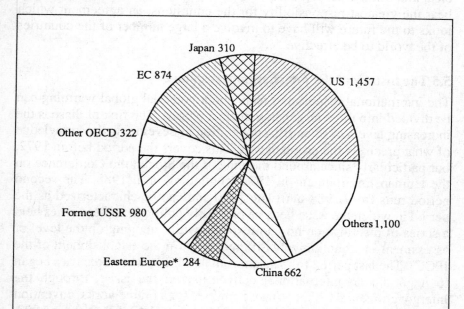

Japan 310
EC 874
US 1,457
Other OECD 322
Former USSR 980
Others 1,100
Eastern Europe* 284
China 662

*Eastern Europe includes Yugoslavia and Albania, but not East Germany

Source: derived from *BP Statistical Review of World Energy*, London, June 1991.

implications. Notably, emissions from developing countries are likely to rise sharply while those in industrialized countries will probably remain about stable (or decline if policy measures are adopted). In the words of Lashof and Tirpak, 'Per capita emissions in developing countries are currently very low, but the share of total emissions contributed by the developing countries is expected to increase significantly in the future and becomes more than 50% by 2025 in the scenarios analyzed'.[51] The relative importance of population growth and industrialization in

[51]D.A.Lashof and D.A.Tirpak (eds), *Policy Options for Stabilizing Global Climate - Draft Report to Congress*, Executive Summary, United States Environmental Protection Agency, Washington DC, 1989, pp.87-88.

contributing to this dynamic is unclear, but both are involved. Thus it is clear that while at the present time, it is the industrialized countries which bear the greatest responsibility for the emissions, an agreement which looks to the future will have to involve a large number of the countries of the world to be effective.

5.5 The history of the international response

The international response to fears about potential global warming can be divided into three reasonably distinct phases. The first of these is the increasing levels of scientific cooperation in developing the knowledge of what precisely the problem was. This covers the period before 1972, but particularly since around the time of the Stockholm Conference on the Human Environment in 1972, continuing until 1988. The second period runs from 1988 until late 1990 and can be characterized as the period in which the issue became explicitly political, and countries held a series of meetings on how to respond, while stepping up the level of assessment in a qualitatively different way (in the establishment of the IPCC). The last period follows on from late 1990, when countries began to negotiate an international convention on the issue, through the Intergovernmental Negotiating Committee for a Framework Convention on Climate Change (INC). This will run up to UNCED in June 1992, when a convention of some sort is likely to be signed, but negotiations will continue after that, since many of the issues will be unresolved during the first round.

The first point at which the international community formally cooperated on climate-related issues was with the establishment of the International Meteorological Organization (IMO) in 1853, at the International Meteorological Congress in Brussels.[52] The primary aim of this Congress was to standardize measurements made from ships by different countries, and exchange information about weather patterns.[53]

The next significant change was not until the establishment of the United Nations, which provided an impetus for the development of international cooperation on scientific and technical questions. In the meteorological field, the World Meteorological Convention was signed

---

[52]Cain, op.cit, p.80, from which much of this section up until 1983 derives; see also Soroos, op.cit, and D.A.Davies, 'The Role of the WMO in Environmental Issues', *International Organization*, Vol.26, No.2, 1972, pp.327-36.
[53]Cain, op.cit.

in 1947, which established the World Meteorological Organization (WMO), replacing the IMO. Two main factors which drove cooperation within the WMO in the early Post-War period were the increase in jet aircraft travel, which required monitoring of weather conditions at high altitude, and the development of satellites, computers and radio communications, which facilitated much more sophisticated monitoring of atmospheric conditions.[54]

As noted above, an eighteen-month period in 1957-8 was International Geophysical Year (IGY), the first major international plan to develop the understanding of the atmosphere, co-organized by WMO and the International Council of Scientific Unions (ICSU). The IGY was deemed a success and led to much greater cooperation on the scientific aspects of the atmosphere.[55] The WMO has since been organized into two aspects; the Global Atmospheric Research Program (GARP), established in 1967, which aims to 'develop the underlying scientific knowledge as a base for improving the services to be provided by WWW and the scientific understanding of climate',[56] and the World Weather Watch (WWW), established in 1968, which aims to help national meteorological services improve weather forecasts.

While the Stockholm Conference in 1972 is widely regarded as the starting point for international efforts better to understand climate and possible problems of climate change, according to Cain the real 'turning point' occurred at the meetings organized in the United States, which resulted in the publications of the *Study of Critical Environment Problems*, and the *Study on Man's Impact on the Climate*.[57] These highlighted the impact of CO_2 on climate as a potentially significant problem, and caused it to be included in the considerations of environmental problems by national and international bodies.

A series of conferences on climate-related problems, coinciding with an apparently significant increase in such problems as drought and desertification, resulted in a qualitative change in the level of international scientific cooperation. These conferences, including the Stockholm Conference in 1972, the UN World Food Conference in 1974,

---

[54] ibid, pp.80-1.
[55] Soroos, op.cit, p.201.
[56] Cain, op.cit, p.81.
[57] *Study of Critical Environmental Problems*, MIT, Cambridge MA, 1970; *Study on Man's Impact on the Climate*, MIT, Cambridge MA, 1971; Cain, op.cit, p.91.

the UN Water Conference in 1976, and the UN Desertification Conference in 1977, highlighted various aspects of severe problems associated with climatic variations and made clear the possible consequences of significant human-induced climate change. The events, such as the Sahel five-year drought in the late 1960s and early 1970s, the 1962 drought in the former Soviet Union, the monsoon failure in India in 1974, and finally the drought in Europe in 1976, all made human dependence on climate more acutely visible.

The increase in international cooperation on scientific aspects of climate was largely organized through WMO, with US scientists playing a leadership role, and UNEP also being influential, through its 'Earthwatch' Program, which was very important in the global monitoring of CO_2. A further significant step was taken at the World Climate Conference in 1979 in Geneva, organized by WMO, which stated that:

It can be said with some confidence that the burning of fossil fuels, deforestation, and changes of land use have increased the amount of carbon dioxide in the atmosphere by about 15 percent during the last century and it is at present increasing by about 0.4 percent per year. It is likely that an increase will continue in the future. Carbon dioxide plays a fundamental role in determining the temperature of the earth's atmosphere, and it appears plausible that an increased amount of carbon dioxide in the atmosphere can contribute to a gradual warming of the lower atmosphere, especially at high latitudes.[58]

The other outcome of this increase in cooperation was the establishment of the World Climate Program[59] (WCP), which was planned during 1977-9, and launched at the World Climate Conference.[60]

[58]World Meteorological Organization, *World Climate Conference Declaration and Supporting Documents 2,* Geneva, 1979, quoted in Cain, op.cit, p.75.

[59]The WCP has four main components; the World Climate Data Programme, which is concerned with 'the assembly and availability of climate data sets'; the World Climate Application Programme, with 'the use of knowledge about climate to increase the safety and economy of human activities'; the World Climate Research Programme, with the influence of changes in the composition of the atmosphere on climate; and the World Climate Impact Studies Programme, with the 'effect of climate change on ecosystems and human activities'. See Sixth Report of the House of Commons Energy Committee (Session 1988-89), *Energy Policy Implications of the Greenhouse Effect*, HMSO, London, HC192, Memorandum by the Department of Energy, paragraph 2.2; also Cain, op.cit, p.83.

[60]Cain, op.cit, p.83..

Several workshops were held under WMO/UNEP auspices, which clarified further the perception among the scientific community of how serious a problem climate could be. The major of these was the 'International Conference on the Assessment of the Role of Carbon Dioxide and Other Greenhouse Gases in Climate Variations and Associated Impacts', held in Villach, Austria, during 9-15 October 1985 under WCP auspices.[61] The Conference established some sort of scientific consensus on the degree of responsibility for global warming of each gas, and on a preliminary prediction of what sort of warming the world was likely to see. There were also some generalized reports on what might happen to different specific parts of the world. Following this, two workshops entitled 'Developing Policies for Responding to Climate Change', were held in Villach, and Bellagio, Italy, in October and November 1987. These became known as the 'Villach-Bellagio workshops'.[62]

Gradually during the 1980s a sort of consensus had emerged among the scientific community concerning the likely range of how much global warming could occur given 'business-as-usual' assumptions about the development of world energy use. The second phase of international cooperation on the climate issue began in 1988. At this point it became increasingly realized that a political response to the issue was necessary. This development occurred partly because of the increasing realization among scientists of the potential scale of the problem and their increasing internal consensus about the definition of the problem,[63] and partly because of the increasing public perception of freak weather conditions,

---

[61]United Nations Environment Programme, World Meteorological Organization, and International Council of Scientific Unions, *Report of the International Conference on the Assessment of the Role of CO_2 and Other Greenhouse Gases in Climate Change and Associated Impacts*, WMO, 1986.

[62]World Meteorological Organization, and United Nations Environment Programme, *Developing Policies for Responding to Climatic Change* (Summary of Workshops held in Villach, Austria, 28 September-2 October 1987, and Bellagio, Italy, 9-13 November, 1987 under the auspices of the Beijer Institute, Stockholm), 1988.

[63]See the views of Peter Haas for a discussion of how consensus on scientific issues helps in bringing about international cooperation; P.M.Haas, 'Obtaining International Environmental Protection through Epistemic Communities', *Millenium*, Vol.19, No.3, Winter 1990, pp.347-364.

such as the US drought in 1988, including the documentation of the fact that the 1980s contained the six hottest years, globally, ever recorded.[64]

Of course suggestions that a political response to global warming was necessary were not totally new, and these phases are partly over-emphasized. As early as 1978, the International Institute for Applied Systems Analysis (IIASA), WMO, UNEP and the Scientific Committee of Problem of the Environment (SCOPE) had organized a workshop at which energy policies were considered in the light of potential global warming. Many individuals had also written books on the need to respond politically.[65]

As scientific knowledge has increased about the likelihood of global warming, the types of gas involved and their anthropogenic sources, and about the severity of the possible changes, the activities of the scientists involved in the WCP and in national programmes have become inherently more political because of the implications of the necessary responses. From about 1985 onwards, scientists therefore started to call on politicians to act. This process started at the Villach Conference. A major part of the Conference's report involved detailed description of what the priorities for further scientific research should be. However, the last recommendation was that a small task force set up by UNEP, WMO and the International Council of Scientific Unions (ICSU) should 'initiate, if deemed necessary, consideration of a global convention'.[66] One of the speakers at the conference reveals the change in attitude which was occurring: 'As a reversal of a position I held a year or so ago, I believe it is timely to start on the long, tedious and sensitive task of framing a *Convention* on greenhouse gases, climate change and energy'.[67] A shift of emphasis away from solely the need for more research, towards including assertions of the need for political action, had started.

The Villach-Bellagio workshops came to similar conclusions, calling for the 'examination ... of the need for an agreement on a law of the

---

[64]R.A.Houghton and G.M.Woodwell, 'Global Climate Change', *Scientific American*, Vol.260, No.4, April 1989. The years were, in order, 1988, 1987, 1983, 1981, 1980, and 1986.

[65]See for example: C.Tickell, *Climatic Change and World Affairs*, Harvard Studies in International Affairs, Cambridge, Mass., 1977; A.Lovins, L.Hunter Lovins, F.Krause and W.Bach, *Least-Cost Energy: Solving the CO_2 Problem*, Brick House, Andover Mass., 1981.

[66]*Report of the Villach Conference*, op.cit, para.5.

[67]ibid, p.33.

atmosphere as a global commons or the need to move towards a convention along the lines of that developed for ozone'.[68] For the political community at large, however, there was still considerable inertia about the issue, and the idea of a convention or any sort of political agreement on greenhouse gases was certainly not being addressed.

Thus politics had been considered in deliberations (mainly by scientists), increasingly during the 1980s. The watershed, however, when the issue first really hit the political agenda of governments and policymakers, was in 1988 at the Toronto Conference on 'The Changing Atmosphere: Implications for Global Security', held in Toronto, Canada, on 27-30 June 1988. 'More than 300 scientists and policy makers from 48 countries, United Nations organizations, other international bodies and non-governmental organizations participated in the sessions'.[69] This was the meeting at which ideas about the sort of international response which was needed became strongly expressed. It was also then that the controversy started, because some of the underlying issues involved in that international response raised serious problems, material and ideological, for many countries.

The Toronto Conference made many recommendations for action. The most basic was a proposal to aim to reduce global CO_2 emissions by 20% by 2005, with an eventual aim to cut emissions by 50%. It called upon governments 'to work with urgency towards an Action Plan for the Protection of the Atmosphere. This should include an international framework convention ... The Conference also called upon governments to establish a World Atmosphere Fund financed in part by a levy on the fossil fuel consumption of industrialized countries ...'.[70]

A series of international and intergovernmental conferences were held during the period after the Toronto Conference, starting with the World Congress on Climate and Development in Hamburg in November 1988, which called for a 30% reduction in greenhouse gas emissions by 2000 and a 50% reduction by 2015.[71] In February 1989, a conference on 'Global Warming and Climate Change: Perspectives from Developing

---

[68]WMO, Summary of Workshops, op.cit.

[69]Statement issued by the participants at the World Conference on 'The Changing Atmosphere: Implications for Global Security', Toronto, June 1988.

[70]ibid.

[71]Boyle and Ardill, op.cit, p.158.

Countries' was held in New Delhi.[72] Also in February 1989 the Canadian government hosted an 'International Meeting of Legal and Policy Experts on the Protection of the Atmosphere' in Ottawa. This produced a statement which comprised a series of elements to be included in a framework convention on the protection of the atmosphere.[73] It included the provision that 'States should consider the possibility of establishing a World Atmosphere Trust Fund'.[74] In March a meeting at the International Court of Justice in the Hague was organized by the governments of France, the Netherlands and Norway and attended by representatives, most of whom were Heads of State, of 24 countries.

In July 1989 the Group of Seven major industrialized countries annual summit was held in Paris, and was widely dubbed the 'green summit'.[75] This called for 'common efforts to limit emissions of carbon dioxide', and stated that a 'framework or umbrella convention' was 'urgently required'.[76] Other conferences such as the Meeting of Non-Aligned Countries in Belgrade in September 1989, the Tokyo Conference on Global Environment and Human Response Towards Sustainable Development in September 1989, and the Commonwealth Heads of Governments Meeting of October 1989, also issued declarations on the need to 'address the serious deterioration of the environment, including climate change'.[77]

In November 1989 a large 'Ministerial Conference on Atmospheric Pollution and Climatic Change' was held at Noordwijk in The Netherlands, attended by representatives from 72 countries. The conference agreed that industrialized countries should stabilize their CO_2 emissions at levels to be set by the IPCC in its preliminary report to the second World Climate Conference in 1990, 'at the latest by the year 2000'.[78]

---

[72]*International Conference on Global Warming and Climate Change: Perspectives from Developing Countries*, New Delhi, 21-23 February 1989.
[73]Meeting Statement of 'Protection of the Atmosphere: International Meeting of Legal and Policy Experts', Ottawa, Canada, 20-22 February 1989.
[74]ibid, p.7.
[75]*Scientific American*, September 1989, p.12; *The Economist*, July 15 1989, pp.14-15.
[76]*Scientific American*, September 1989, p.10.
[77]*Declaration for the Ministerial Conference on Atmospheric Pollution and Climatic Change*, Noordwijk, November 1989.
[78]ibid.

In 1988, as a response to the Toronto Conference, the Intergovernmental Panel on Climate Change (IPCC), was established by UNEP and WMO at the instigation of the United States government. It had been around as an idea since the Villach-Bellagio workshops,[79] and was regarded by many as the primary forum for coordinating policy research and negotiations related to climate change.[80] It made its first full report to the Second World Climate Conference in 1990.

The IPCC first met in November 1988, in WMO offices in Geneva. It set up three working parties, one to assess scientific information, one for environmental and socio-economic impacts and one to look at possible response strategies. These working parties were chaired by the UK, the former Soviet Union and the US respectively, and the vice-chairs were: Brazil and Senegal for the scientific group; Australia and Japan for the socio-economic impacts group; and Canada, China, Malta, the Netherlands and Zimbabwe for the response strategies group.[81]

Throughout 1989 and 1990 the IPCC continued meeting. In 1990 it produced large reports from each of its three working groups,[82] starting with the report of Working Group 1, published in draft form on 25 May. These produced the scientific consensus on what the problem of global warming entailed, and produced a policy response document on possible responses in each of the relevant areas of policy.

Throughout 1990, international meetings continued. On January 15-19 the Soviet government organized the Global Forum on Environment and Development in Moscow, at which President Gorbachev suggested that the UNCED Conference in Rio in 1992, should be held at 'summit level'.[83] Also in January, the small island states held a conference in the Maldives to discuss their position. Further substantial conferences were held at the White House in Washington DC on April 17-18, in Nairobi

---

[79] WMO, Summary of Workshops, op.cit, para.17.

[80] *The Greenhouse Effect - the UK Government View*, HMSO, London, 1989; J.B.Smith and D.A.Tirpak, *The Potential Effects of Global Climate Change on the United States, Draft Report to Congress*, United States Environmental Protection Agency, Washington DC, 1988, Executive Summary, pp.1-2. See W.Nitze, 'The Intergovernmental Panel on Climate Change', *Environment*, Vol.13, No.1, January/February 1989, pp.44-45, for a general discussion of the IPCC.

[81] Nitze, op.cit.

[82] Houghton et al (eds), op.cit; IPCC, *The Potential Impacts of Climate Change*, WMO/UNEP, 1990; IPCC, *Formulation of Response Strategies*, WMO/UNEP, 1990.

[83] *Keesings Record of World Events*, Vol.36, No.1, 1990, p.37202.

on 2-4 May (to discuss African perspectives on global warming), and in Bergen on 8-16 May.

The other significant development during 1990 was that many industrialized countries began to make unilateral commitments in relation to their CO_2 emissions. By March 1992 these commitments were as outlined in Table 5.2 (pp182-183). By the time the negotiations started in early 1991, all industrialized countries apart from the United States had declared a target to stabilize their fossil CO_2 emissions at some date (most commonly 2000 or 2005), or were part of a regional stabilization target such as those set by the EC or the European Free Trade Association (EFTA), and many had committed themselves to actual reductions in their emissions.

The developments between 1988 and November 1990, when the Second World Climate Conference (SWCC) was held in Geneva, built up sufficient pressure that the SWCC statement announced the beginning of formal negotiations on climate change (as it increasingly was called), taking us into the third period. The formal establishment of the Intergovernmental Negotiating Committee for a Framework Convention on Climate Change (INC) was declared in the UN General Assembly Resolution 45/212 on 21 December 1990,[84] and it unexpectedly took control of the negotiation process away from UNEP/WMO and under the direct control of the UNGA.

The US government had offered to host the first session of the INC, which was held on 4-14 February 1991, at Chantilly, near Washington DC. Five sessions were held in all: in Geneva on 19-28 June, in Nairobi on 9-20 September, in Geneva again on 9-20 December, and in New York on 18-28 February 1992. The fifth New York Session resumed on 30 April-8 May.

Some worried about the fact that the negotiations had been taken over by the UN General Assembly, rather than being organized by UNEP as much of the precursor work had been done by UNEP, and it had also organized the negotiations for the Vienna Convention and Montreal Protocol. They felt that it would encumber the process unduly, by getting more countries involved than needed to be at this stage, and argued that what they saw as the failure of the UN Conference on the Law of the Sea

---

[84]United Nations General Assembly, Resolution 45/212 (*Protection of Global Climate for Present and Future Generations*), 21 December 1990.

was an example of how UN multilateral diplomacy might not be best suited to hugely complex environmental problems.[85]

As with many UN negotiations, much time is spent on formal aspects, such as the election of Officers. Subsequently there was much criticism from environmental NGOs that time was being wasted on these procedural points rather than getting down to serious negotiations. The First Session in Chantilly, and much of the Second Session in Geneva, were taken up largely by procedural questions, and the formal submission of papers by delegations from states.[86] Substantive negotiations started on 23 June,[87] when the principles to be incorporated into a convention were discussed.

While some progress has been made in the negotiations, they have not lived up to the expectations and hopes of those in the environmental community. In some ways, global warming and the environment has declined on the political agenda in many countries during 1991 and 1992, and subsequently the negotiations have not received significant media coverage. The nature of the agreement planned to be ready for signing at UNCED in June 1992 remains to be seen. Now we turn to the international politics of the negotiations.

5.6 The politics

International cooperation remains fraught with problems, and a subject of much study by international relations scholars. The essence of successful cooperation is about trying to find 'politically feasible ways to increase the incentives for collectively rational behaviour'.[88] Many factors may make it difficult for governments to cooperate with each other on specific issues. Governments often do not perceive it to be in their best interest to cooperate, or each may be concerned with a different

---

[85]K.Ramakrishna, 'North-South Issues, Common Heritage of Mankind and Global Climate Change', *Millenium*, Vol.19, No.3, Winter 1990, pp.429-446; J.K.Sebenius, 'Negotiating a Regime to Control Global Warming' in R.E.Benedick et al, *Greenhouse Warming: Negotiating a Global Regime*, World Resources Institute, Washington DC, 1991.

[86]See, for example, the issues of *ECO* for 14 February and 20 June, 1991. *ECO* is a magazine produced collectively by NGOs at environmental negotiations.

[87]*ECO*, 24 June 1991.

[88]P.Sand, *Lessons Learned in Global Environmental Governance*, World Resources Institute, Washington DC, 1990, quoting M.Olson, 'Increasing the Incentives for International Cooperation', *International Organization*, Vol.25, 1971, pp.866-874.

Table 5.2 Status of commitments of OECD countries on global climate change

Country	Type of commitment	Gases include	Action	Base year	Commit-ment year	Conditions/Comments
Australia	Target	NMP GHG	Stabilization	1988	2000	Interim planning target; to be implemented
			20% reduction	1988	2005	if others take like action
Austria*	Target	CO$_2$	20% reduction	1988	2005	Still needs parliamentary approval
Canada	Target	CO$_2$ & other GHG	Stabilization	1990	2000	
Denmark**	Target	CO$_2$	20% reduction	1988	2005	Implementation plan adopted
Finland*	Target	CO$_2$	Stabilization	1990	2000	Policy goal, not a formal target
France**	Target	CO$_2$	Stabilization	1990	2000	This is a per capita per year target of less than 2 tonnes of carbon
Germany**	Target	CO$_2$	25% reduction	1987	2005	Larger % reductions in eastern Länder
Italy**	Target	CO$_2$	Stabilization	1988	2000	Non-binding resolution
			20% reduction	1988	2005	
Japan	Target	CO$_2$	Stabilization	1990	2000	On a per capita basis; implemented if others act likewise
Luxembourg**	Target	CO$_2$	Stabilization	1990	2000	
			20% reduction	1990	2005	
Netherlands**	Target	CO$_2$	Stabilization	89/90	1995	Unilateral action committed
			3-5% reduction	89/90	2000	
"	Target	All GHG	20-25% reduction	89/90	2000	Unilateral action committed

New Zealand	Target	CO$_2$	20% reduction	1990	2000	Conditional on measures to achieve the target, being cost-effective and providing a net benefit for New Zealand society.
Norway*	Target	CO$_2$	Stabilization	1989	2000	Preliminary
Spain**	Target	CO$_2$	Limit to 25% growth	1990	2000	Target approved but still pending Parliamentary approval
Switzerland*	Target	CO$_2$	At least stabilization	1990	2000	Interim target
UK**	Target	CO$_2$	Stabilization	1990	2000	Conditional on like action.
US	Commitment to set of policies	All GHG	Stabilization	1990	2000	Stabilization achieved in part by CFC phase out
EC	Target	CO$_2$	Stabilization	1990	2000	Target is for Community as a whole

Key: * EFTA Member; ** EC Member; NMP- Gases not covered by the Montreal Protocol; GHG- greenhouse gases; GWP- global warming potential. Note: EC countries not mentioned (Belgium, Greece, Ireland and Portugal) have agreed to be part of the EC target, but have not yet developed their own targets. EFTA countries not mentioned (Iceland and Sweden) have agreed to meet the EC target together with the EC.

Source: IEA, *Climate Change: Policy Update, March 1992*, IEA, Paris, March 1992; *Guardian*, 1 May 1992, for revised UK target of 2000 (previously 2005).

aspect of a problem. Within negotiations on a particular issue each government will want to protect its own interests, which may often be diametrically opposed to those of others. In particular in relation to environmental problems, there can often be a 'tragedy of the commons' problem, or as Robert Dorfman points out, a situation which is 'an aggravated instance of the Prisoners' Dilemma game',[89] whereby it would be in everyone's interest if all cooperated, but in the individual interest of each to 'free-ride', and rely on the efforts of others. As Soroos points out, Intergovernmental Organizations (IGOs), unlike national governments or the town council in Garrett Hardin's mythical village, do not have the 'authority to impose rules, but must induce the willing cooperation of sovereign states'.[90] However, international cooperation is vital to solving these problems because of their transboundary nature. One state can reduce its own emissions but unless all (or at least most) do the same, little significant overall amelioration of the problem will be experienced.

Thus the likelihood of a successful agreement being reached on global warming depends on countries being able to work round any opposed interests which exist, and integrate all the special interests of each state, while providing strong disincentives to free-ride. This section will begin by looking at the current positions of the various countries and groups of countries active in the negotiations. The most noticeable divide, although much more differentiation does exist, is that between industrialized and developing countries. The negotiations have been characterized by what could be seen as a set of irreconcilable positions. It will then look at various issues which, it has become clear, are important in the process of negotiating an agreement on global warming.[91] These issues include that of equity, differential cost/benefits

[89]R.Dorfman, 'Protecting the Global Environment: An Immodest Proposal', *World Development*, Vol.19, No.1, 1991, pp.103-110. The politics of global warming at the international level is in fact more analogous to the game of 'chicken'. See H.Ward, 'Game Theory and the Politics of the Global Commons', Department of Government, University of Essex, January 1992.

[90]Soroos, op.cit, p.197. G.Hardin, 'The Tragedy of the Commons', *Science*, Vol.162, 1968, pp.1,243-8.

[91]Global warming has fostered a number of special issues of journals which look at the implications for international relations. These include *Millenium* (Vol.19, No.3, Winter 1990), *Policy Studies Journal* (Vol.19, No.2, 1991), *International Challenges* (Vol.11, No.1, 1991), and *International Social Science Journal* (Vol.121, August 1989).

between countries, the role of science in the negotiations, and sovereignty.

Groups of countries and their positions

The positions of various countries in the negotiations have often been strongly in opposition to each other, making it possible that no universal substantive agreement will be reached on tackling climate change. The problems of trying to reach agreements among all the countries of the world are amply illustrated by looking at the global warming negotiations.

The United States has made it clear that it is not currently prepared to countenance any targets for the stabilization of, or reductions of, their CO_2 emissions. Initially, the US justified its position on grounds of scientific uncertainty, highlighting sceptical scientists such as Lindzen (see above). However, the rationale has moved towards being partly based on their perception of the costs which the US economy would incur if reductions were made, partly on their perception of the costs which the US would incur under most scenarios of global warming, and partly on the argument that 'if only industrialized countries take these short-term actions, the effect ... is likely to be small and transitory'.[92] However, the US has outlined a series of policy measures which it plans to implement, which it projects will stabilize overall greenhouse gas emissions at 1990 levels by 2000.[93]

The rest of the industrialized world (ie. the European Community, Japan, the Scandinavian countries, Canada, Australia and New Zealand) has made specific commitments to stabilize and in some cases reduce CO_2 emissions (see above, section 5.5), largely because their perception of the costs of abating their emissions are less severe. However, it is

[92]US Chief negotiator Robert Reinstein, quoted in *ECO*, 13 September 1991. For a US estimate of costs, see A.S.Manne and R.G.Richels, 'CO_2 Emission Limits: An Economic Cost Analysis for the USA', *The Energy Journal*, April 1990.
[93]US Department of Energy, *National Energy Strategy: First Edition 1991/1992*, Washington DC, February 1991; The White House, *America's Climate Change Strategy: An Action Agenda*, Washington DC, February 1991. For an overview of OECD countries responses, see International Energy Agency, *Climate Change Policy Implications: Update*, International Energy Agency/Organization for Economic Cooperation and Development, Paris, July 1991, or Karen Schmidt, *Industrial Countries Responses to Global Climate Change*, Environment and Energy Study Institute Special Report, Washington DC, July 1991. On the US position, see, S.Andresen, 'US Climate Policy: Reactionary or Realistic?', *International Challenges*, Vol.19, No.3, 1991, pp.17-24.

worth contrasting their proposed targets with the levels of reductions estimated by the IPCC to be necessary. Their positions also vary on the question of technological and financial transfers to developing countries, which would be designed to help them develop while minimizing their increases in emissions. The EC and Scandinavian countries have been clear that 'new and additional' financial commitments must be made by industrialized countries to facilitate these transfers, while the US, Canada and Japan have showed 'distinct unwillingness to discuss 'new and additional' funding to developing countries'.[94]

In contrast developing countries have been united, perhaps not surprisingly, on the question of technology transfers and new funding and also (with the exception of one group, the oil producers) on the point that industrialized countries should make significant cuts in their emissions. However, beyond that, there have been a number of different groups of developing countries.[95]

There are the developing countries, who by the very nature of their size, have been able to be influential in the negotiations. The most obvious of these are China, India, Mexico and Brazil. Some of their influence is through their historical role as leaders of the developing countries in other negotiations. But also it derives from the inherently important role which they play in a greenhouse convention, since they, if they do not have particularly high emissions at present, will account for an increasing proportion of world CO_2 emissions during the next few decades (see above, section 5.4). This arguably gives them significant leverage,[96] and correspondingly their position has been uncompromising; all developing country commitments can only be conditional upon provision of technology and finance from industrialized countries.

Another important subgroup of developing countries is the small island states, organized into the Alliance of Small Island States (AOSIS). This

---

[94]*ECO*, 16 September 1991, 'All Mouth, Too Little Money'; A.K.Sydnes, *Developing Countries in Global Climate Negotiations*, Energy, Environment and Development Report 1991/4, Fridtjof Nansen Institute, Oslo, 1991, pp.9-12.
[95]For studies which look at different groups of countries in relation to global warming, see K.Ramakrishna, 'Third World Countries in the Policy Response to Global Climate Change', in Leggett (ed.), op.cit, pp.421-437; W.Nitze, *The Greenhouse Effect: Formulating a Convention*, Royal Institute of International Affairs, London, 1990, pp.5-9; M.Paterson and M.Grubb, 'The international politics of climate change', *International Affairs*, Vol.68, No.2, April 1992, pp.293-310.
[96]O.Young, 'Global Environmental Change and International Governance', *Millenium*, Vol.19, No.3, Winter 1990, pp.337-346.

has been widely acclaimed as being extremely successful at getting its message across in the negotiations. For obvious reasons, its primary preoccupation is with the impact of sea level rise (see Chapter 4 for details).

The major oil producing developing countries also form a significant group. This group has been led in the negotiations on global warming by Saudi Arabia and Kuwait, but has included the other Middle Eastern oil producers, as well as Algeria, Venezuela, and to an extent, Nigeria. For obvious reasons, this has been the group which has opposed suggestions that industrialized countries should set targets to reduce CO_2 emissions. Their focus has consistently been on the need for increased scientific research, and on increasing sinks for CO_2.

The least developed countries, largely of Sub-Saharan Africa, have formed another distinct group within the negotiations, focusing not only on the general problems of developing countries in relation to financial and technology transfers, but more strongly on their needs in relation to adapting to global warming, and their generally greater susceptibility to whatever increased levels of freak weather conditions there may be. The fact that they do not, and are not likely to in the immediate future, contribute significantly to global greenhouse gas emissions, causes their focus to be on impacts.

The Newly Industrialized Countries (NICs), mainly of East Asia, form another group. They have argued in the negotiations for recognition of their special circumstances due to their recent industrialization and their subsequent dependence on energy-intensive patterns of production. Their general motive has, according to Ramakrishna, been to ask 'how does participation in an international debate help hasten their economic development?';[97] their focus has correspondingly been on securing finance and advanced energy-efficient technology for their industries.

The final group of countries is the former centrally-planned economy countries of eastern Europe, in particular the former Soviet Union, known in the negotiations as the countries with 'Economies in Transition'. Because of the peculiar problems of these countries and the great uncertainties surrounding the general political character of their futures, it is difficult to make generalized statements about them. On the one hand they have highly inefficient industry and, related to this, very high per capita emissions compared to their GNP, which means that in

---

[97]Ramakrishna, 'Third World Countries', op.cit, p.430.

principle, significant reductions in their emissions are possible. On the other hand, the political turmoil within those countries means that it is not always clear that the effective decisionmaking capacity is there to put this possibility into effect. Also, this often means that CO_2 emissions are by no means near the top of the political agenda. What may well happen is that the east European and most of the non-Russian republics will become more favourable towards controlling CO_2 emissions since they will be dependent on fuel imports primarily from Russia; in contrast Russia's position is likely to stay close to that of the oil producers as it becomes increasingly dependent on energy for its export income. The contradictory messages which come across from this group, with the Russian Republic[98] joining the US in refusing to set targets for emissions stabilization, and Romania announcing at the Third Session of the INC its intention to stabilize its emissions at 1988/9 levels by 2005,[99] may be an early example of this.

The equity issues

Equity issues have been widely recognized by analysts and many negotiators as possibly the most crucial issue to be resolved in negotiating an agreement on global warming.[100] If an agreement is not seen to be fair by countries, then they will not sign or participate in it, and, since a global warming agreement requires the participation of a great number of countries, in principle all in the world, an inequitable agreement will fail as an environmental agreement. The issue of equity becomes not simply an ethical consideration, but a practical one in relation to the effectiveness of an agreement.[101] For example, with the Montreal Protocol, China and India initially refused to participate because they felt it was an unfair agreement due its lack of provision for technology and financial transfers to developing countries, and their lack

[98]In formal negotiations the Russian Republic has taken over the USSR's seat in the UN. The disintegration of the former Soviet Empire has yet to work itself through the UN system.

[99]Personal notes, INC Session, Nairobi, 12 September 1991.

[100]For example, UNEP/Beijer Institute, *The Full Range of Responses to Anticipated Climatic Change*, Beijer Institute, Stockholm, 1989; W.Nitze, *The Greenhouse Effect*, op.cit, pp.14-15; J.MacNeill, 'The Greening of World Politics', *International Journal*, Vol.XLV, Winter 1989-90; Grubb, op.cit. (1990), pp.280-283.

[101]O.Young, 'The politics of international regime formation: managing natural resources and the environment', *International Organization*, Vol.43, No.3, Summer 1989, pp.349-375, at p.368.

of participation was regarded as likely to cause the agreement to fail to reduce CFC emissions by the necessary amount. Provision of such transfers in a fund set up at the London Revision of the Montreal Protocol was at aimed to procure their accession (see Chapter 6 for details).

A number of analysts have written on the approaches which could be used to deal with the question of whether or not the mechanisms in an agreement for burden sharing would be equitable.[102] Defined simply as fair, or just, equity considerations clearly leave much room for scope both in terms of its meaning and in terms of how it should be implemented. Grubb, Sebenius et al give a summary of the various possible positions. These are as follows: egalitarianism, whereby it is argued that 'all human beings should be entitled to an equal share in the atmospheric commons';[103] historical responsibility, whereby an equitable solution would be based on the idea that those who have caused the global warming problem should compensate those who suffer from it and should bear the main burden for responding;[104] a status quo and comparable burdens position, which holds that current levels of emissions of countries have established some sort of common law right to emit at that level, so that any burden for reducing global emissions would be equally met by countries irrespective of their starting point in terms of emissions; a willingness-to-pay based argument derived from welfare economics which suggests that it is fair for those who are most concerned to solve a problem should bear the burden; and finally, an

---

[102]M.Grubb, J.K.Sebenius, A.Magalhaes and S.Subak, 'Sharing the burden', in I.Mintzer (ed.), *The Challenge of Responsible Development in a Warming World*, Stockholm Environment Institute/CUP, Cambridge, 1992; H.P.Young, *Sharing the Burden of Global Warming*, University of Maryland, 1991; F.Krause, J.Koomey, and W.Bach, *Energy Policy in the Greenhouse: From Warming Fate to Warming Limit*, International Project for Sustainable Energy Paths, El Cerrito, 1989; E.Brown Weiss, 'Climate Change, Intergenerational Equity and International Law: An Introductory Note', *Climatic Change*, Vol.15, 1989, pp.327-335; H.O.Bergesen, 'A Legitimate Social Order in a "Greenhouse" World: Some Basic Requirements', *International Challenges*, Vol.11, No.2, 1991, pp.21-29; A.Agarwal and S.Narain, *Global Warming in an Unequal World: A Case of Environmental Colonialism*, Centre for Science and Environment, New Delhi, 1990.

[103]Grubb, Sebenius, Magalhaes and Subak, op.cit, p.8.

[104]Existing generations in industrialized countries can be easily shown to benefit not only from existing high levels of emissions, but from past emissions in those countries, for example through the past development of industrial, transport or housing infrastructure which they still use.

equity argument based on the distributional consequences of the scheme. In this last version, what matters is that an agreement would be equitable to the extent that it mitigates the international distribution of wealth (a basically Rawlsian argument that to be just, social institutions must improve the lot of the poorest.)[105]

The arguments which have been most vocally expressed in the negotiations have been those advocating equal per capita entitlements in combination with that about historical responsibility. This combination has been consistently used by most developing countries, most prominently by the Indian delegation, to argue that for an agreement to be just, the industrialized countries must both reduce their emissions drastically, and provide new technology and finance for developing countries so that they can develop while minimizing the growth in their emissions. This argument has been explicitly based on the historical and current level of emissions in the North, and the subsequent responsibility of the North to deal with the problem. Correspondingly, India in particular has held that developing countries have no obligations whatsoever to deal with global warming since they have not contributed to the problem. All developing country commitments would therefore be completely conditional on finance and technology from the North.[106] They have also used the egalitarian per capita entitlements argument as a key to how the distribution of emissions should, in their view, evolve.

However, this argument is clearly not accepted by the great majority of industrialized countries (New Zealand being an exception at the Third INC Session). While there is a general recognition that industrialized countries must bear the greatest burden in reducing their own emissions, by no means has this extended to accepting something approaching an

---

[105]J.Rawls, *A Theory of Justice*, OUP, Oxford, 1973.
[106]See Sydnes,op.cit; *Beijing Ministerial Declaration on Environment and Development*, Beijing, 19 June 1991. For more general information on developing countries in relation to global warming, see: P.Usher, 'Climate Change and the Developing World', *Southern Illinois University Law Journal*, Vol.14, 1990, pp.257-262; A.K.Sydnes, 'Global Climate Negotiations: Another Twenty Years of Fruitless North-South Bargaining?' *International Challenges*, Vol.11, No.1, 1991, pp.58-60; K.Ramakrishna, 'North-South Issues, Common Heritage of Mankind and Global Climate Change', *Millenium*, Vol.19, No.3, Winter 1990, pp.429-446; J.A.Sathaye, *Developing Countries and Global Climate Change*, Energy, Environment and Development Report 1990/8, Fridtjof Nansen Institute, Oslo, 1990; L.Lunde, *The North/South Dimension of Global Greenhouse Negotiations: Conflict, Dilemmas, Solutions*, Fridtjof Nansen Institute, Oslo, 1991.

equal per capita rights formula. Much of the Northern reluctance is because of the anticipated scale of the transfers involved. Some estimate that up to $100bn annually would be necessary to limit developing country emissions while enabling them to develop.[107] As Morrisette and Plantinga argue, 'it is this final point [the scale of the transfers] that will prove to be the most difficult to resolve'.[108] Currently no consensus is emerging as to what method for burden sharing in relation to reducing emissions is the most equitable and acceptable.

Equity arguments are clearly complicated by differing assessments about the costs and benefits of global warming. These make it difficult to have significant underlying agreement on how to define precisely what the problem is.[109] Notably, the US position can be explained largely in terms of their assessment of the costs of emissions reductions and of the costs of the projected impacts of global warming *on the US*. The fact that the projected impacts differ widely over the globe, and that industrialized countries in general will be more easily placed to adapt to global warming, exacerbates this problem. At the other end of the extreme to the United States, AOSIS members face huge costs from the projected impacts (to the extent of their possible physical disappearance), while their ability to make any contribution to the global effort to abate emissions is negligible. Governments have arguably used equity-based arguments to mask their own perceived self-interest.

Illustrating the last point, the use of science to support one's position and perceived self-interest has also clearly emerged in the negotiations. As noted above, during 1990 and some of 1991 the US also used scientific uncertainty to justify its position. Some governments, notably those from oil-producing countries, have continued to do so. Even before the INC began meeting, the science had become politicized. In the IPCC, delegates were appointed by their governments and many worked in government ministries.[110] The disparity between the reports of Working Group I and Working Group III were widely commented on by NGOs.[111]

---

[107]L.R.Brown et al, *State of the World 1988*, Norton, New York, 1988; Grubb, op.cit, (1990), p.288.

[108]P.M.Morrisette and A.J.Plantinga, 'Global Warming: A Policy Review', *Policy Studies Journal*, Vol.19, No.2, Spring 1991, pp.163-172 at p.171.

[109]UNEP/Beijer Institute, op.cit, p.32.

[110]Ramakrishna, 'Third World Countries ...', op.cit, p.424.

[111]Grubb, op.cit, (1990), pp.6-7.

Working Group III was much more highly politicized than Working Group I because of its more direct policy-related nature.

In the negotiation process proper, differing interpretations of scientific evidence have been clearly used by states. Perhaps the most obvious has been the United States' use of those scientists who remained sceptical about the problem of global warming to justify its refusal to commit itself to any targets on its CO_2 emissions. Another tactic of the US has been the 'comprehensive approach', through which it has argued, and gained support from several states (usually for what can be interpreted as political reasons) that there should not be such a great focus on CO_2 as was being generally given, that all gases should be considered, and that sources and sinks should be considered together.[112] Irrespective of the desirability or otherwise of this approach, it seems clear that it was introduced by the US as a way of trying to take the focus off its refusal to set targets on CO_2.

The problems inherent in trying to measure emissions and sinks of greenhouse gases have produced much controversy on how best to go about these measurements, and how to interpret them as a guide for policy and action. What has possibly been the most significant controversy was over the measurements used in the World Resources Institute's report World Resources 1990-91,[113] which provoked a violent response from analysts at India's Centre for Science and Environment. In their report *Global Warming in an Unequal World - A Case of Environmental Colonialism*, Agarwal and Narain went so far as to state that WRI's report was 'based less on science and more on politically motivated jugglery. Its main intention seems to be to blame developing countries for global warming and perpetuate the current global inequality in the use of the earth's environment and its resources'.[114] The controversy centred around how to measure and make estimates for calculating countries' net emissions of CO_2, which depends on how the

---

[112]*A Comprehensive Approach to Addressing Potential Climate Change*, US Task Force on the Comprehensive Approach to Climate Change, US Department of Justice, February 1991. See M.J.Grubb, D.G.Victor, and C.Hope, 'Pragmatics in the Greenhouse', *Nature*, 5 December 1991, for a discussion of the Comprehensive Approach and some of its problems.
[113]World Resources Institute, *World Resources 1990-1: A Guide to the Global Environment*, OUP, New York, 1990. WRI is an independent Washington based environmental research and lobbying organization.
[114]Agarwal and Narain, op.cit, p.1.

natural 'sinks' are allocated. They also roundly criticized WRI's estimates of CO_2 from deforestation, and methane releases from developing countries, as far too high.

Another issue which has gained attention is the problem of how to impose international obligations on countries without breaching the principle of sovereignty, regarded as the 'basic element in the compact of coexistence'.[115] The principle of sovereignty as outlined in the Stockholm Declaration of 1972, that states have sovereign use of their natural resources, and have obligations to make sure their activities do not harm other countries (arguably two mutually inconsistent principles), has been widely cited. Some have also tried to get this incorporated into a Framework Convention, although this has been resisted by other countries (particularly the US) as it would turn it into a formal principle of international law.

Early on, before the negotiations started, controversy around the issue of sovereignty had emerged. Some countries strongly advocated the development of new institutional bodies (including a widely mentioned 'climate fund') within the UN system, to administer and enforce any agreements on global warming, while others felt that this heavily compromised the sovereignty of states. For example, the Hague Conference in March 1989 (see above, section 5.5), called for the development within the UN framework of a 'new institutional authority, either by strengthening existing institutions or creating a new institution', with responsibility for combatting global warming, and with 'power to monitor governments performance ... and to enforce compliance through the International Court of Justice' and also for an atmospheric fund to assist developing countries.[116]

In contrast, Margaret Thatcher, the then UK Prime Minister, argued at a conference in London in March 1989 to get new signatories to the Montreal Protocol, that 'no new international bodies were needed to protect the world from a thinning ozone layer or the greenhouse effect'.[117] In a similar vein, at the Helsinki conference, the 'First Meeting of the Parties to the Montreal Protocol on Substances that Deplete the Ozone Layer', Nicholas Ridley, the then UK Secretary of State for the

[115]H.Bull, *The Anarchical Society*, MacMillan, London, 1977, p.31.

[116]*Declaration of The Hague*, 11 March 1989.

[117]*New Scientist*, 18 March 1989, p.33; *Keesings Record of World Events*, Vol.35, No.3, 1989, p.36540.

Environment, said that a climate fund 'implies a degree of sovereignty over sovereign nations that there can never really be'.[118]

Since then, the debate appears to have subsided to an extent, but so have the radical calls for new UN bodies with strong powers of enforcement. The debate over sovereignty has become largely a North-South one, with developing countries making clear their objections to any review bodies having the right to inspect their national policies on energy, land-use, etc, with deforestation being a particularly thorny issue in the negotiations. This has encompassed many of the issues briefly discussed here: the Brazilian government proclaiming its sovereignty over Amazonia; the North-South equity problem; and the science question, since the estimates of the extent of deforestation made by the Brazilian government and by the World Resources Institute differed greatly.[119]

Equity issues, along with the others mentioned, may therefore of course be a front for states to justify their positions which are in reality simply determined by their own perceived self-interest. The negotiations will thus be guided to a great extent by power relations between countries. However, while in the North-South context, negotiations and other developments have historically reflected the power of the North, there are reasons for believing that in relation to global warming, this may not be so simple. Developing countries now have a new type of bargaining chip; their increasing ability, as their emissions grow as a proportion of total world emissions over the next few decades, to have a significant effect on the pace and extent of global warming. Therefore, while 'The South has a strong case for demanding compensation for refraining from replicating the Northern experience of destroying its own environment in the quest for rapid economic growth',[120] the North has a corresponding incentive to provide the South with the technology and finance necessary to ensure that its development does not involve massive increases in emissions. In Susan George's words, 'Biospheric solidarity may yet be forced upon the governments of the North; like it or not, they may finally

---

[118]The Guardian, 4 May 1989.
[119]A.K.Sydnes, op.cit, 1991, p.7.
[120]J.Ravenhill, 'The North-South balance of power', *International Affairs*, Vol.66, No.4, October 1990, pp.731-748.

have to recognize that debt relief and real contributions to sustainable development in the South are vital to their own survival'.[121]

5.7 Conclusions

Many of these problems are simply symptoms of the general problem of states, in an essentially anarchic world system, having to cooperate in order to meet certain objectives. States, while recognizing the need for cooperation and the development of international organizations to facilitate this cooperation, still try to maximize their own self-interest within that process. Hence uncertainties over the science, or differing interpretations of equity principles, or differing perceptions of costs and benefits of greenhouse gas abatement, are used by different states to further their ends and try to make the form of an agreement as beneficial to themselves as possible. Even the definitions of the objectives of the agreement are not fixed. Negotiations have revealed clear differences on how the problem is to be defined, ie. whether it is to be limited very strictly to greenhouse gas abatement and adaptation to the impacts of global warming, or whether it has necessarily to be widened out to issues of global economics, and how this might affect the efforts, in particular those of developing countries, to alter their emissions path.

However, several possible ways out of this apparent impasse can be seen. Thus, the prospect for successful international cooperation on the global warming issue is less bleak than at first it might seem. Firstly, the perception about the costs of CO_2 abatement is continually evolving. While in Europe and among NGOs, the estimates of costs have always been lower than in the US, the position in the United States seems to be changing, albeit slowly. At the Third Session of the INC in Nairobi, the US delegation explicitly recognized that 'other studies [than their own] seem to show that the costs [of CO_2 abatement] could be lower',[122] and it seems to be the strategy of both US NGOs and parts of the US administration (notably the Environmental Protection Agency) to pursue this approach. This may cause the US position to change significantly if their perception of costs changes. If a consensus on costs emerges then

---

[121] S.George, 'Managing the Global House: Redefining Economics in a Greenhouse World', in Leggett (ed.), op.cit, pp.438-456.
[122] Reinstein, quoted in *ECO*, 13 September 1991.

agreement may be noticeably easier,[123] since one of the roots of differences over how to respond most effectively will have disappeared, or at least lessened.

Secondly, the analysis so far has largely assumed that the only relevant actors in the global warming negotiations are governments. While it true that only states can formally sign a convention, this does not mean that they necessarily drive changes. Some analysts looking at environmental negotiations have focused on what Peter Haas calls 'epistemic communities' - 'transnational networks of knowledge-based communities that are both politically empowered through their claims to exercise authoritative knowledge and motivated by shared causal and principled beliefs'.[124] Thus it is clear that the scientists who have been involved in the work on global warming (in the IPCC, for example), have come from various government departments, NGOs, universities, and international organizations, across national boundaries, and arguably that their the primary allegiance has been to the issue and to their professional position, rather than to the states they have formally represented. As Sand points out, 'Since transnational contacts enhance the professional status of participants, they create strong incentives for continuing and expanding international agreements'.[125] The way that these groups have caused knowledge to evolve on the global warming issue has clearly acted as a spur to international cooperation, and may continue to make it easier for states to cooperate as knowledge evolves further.[126]

A traditional response to global environmental problems has often been to hanker after some sort of world government.[127] The problems involved in enforcing agreements on sovereign states may seem insuperable without establishing some sort of international Leviathan.

---

[123]Haas, op.cit, p.360, note 27.

[124]Haas, op.cit, p.349.

[125]Sand, op.cit, p.29.

[126]See also on this idea, E.Haas, *When Knowledge is Power: Three Models of Change in International Organizations*, University of California Press, Berkeley, 1990; E.Haas, 'Why Collaborate? Issue Linkage and International Regimes', *World Politics*, Vol.32, 1980, pp.357-405; P.M.Haas, 'Do Regimes Matter? Epistemic Communities and Mediterranean Pollution Control', *International Organization*, Vol.43, 1989, pp.377-403.

[127]L.P.Shields and M.C.Ott, 'The Environmental Crisis: International and Supranational Approaches', *International Relations*, November 1974, pp.629-648; Sand, op.cit.

However, as Sand shows, there are many other ways in which problems can be resolved. International regimes can be used to diffuse information about national regulatory models among states, public review procedures can often be as effective as litigation in getting states to comply with agreements, and, as noted above, 'epistemic communities' can often enhance cooperation because those formulating and implementing an agreement can share a primary commitment to the goals of that agreement rather than to the country where they are based.[128] With many of these approaches, what becomes important is the dissemination of information and knowledge, and the strong involvement of NGOs.

Looking particularly at global warming, some of these factors can be seen to be at work, while others do not appear to be present. NGO involvement is very evident and strong, as are a series of 'epistemic communities'; many of the delegates in the negotiations are scientists rather than diplomats, and the links between those involved in the INC, the IPCC, and national scientific programmes are clear. On the other hand, some of the sort of sophisticated bargaining outlined by Sand,[129] using selective incentives, differential obligations, side payments, and so on to get countries to participate, do not seem to be much in evidence so far. In the formal sense, the negotiations on global warming still seem in a stalemate, with strong differences between the parties.

Unless more sophisticated bargaining strategies are adopted, or unless greater consensus develops over the nature of the issue and the costs involved, we may be left with the following possible lines of development during the 1990s. The convention signed at UNCED will be in all likelihood purely a framework convention, setting out the conditions for further cooperation. Beyond that, international cooperation could remain at the lowest common denominator level; simply stating the existence of the problem of global warming and a general intention to do something about it, but without committing governments to anything specific, thereby succeeding in getting near universal participation. Secondly, there could be cooperation which commits industrialized countries to stabilization and possibly to

---

[128] Sand, op.cit; see also M.Grubb and N.Steen, *Pledge and Review Processes: Possible Components of a Climate Convention*, Workshop Report, Royal Institute of International Affairs, London, 1991, especially O.Greene, 'Building a Global Warming Convention: Lessons from the Arms Control Experience?', in ibid, pp.xxi-xxxiii.
[129] Sand, op.cit.

reduction targets (thereby making it highly unlikely in the short term that the US will join in), but which fails to make sufficient commitments on North-South transfers to gain the accession of many developing countries, for example China. Lastly, the ongoing negotiations could lead to an agreement which has both industrialized country targets and commitments on North-South transfers, and achieves wide participation, but almost certainly would not include the US. Any of these developments seems possible in May 1992. Looking at the present position of the United States, it seems difficult to envisage an emerging regime which will simultaneously commit governments to significant action on global warming and gain the participation of the US. However, an agreement which includes all the major states except the US, would put massive pressure on the US, with its self-perception as the world's leading power, possibly contributing to a re-evaluation of its position.[130]

---

[130]For an elaboration of this argument, see Paterson and Grubb, op.cit, pp.305-310.

The ozone layer in the stratosphere performs a vital job in protecting life on earth by absorbing harmful ultraviolet rays. In 1985, Joe Farman, head of the British Antarctic Survey Team, published alarming findings of massive thinning of the ozone concentration over the Antarctic, commonly referred to now as the 'ozone hole'.[1] This has massive implications for life on Earth. The debate ongoing since the early 1970s over whether ozone depletion results from natural or human activity intensified, and a flurry of diplomatic and pressure group activity resulted. Within the space of a few years a Convention and a Protocol were formulated to regulate production of chlorofluorocarbons (CFCs), targeted as the primary man-made ozone depleter. This chapter examines the ozone problem from scientific, legal and political angles to understand the response of the international community to the common challenge presented by this environmental problem.[2]

6.1 The scientific problem

The lower atmosphere around the earth is divided into two layers - the troposphere below and the stratosphere above - and the concentration, source and function of ozone varies in each layer.[3]

[1] J.C.Farman, B.G.Gardiner and J.D.Shanklin, 'Large Losses of Total Ozone in Antarctica Reveal Seasonal ClOx/NOx Interaction', *Nature*, Vol.315, 1985, pp.207-210.
[2] For a general work on ozone diplomacy, see R.Benedick, *Ozone Diplomacy: New Directions in Safeguarding the Planet*, Harvard University Press, Cambridge, Mass., and London, 1991.
[3] This section draws heavily on the excellent exposition of the scientific aspect by the German Bundestag, *Protecting the Earth's Atmosphere: An International Challenge*,

The troposphere contains 10% of the lower atmosphere's ozone. It used to be thought that the ozone here had wafted down from the stratosphere. However, scientists now know that man-made pollution, especially smog, is largely responsible. These pollutants react photochemically to increase the concentration of ozone in the troposphere. This has adverse consequences for flora and fauna and is thought to contribute to forest dieback. The increase in tropospheric ozone is also thought to contribute to greenhouse warming, but the extent of this effect remains unknown.

Ninety per cent of lower-atmospheric ozone is found in the stratosphere where its natural distribution depends on latitude and season. In a continual process of creation and destruction, it is formed by the reaction of oxygen in the lower stratosphere under the influence of ultraviolet radiation. Normal oxygen molecules are acted on by UV to break down into monatomic oxygen. These single oxygen atoms are sufficiently agitated by the UV to combine in rather fragile fashion to form O_3, alias ozone. Ozone is a molecule formed from three oxygen atoms, compared with the two atoms in the molecular oxygen we breathe on earth. This soon breaks down again to oxygen and monatomic oxygen. The cycle is repeated ad infinitum.

Most ozone formation takes place above the equator and the tropics, for this is the area where the atmosphere is most deeply penetrated by solar radiation. It is then carried by winds around the earth to the polar regions. While the ozone 'layer' is the common term of reference, ozone actually exists in the form of very small quantities of trace gases distributed throughout the stratosphere. If all the ozone here were compressed across the planet, the layer formed would probably not be more than 3mm thick. The ozone layer in the stratosphere acts as a filter for shortwave ultraviolet radiation, or UV-B. Thereby, it plays a very important role by preventing harmful shortwave radiation (which tends to be penetrative of living tissues) in the 290-310nm (nano-metre) range from reaching the earth's surface.

The natural distribution and amount of stratospheric ozone has been altered significantly by anthropogenic activity, in particular the release

Interim Report of the Study Commission of the 11th German Bundestag 'Preventive Measures to Protect the Earth's Atmosphere', Deutscher Bundestag, Referat Offentlichkeitsarbeit, Bonn, 1989.

of CFCs into the atmosphere.[4] (See below for details). This has resulted ultimately in a decrease in the amount of ozone in the stratosphere. As the amount of ozone in the stratosphere diminishes, the amount of UV-B reaching the earth's surface will increase. This will probably result in a higher incidence of skin cancer, cataracts and infectious diseases among animal life, genetic mutations and lower productivity of plants, disruption of the aquatic food chain, increased global warming and deterioration of synthetics such as plastics. Until further investigations are carried out, we cannot know the full range of consequences. Effects on the earth's climate are anticipated, as are changes in the stratosphere's chemical composition. It is with the fate of stratospheric ozone that we are primarily concerned in this section.

In 1974, Molina and Rowland published an article in *Nature* in which they theorized about the depletion of stratospheric ozone due to the catalytic action of free chlorine atoms that were released by the breakdown of CFCs in the stratosphere.[5] Their findings were alarming, for hitherto CFCs had been praised ever since they were first used commercially in the 1930s for their non-toxicity and their general positive contribution to human health, for example via refrigeration. They suggested that CFCs, which have a very long atmospheric lifetime of 65-120 years, when released into the atmosphere move upwards from the troposphere to the stratosphere over a period of about six to eight years. Once there, when exposed to ultraviolet light, they are finally broken down. The chlorine atoms contained in CFCs are then released, and they combine with ozone molecules in the beginning of a chain of catalytic reaction cycles which lead to destruction of further ozone molecules. Indeed, later studies showed that one chlorine atom can destroy 100,000 ozone molecules before it becomes inactive and moves back to the troposphere.[6]

---

[4] An authoritative statement on stratospheric ozone depletion was first issued by the WMO in 1975. Updates were prepared in 1978 and 1982, and comprehensive reports in 1981, 1985, 1988, 1991. For the most recent analysis, see *WMO Ozone Report No.25*, WMO, Geneva, January 1992. For an executive summary, see 'WMO/UNEP Scientific Assessment of Stratospheric Ozone - 1991', WMO/UNEP, Geneva, released on 22 October 1991; and WMO, 'WMO/UNEP Scientific Assessment of Stratospheric Ozone - 1991', Press Release, WMO, No.473, 22 October 1991.

[5] M.J.Molina and F.S.Rowland, 'Stratospheric Sink for Chlorofluoromethanes: Chlorine Atom Catalyzed Destruction of Ozone', *Nature*, Vol.249, 1974, pp.810-814.

[6] R.S.Stolarski, 'The Antarctic Ozone Hole', *Scientific American*, Vol.258, No.1, 1988, p.22.

More recently, the theory has been supported by data obtained from sampling stations and by satellite. Ozone has been measured since the 1920s by use of the Dobson Spectrometer, named after its inventor. He also lent his name to the units of measurement of ozone - Dobson Units. In the International Geophysical Year (1957-58), several atmospheric sampling stations using Dobson spectrometers were set up in Antarctica. There are at least 85 such ground stations in operation now, but these are concentrated in the northern mid-latitudes, with only a sparse coverage in the tropical and subtropical regions or in the southern hemisphere outside the Antarctic region. Since 1979, ground-based measurements have been supplemented by continuous recording of global ozone distribution by instruments mounted on the Nimbus 7 satellite: the Total Ozone Mapping Spectrometer (TOMS) and the Solar Backscatter Ultraviolet Unit (SBUV).

Global atmospheric models in the 1970s predicted a slow downward trend in stratospheric ozone levels. In the early 1980s, scientists began to revise earlier estimates upwards. However, in 1985, Joe Farman's team working out of the British Halley Bay Station reported that a hole had been appearing in the ozone layer over Antarctica each year since 1979. They also reported a current 40% loss in springtime ozone over Antarctica. They had been aware of the situation since 1982, but given that their results went against the scientific convention, they had decided to exercise caution and re-check their observations of this annual phenomenon before making public their findings.

Surprised at this new feature, scientists checked the findings from ground stations against Nimbus 7 satellite data. The satellite sensors had not merely picked up the fall in ozone levels, but had even flagged the lowest values.[7] Analysts, trained to monitor and interpret within given limits, had ignored them as freak measurements. Both the framework of analysis which discounted unexpected developments, and the attitude of the analysts, indicate clear examples of tracked thinking. None of the global atmospheric models had predicted these massive ozone losses. Ozone depletion due to chlorine build up had been expected to occur in a slow, linear fashion. Scientists hypothesized as to whether the current losses were due to natural activity or chemical reactions resulting from human activity. Ozone research was stepped up, and in 1986 the USA

---

[7]C.P.Shea, 'Protecting Life on Earth: Steps to Save the Ozone Layer', *Worldwatch Paper*, No.87, The Worldwatch Institute, Washington DC, December 1988, p.7.

conducted NOZE - National Ozone Expedition - at its McMurdo station in the Antarctic. In 1987 conclusive evidence was provided by NASA (National Aeronautical and Space Administration). Measurements were made from a converted U2 spy plane which, flying from Punta Arenas in Chile, flew into the centre of the ozone hole. The hole now displayed a general 50% ozone loss, and at certain altitudes 97.5% of ozone was missing. It covered an area larger than the USA and deeper than Everest. A huge rise in chlorine monoxide was monitored as soon as the hole had been entered. A combination of other factors contributed to this strange phenomenon, notably the unique meteorological conditions existing over Antarctica. High concentrations of active chlorine were the primary cause.

The next question which scientists had to address was whether this hole was a localized phenomenon. The NASA Ozone Trends Panel report of March 1988 was drawn up by over 100 international scientific experts. It suggested that the entire ozone layer around earth was eroding much faster than scientific models had predicted. Drawing on the report, Shea remarks that:

Between 1969 and 1986, the average concentration of ozone in the stratosphere had fallen by approximately 2%. The magnitude of the decline varied by latitude and by season, with the most heavily populated regions of Europe, North America, and the Soviet Union suffering a year-round depletion of 3% and a winter loss of 4.7%.[8]

Disturbingly, the report also states that between latitudes 30 degrees north and 64 degrees north, where the majority of the world's population lives, the total amount of ozone above any particular point had decreased by between 1.7% and 3% in the period 1969-86.[9] The natural chlorine content of the stratosphere is changing too, providing more corroboration for the argument that chlorine is the major human-induced cause of ozone depletion. Estimated by scientists to be about 0.6 parts per billion (ppb) in its natural concentration in the stratosphere, the concentration stands now at about 2.5-3.5ppb. This represents a very substantial increase.

The NASA report was followed in October 1988 by the second report of the UK Stratospheric Ozone Review Group, set up by the UK Department of the Environment and the Meteorological Office. It

---

[8] ibid., p.6.

[9] 'Saving the Ozone Layer: London Conference', Reference Services, Central Office of Information, London, July, 1989, p.3.

confirmed the view that significant stratospheric ozone depletion was resulting from human activities. It also predicted that:

... in the absence of other changes, the Antarctic hole will continue to appear each year until stratospheric chlorine levels fall to those of the mid-1970s. This would take many decades, even if no more man-made chlorine were to be released into the atmosphere.[10]

Evidence provided by NASA flights over the North Pole in 1988-9, and more recently from balloon measurements in the Arctic winter of 1989-90,[11] points to the wintertime loss of ozone over the Arctic. This suggested the possible future development of a hole similar to that revealed over the Antarctic in springtime.

Reports published in 1991 by the UK's Stratospheric Ozone Review Group[12], WMO/UNEP/[13], and UNEP[14] gave further cause for concern.[15]

In October 1991, the European Arctic Stratospheric Ozone Experiment (EASOE) was launched in London to study ozone destruction over the northern hemisphere.[16] Its early findings suggest that ozone depletion over northern Europe is occurring faster than expected. A shrinkage of up to 20% occurred in the first two months of 1992.[17] Dr Neil Harris of EASOE, and Joe Farman, attribute the loss to three causes: high levels of CFCs; repercussions of the eruption of Mount Pinatubo in July 1991; and unusual sustained high pressure over the north Atlantic which naturally 'thawed' the ozone layer in the period December 1991-February 1992.

Looking to the future, it is possible that information-gathering on the ozone layer by satellite will be interrupted. The German Atmos satellite,

[10]ibid., p.3.
[11]See D.Hofmann and T.Deshler, 'Evidence from Balloon Measurements for Chemical Depletion of Stratospheric Ozone in the Arctic Winter of 1989-90', *Nature*, Vol.349, January 1991, pp.300-5.
[12]Stratospheric Ozone Review Group, *Stratospheric Ozone 1991*, HMSO, London, 1991.
[13]WMO/UNEP, *Scientific Assessment of Stratospheric Ozone 1991*, WMO/UNEP, Geneva, 1991.
[14]UNEP, *Environmental Effects of Ozone Depletion: 1991 Update*, UNEP, Geneva, 1991.
[15]See Greenpeace, *Danger Overhead: Britain's Vanishing Ozone Layer*, Greenpeace, London, 1991.
[16]C.Cookson, 'Ozone Hole Set to Grow', *Financial Times*, 16 October 1991.
[17]T.Radford, 'Ozone Layer Shrinks By Up To 20%', *The Guardian*, 8 April 1992.

due for launch in 1995, may be cancelled for financial reasons. NASA's Upper Atmosphere Research Satellite ends its useful life in 1995, while the US earth Observation System is not scheduled to be launched until 1998. This represents a real international failure to coordinate policy.[18]

It would be premature to dismiss the possible role of natural phenomena such as volcanic activity or cyclical changes in solar activity in altering ozone concentration. Scientists do not yet fully understand the part they play. However, scientists are united in the significance of compounds containing chlorine, and also those containing bromine. These play a major role in depleting the ozone layer. CFCs are the main source of chlorine in the stratosphere, while the halons used in fire extinguishers are the main source of bromine. These harmful chemicals result from industrial processes and products. In an excellent summing up, the report of the German Bundestag on *Protecting the Earth's Atmosphere* states that:

> The total ozone content is influenced by at least three natural cyclical phenomena: the seasons, the quasi-biennial oscillations (QBO), and the eleven year solar cycle. In addition, stratospheric ozone distribution is affected by irregular phenomena such as volcanic eruptions[19] and the 'El Nino event'[20]. It is only after filtering out this natural variability that one can try to assess the effects of human activities. Man-made ozone destruction is caused by emissions of trace substances. In this context, industrially produced CFCs as well as other chlorinated and brominated substances and halons are a major threat for the ozone layer. In addition, trace gases that form during the extraction and combustion of fossil fuels, during the burning of biomass, in large-scale animal husbandry, through the use of nitrogen-based fertilizers and during rice paddy cultivation also play a major role in ozone change.

---

[18] *The Environmental Digest*, February 1992, No. 56, p. 11.

[19] A.Robock, 'Volcanoes and Climate', in A.Berger, S.Schneider and J.Duplessy, (eds), *Climate and Geo-Sciences: A Challenge for Science and Society in the 21st Century*, Kluwer Academic Publishers, Dordrecht/Boston/London, 1989. See also German Bundestag, op.cit., p.152.

[20] The El Nino event refers to an ocean current, as yet not fully understood, which disrupts otherwise rich fishing grounds and probably also effects weather. It is the subject of a large-scale international project: Tropical Oceans Global Atmosphere experiment, or TOGA. This aims to find out why the El Nino event occurs and to predict when it will occur.

What is certain is that the ozone hole which forms in the early Antarctic spring is caused primarily by man-made CFC emissions. Global ozone depletion is much less pronounced than the Antarctic phenomenon. Nevertheless, there is still a significant loss, even if one makes allowance for natural ozone variations, and this reduction is most probably due to the effects of man-made CFC emissions ...

If CFC emissions remain at their current level, man-made concentrations (of chlorine) will reach about twelve times the natural concentration in a few decades. A fourfold or fivefold increase in the natural concentration has already led to massive ozone destruction in the Antarctic region. Even if CFCs were banned, the ozone layer would not recover immediately. Instead, the effects would first of all become more pronounced, and all the more so the later countermeasures are adopted.[21]

The hazards associated with their emission go far beyond even the threat to life on earth posed by destruction of the ozone layer. Scientists are in general agreement on the formidable role played by CFCs in the greenhouse warming problem. While carbon dioxide is regarded as the most important single anthropogenic greenhouse gas, one molecule of the compound CFC-12 is 10,000 times more effective as a heat trapper than a molecule of carbon dioxide. Clearly, then, the scientific case for action to stop emission of CFCs is watertight; we are altering the atmosphere in a way which we do not fully understand, and doing untold damage.

6.2 Implications on earth

Some of the implications of increased UV-B radiation at the earth's surface have already been established, at least at a general level. However, there is still a long way to go in predicting likely effects on living and non-living matter and outlining responses. Many of the predictions are based on laboratory studies, and caution is required when extrapolating these results onto field conditions. To date, most of the research has been carried out by US government agencies and to a much lesser extent by west Europeans. In February 1992, UNEP published a full report on 'The Environmental Effects of Ozone Depletion'.[22] The effects of ozone depletion will surely be felt across the globe, and it is

[21]German Bundestag, op.cit., pp.149-50.
[22]See UNEP, Geneva, 1992.

imperative that work is done to assess potential difficulties facing the poorer regions of the world which are least able economically and technically to meet the new challenges. The increase in UV-B radiation is expected to be greatest in tropical and subtropical regions, and hence the problems posed for animal and plant life will probably be most acute there.

Increased incidence of skin cancer is the most frequently cited likely repercussion of ozone depletion in the stratosphere. The occurrence, particularly amongst Caucasians, of the most common but rarely fatal types of skin cancer - squamous and basal cell carcinoma - has been linked directly to cumulative exposure to ultra-violet radiation.[23] Shea reports that globally those most at risk are people with light colouring living nearest the equator, and Argentinians, Australians, Chileans and New Zealanders who live in areas under the springtime reach of the Antarctic hole.[24]

In October 1991 a WMO/UNEP report[25] suggested that the ozone layer is disappearing faster than expected, and the depleting area is extending from Antarctica to other areas of the earth. Whereas ozone depletion was originally confined to Antarctica and the northern hemisphere in winter, it now seems to have reached middle and high latitudes in both hemispheres in spring and summer. Thus the cancer risk (as well as other risks such as effects on crops) is already likely to be increasing.[26]

Eye problems, particularly cataracts (a disease usually of old age) which can lead to blindness, will probably increase with more UV radiation at the earth's surface. It has been estimated that a 1% decrease in total ozone could increase the incidence of cataracts by 0.6%, resulting in 100,000 additional cases. While in the industrialized countries treatment is by a routine operation, in developing countries millions of people suffer blindness already because of lack of access to remedial treatment. There is little hope that treatment will be available for the

---

[23]See for example, R.R.Jones, 'Ozone Depletion and Cancer Risk', *The Lancet*, 22 August 1987, pp.443-47. Also J.C.Van der Leun, 'Health Effects of Ultraviolet Radiation', draft report to the UNEP Coordinating Committee on the Ozone Layer, Effects of Stratospheric Modification and Climate Change, Bilthoven, Netherlands, 19-21 November, 1986, cited by Shea, op.cit., p.14.
[24]Shea, op.cit, p.14.
[25]WMO, op.cit, 1991 for executive summary; WMO, op.cit, 1992 for full report.
[26]'UN Finds Ozone Depletion and Cancer Increasing', *International Herald Tribune*, 23 October 1991.

millions more who develop cataracts in the future because of depletion of the ozone layer.[27] In 1980 half of the world's elderly population was in the developed world, but by the year 2000, two-thirds of the elderly will inhabit developing countries.[28] Their chance of treatment will be negligible.

General suppression of the immune system may well be another result, thus leading to an increase in infectious diseases and reduced effectiveness of vaccination programmes. Indeed the 1992 UNEP report on the environmental effects of ozone depletion warns of 'profound influences' on the human immune system, and says that the 'activation of HIV-1 by UV radiation is a cause for concern'. Bacterial infections, such as leprosy and tuberculosis, viruses like herpes, parasitic invasions such as malaria and leishmaniasis, and fungal infections such as candidiasis could become far more common.[29] Again, the developing world will be the hardest hit. Inoculation may become inappropriate with respect to certain diseases, such as diphtheria and tuberculosis, as it could result in enhancement of the disease in the body rather than protection against it. While research still has a long way to go in terms of quantifying the level of immuno-suppression caused by increased ultraviolet radiation, Australian work suggests that the trigger levels may well be lower even than those required to stimulate skin cancer.[30]

We can expect other forms of animal life to be affected in similar ways. Work on cattle already indicates susceptibility to eye problems such as pink eye and cancer eye; indeed it has recently been suggested that an increase in blindness in Argentine sheep may well be due to ozone depletion. Further research may well reveal general suppression of the immune system. This area needs greater exploration. The implications for communities who depend on animal husbandry for their livelihood cannot be over-stressed. Throughout the developing world peasants rely to a greater or lesser extent on cattle for milk products, meat, dung, clothing and utensils.

---

[27] EPA, *Regulatory Impact Analysis: Protection of Stratospheric Ozone*, Vol.1, Washington DC, 1987, cited in Shea, op.cit, p.15.
[28] Friends of the Earth, *Funding Change: Developing Countries and the Montreal Protocol*, London, 1990, p.5.
[29] ibid, p.6.
[30] Shea, op.cit, p.14.

Of over 200 plant species tested under UV radiation, the majority being food crops, two-thirds showed stunted growth.[31] Crops like peas and beans fared particularly badly. Research on protein rich soya beans by Alan Teramura of Maryland University showed that ozone loss of 25% led to a 25% reduction in yield. Moreover, he discovered that plant sensitivity to increased UV-B radiation was heightened as the level of phosphorous (a fertilizer) in the soil increased.[32] Plant ecosystems which rely on nitrogen, such as rice paddies, may be affected drastically as the organisms which fix nitrogen in tropical countries are very sensitive to UV-B levels. Clearly, in the absence of a complete and immediate ban on ozone depleters, it is imperative that more research is undertaken to develop remedial chemical supplements or, alternatively, ultra-violet resistant crop strains which are nutritionally, economically and culturally acceptable. Even with such a ban, we may well experience genetic mutations in the years ahead on account of damage already done to the ozone layer and due to the life-span of ozone depleters in the atmosphere. There is a great need for more systematic and comprehensive research on *all* terrestrial ecosystems.

The basis of the marine food chain may well be under threat. Phytoplankton, the sole food source of many zooplankton and fish larvae, must live at the surface of the sea to receive necessary sunlight for photosynthesis. This means they will also receive more ultraviolet radiation. Studies show that a 25% reduction in ozone is likely to result in a 35% drop in the productivity of phytoplankton.[33] Shea remarks that:

Exposure resulting from ozone loss of 10% corresponds to moving 30 degrees closer to the equator ... Ultimately, entire ecosystems may become more unstable and less flexible.[34]

The future composition of fish populations, and the related issue of commercial fish harvests, remains unclear.

The importance of phytoplankton extends far beyond their role in the aquatic food chain. These single-cell organisms are responsible for fixing over half of the carbon dioxide produced globally annually. Their fate

[31]Greenpeace, 'Life Without Ozone', *Air Pollution Briefing*, Greenpeace, London, October 1987.
[32]A.H.Teramura and N.S.Murali, 'Intraspecific Differences in Growth and Yield of Soybean Exposed to Ultraviolet-B Radiation Under Greenhouse and Field Conditions', *Environmental and Experimental Botany*, Vol.26, No.1, 1986.
[33]Shea, op.cit, p.16.
[34]ibid, p.17.

will therefore be reflected crucially in the amount of carbon dioxide removed from the atmosphere, and that in turn will affect the pace of global warming.

Increased UV-B radiation affects not only living matter but certain types of synthetics. For example, some plastics are particularly vulnerable to degradation if inhibitors are not used in their manufacture. Again, susceptibility is likely to be highest in the tropics.

Much more research is needed across the globe to establish causal relationships. Some investigations will be carried out by satellite; others need to be done on site. Thorough investigation of, for example, medical effects on humans and cattle, will require immense effort, and it is highly unlikely that many countries will feel that their meagre resources can be spent on such a study.

6.3 Who is responsible?

The main anthropogenic source of stratospheric chlorine is chlorofluorocarbons. Other sources include halons, carbon tetrachloride, methyl chloroform and HCFCs. (See Table 6.1 for sources, uses, and life-span in the atmosphere of various anthropogenic chemical ozone depleters). CFCs were first produced in the laboratory in around 1892 by Swarts in Belgium. It was not until the 1930s that they were brought into industrial use. They were hailed for their non-toxic, non-flammable, non-corrosive properties and the fact that they were stable ie. they did not react with other substances. Moreover, they were cheap to produce and consume. In 1929, Midgeley of General Motors discovered the use of CFC-11 and CFC-12 as refrigerants.[35] Later other refrigerants emerged: CFC-13, CFC-14, and H-CFC-22. During World War II, research began in the USA into using CFCs as sealants. H-CFC-22, for example, is a starting product for Teflon (non-stick coating). After the War, the emphasis shifted to CFC usage in aerosols, air-conditioning systems, coolants for refrigeration, foam blowing agents, and cleaners for plastics and metal.[36] More recently, they have come to be used for cleaning precision electronic appliances and micro chips.

It was not until the 1970s that the production and use of CFCs really got underway. This upward trend was arrested slightly in the mid-1970s when production dipped due to the Rowland and Molina theory that

---

[35]German Bundestag, op.cit, p.168.
[36]ibid.

Table 6.1 Ozone depleting chemicals

Chemical	Use	Life time in atmosphere
CFCs	Refrigerators Car air conditioners Foam cushioning and insulation Solvent to clean electronics Sterilants	100 years
HCFCs	Home air conditioners Plastic food packaging Some aerosols	15 years
Halons	Fire extinguishers Fixed fire suppressant systems	100 years
Carbon tetrachloride	CFC production Laboratory reagent Pesticide production Solvent Chlorine production	50 years
Methyl chloroform	Industrial solvent to clean metal and electronics and as a carrier solvent for adhesives	6 years

Reproduced from the Ministry of the Environment, Canada. Release:
PR-HQ-090-54, 2 November 1990

CFCs would destroy the ozone layer. Prior to fears about the harmful
potential of CFCs, stratospheric ozone depletion had already become an
important environmental, health and political issue in the US.[37] Fears
about the effect of supersonic transport (SST) aeroplanes on the ozone

[37]M.Morrisette, 'The Evolution of Policy Responses to Stratospheric Ozone Depletion', *Natural Resources Journal*, Vol.29, Part 3, Summer 1989.

layer via emissions of hydrogen and nitrogen compounds,[38] and other environmental concerns such as noise pollution and sonic booms, coupled with economic non-viability, had resulted in the Senate cancelling the SST project in 1971. Concern had also been expressed about the possible effects of above ground nuclear testing on ozone depletion, and the consequences of certain agricultural practices such as the use of nitrogen fertilizers.

This early concern in the US, however, had not been matched by similar concern in EC states or Japan. By the mid-1970s, two groups had formed: one, composed of the US, Canada, Sweden, and Norway, supported the precautionary principle and banned the use of CFCs in non-essential aerosols and wanted a global ban;[39] and the other, composed of the EC and Japan, took a much softer line domestically and internationally. Within the EC, Britain and France in particular resisted regulation, calling for more scientific evidence linking CFCs with ozone depletion. Both countries were major producers and users of CFCs, and they were involved in developing a commercial SST. However, they agreed to the EC Decision of 1980.[40] This legally binding Decision placed a duty on member states to take measures to ensure that industry situated on their territories did not increase production capacity for two CFCs, F-11 and F-12. In other words, it amounted to a production cap. It also required a 30% reduction in the use of CFCs in aerosol cans by 31st December 1981 as compared with 1976 levels. Since production in the EC was well below capacity, the cap was really symbolic in nature. However, if industry had not complied voluntarily then governments would have had to put regulatory mechanisms in place to stay within the targets.

Shea argues that the group of countries which first banned CFC propellants in their aerosol products benefited economically as well as environmentally: hydrocarbons, the replacement propellant, are cheaper than CFCs and saved the US economy $165 million in 1983 alone.[41]

---

[38]H.Johnston, 'Reduction of Stratospheric Ozone by Nitrogen Oxide Catalysts from Supersonic Transport Exhaust', *Science*, Vol.173, No.517, 1971.

[39]The US ban on the non-essential use of CFCs in aerosols under the Toxic Substance Control Act and the Federal Food, Drug and Cosmetic Act took effect in December 1978. See Morrissette, op.cit, p.805.

[40]N.Haigh, *EEC Environmental Policy and Britain*, 2nd revised edition, Longman, Essex, 1989, pp.265-270.

[41]Shea, op.cit, p.24.

Figure 6.1 CFC production by region 1984, tonnes

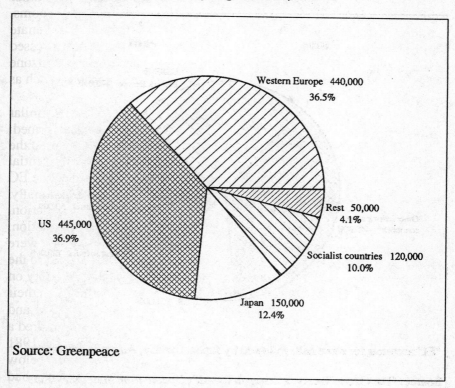

Western Europe 440,000
36.5%

Rest 50,000
4.1%

US 445,000
36.9%

Socialist countries 120,000
10.0%

Japan 150,000
12.4%

Source: Greenpeace

The downward turn in sales of CFCs in the mid-1970s was soon reversed. Obtaining precise figures is very difficult, as there is much secrecy involved throughout industry, and also a lot of ignorance. Figure 6.1 shows estimated levels of CFC production by region in tonnes in 1984. By 1987, global CFC production, excluding China, the USSR and eastern Europe, exceeded 1974 production, and approached one million tonnes.[42] Figure 6.2 reveals that the capitalist industrialized countries account for 70% of total consumption. On a per capita basis, discrepancies between different parts of the world are startling: the US, for example, uses six times the global average per capita. Shea shows that from 1931-86, virtually all CFC-11 and CFC-12 was produced and sold within the northern Hemisphere. However, she adds that:

---

[42] ibid, p.20.

Figure 6.2 CFC consumption by region 1986, tonnes

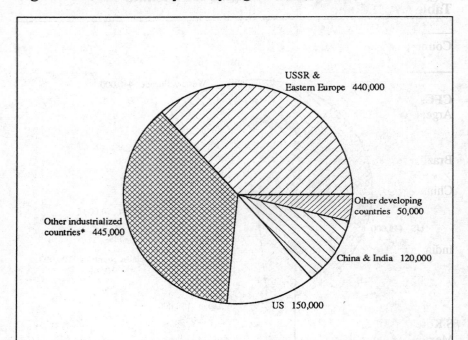

*EC accounts for more half, followed by Japan, Canada, Australia and others

Source: 'The Ozone Treaty: a Triumph for All', *Update from State*, May/June 1988, cited in Shea op.cit.

Since raw chemicals and products made with and containing CFCs were then exported, in part to developing countries, final usage was not quite as lopsided. Indeed, the Third World accounted for 16% of global CFC consumption in 1986.[43]

We can expect the demand for CFCs to rise rapidly in developing countries as they industrialize and as populations and expectations rise. Already, several developing countries are establishing CFC manufacturing capability of their own which will make them less dependent on imports from the developed world. Table 6.2 shows estimated CFC production in developing countries. Brazil, Argentina,

[43]ibid, p.20.

Table 6.2 CFC and HCFC production in developing countries

Country	Plant/Company	Production tonnes (CFC)	Startup year	Source
CFCs				
Argentina	Ducilio, S.A.	7000	running	M
	Fiasa	3000(11,12)	2-88	D
	Irsa	1000(11,12)	delayed	D
Brazil	Dupont do Brasil	17000		
	Hoechst do Brasil	15000 in '88	running	M
China	30 plants (5major)	40000 in '95		D
		22000 in '86		D
		20000 in '88-89		M
		5000		E
India	Gujarat Fluorochemicals	5000	89	M
	Navin Fluorine Industries	7000(11,12)	?88	M
	Industrial Oxygen Co	7000(11,12)	4-89	D
	Mettur Chemicals	3000(11,12)	88	D
	Shri Ram Fibres	4000 (11,12)	3-89	D
S Korea	Ulsan	7000(113)		M
Mexico	Quimobasicos S.A.		90	D
	Halocarburos S.A. (DuPont)	?10000	running	M
Taiwan	Formosa Plastics	12000 (11,12,113)	running	D
Venezuela	Produve (Atochem, France)	5000	90	M
HCFCs				
China		10000 (HCFC 22)	running	E
		100 (HCFC 152a)	running	E
Taiwan		3000 (HCFC 22)	90	D

Sources: D - DuPont, CFC - New Plant Activity; E - Proceedings of the US EPA Workshop on Integrating Case Studis Carried Out under the Montreal Protocol, January 1990; M - A. Markandya, *The Costs to Developing Countries of Entering the Montreal Protocol*, January 1990.
Reproduced from the Friends of the Earth, London, *Ozone Protection Campaign,* 'The Developing Countries and the Montreal Protocol' June 1990.

China, Mexico, Venezuela, Indonesia, and Taiwan already have plants running or planned. Statistics may not be completely accurate; just as in the case of the developed world there are vested business and national interests pitted against telling the whole truth. Also there may be straightforward ignorance of the real picture on the part of the governments concerned. Total developing countries CFC production potential stands at something like 110,000 tonnes. India is the largest developing country producer, followed by China and then Brazil. Despite this growing indigenous capability, at least half the total demand is met by imports.[44] Moreover, high-return products in particular tend to be imported. A Friends of the Earth report notes that 'Two thirds of the $3 billion market for refrigerators and air conditioning systems ... is satisfied by imports.'[45] It states also that local production of CFCs and substitutes meets half the developing countries demand, which in 1989 was estimated at 209,000 tonnes.

The detailed study of the current and future market for CFCs in the developing countries undertaken by Friends of the Earth offers a scenario of rapidly rising demand, seeing developing countries consume perhaps 43.5% of the world total by 2008. They see India and China potentially consuming one third of the global total. Just as in the developed world, the demand in the developing world for certain types of CFCs specific to particular uses can be disaggregated. For the developed world, Europeans use the most CFC-11 because of aerosol usage; the US uses the most CFC-112 because of mobile air-conditioning and other refrigeration, and Japan uses the most CFC-113 due to its use of solvents in the electronics industry.[46] In the developing world, the newly industrializing countries of east Asia will require solvents for their electronics industry, while the Chinese market for refrigeration is expected to grow exponentially. The market in India will probably be more generalized, covering aerosols, air conditioning and refrigeration.

While scientific logic suggests that there should be an immediate ban on CFC production, unfortunately political and economic arguments do not necessarily lead to the same conclusion. It is the developed countries which have created the ozone problem as a side-effect of their industrial development. To the developing countries, it appears grossly unfair that

---

[44]Friends of the Earth, op.cit, p.9.
[45]ibid, p.9.
[46]Shea, op.cit, p.20.

they are now being asked not to produce or consume CFCs because they are harmful to the whole world. China and India, with one-third of the world's population, consume only 2% of the CFCs. The UK by contrast, consumes 6% yet it has a population only one-thirtieth of the combined total of China and India.[47] Greenpeace poses the question:

> Why should they [the developing countries] forego these useful chemicals when the industrialised world has used them for 40 years and was totally responsible for the problem - for making 95% of the main CFCs?[48]

Clearly if they are to be encouraged to forego them, they will have to be given very appealing incentives in terms of finance and/or technology transfer.

The developed countries remain the main culprits in terms of CFC emissions, though it is noteworthy that some of them, such as Sweden, Norway, Australia, New Zealand and Germany, have made far greater efforts at reduction than the rest. Aerosol cans are the largest source of CFC emissions; they are responsible for 224,000 tonnes annually. France, Japan and the countries of eastern Europe are the most tardy in the developed world in terms of phasing these out. Individual countries have adopted different policies, from voluntary industry cutbacks in Belgium, the UK and Germany, to outright bans such as that instituted by Denmark in 1987. Recycling of CFCs by individual companies, such as ICI and IBM, is becoming more widespread, as is capturing CFC emissions from flexible-foam manufacturing.[49] There is room for improvement in the design of refrigeration and air-conditioning systems, where leakage of CFCs is a particularly irksome problem.

The challenge to government and industry is to find environmentally-friendly, non-toxic, reasonably priced alternatives. Some progress has been made, but the process is costly and slow due to the need for five- to seven-year toxicity tests. Shea notes that fourteen CFC producers from the USA, Europe, Korea and Japan have pooled their efforts to cut costs and time.[50] RTZ Chemicals of the UK, and Kali Chemie of Germany, have announced a joint programme to develop substitutes for air-conditioning, refrigeration and foam-blowing

---

[47]Greenpeace, 1987, op.cit.
[48]ibid.
[49]Shea, op.cit, p.26.
[50]ibid, p.30.

applications.[51] Unfortunately some of the substitutes that are being marketed are themselves either ozone depleters, or they contribute to global warming, or both. For example, the US company Du Pont has been producing HFC-134a from a plant in Texas since 1990. ICI, its British competitor, started commercial production at its first HFC-134a plant in Runcorn, UK, in October 1990, and it plans to have another in production in the USA in 1992. While this product is not an ozone depleter, it is a greenhouse gas 3,200 times stronger than carbon dioxide.[52] Table 6.3 shows the ozone depletion potential and global warming potential of these substitutes. It has been estimated that HCFC 22 already contributes 3% of the ozone destroying chlorine in the atmosphere.[53] Friends of the Earth cite UNEP's ozone experts, Dr Robert Watson and Dr Daniel Albritton, who state that HCFCs should only be used as options of last resort.[54] Thus, Friends of the Earth International (FOEI), along with many other environmental groups, is calling for an immediate ban on HCFCs in aerosols, and for use being confined to essential applications where chlorine-free substitutes are not available. Progress to control usage began on a national basis. The US Congress, for example, voted for a phaseout in new HCFC uses by 2015. The Nordic countries, Australia, New Zealand and Switzerland preferred a phase-out date of 2010 to be incorporated in international regulation. They were strongly opposed by the EC and Canada, who argued against any international restriction of HCFC production. Japan and the USA adopted a middle road, accepting the necessity of restrictions but trying to delay them until mid-way through the next century. However, government attitudes can change rapidly, and these positions have been overtaken by the London revision of the Montreal Protocol.

Even though ultimately it is customers who choose which product to use, the fact that the international community is depending on private companies to develop safe alternatives poses major difficulties in terms of incentives. FOEI points out that 'private investment into alternatives is disproportionately controlled by CFC producing companies, who are

---

[51]'Saving the Ozone Layer: London Conference', Reference Services, Central Office of Information, London, January 1989, p.5.
[52]IPCC, *Climate Change - The IPCC Scientific Assessment*, WMO/UNEP, CUP, Cambridge, 1990.
[53]Friends of the Earth, ' "H" CFCs: the Chemical Industry's New Ozone Destroyers', Briefing Sheet, Ozone Protection Campaign, FOE, London, 1990, p.1.
[54]ibid, p.2.

Table 6.3 Ozone and global warming potential of fluorocarbons

	Ozone depletion potential % of CFC11	Global warming potential % of CFC11
Hydrochlorofluorocarbons		
HCFC 22	5%	32%-37%
HCFC 123	2%	1.7%-2%
HCFC 124	2%	9.2%-10%
HCFC 141b	10%	8.4%-9.7%
HCFC 142b	6%	34%-39%
HCFC 225ca	5%	n.a.
HCFC 225cb	5%	n.a.
Hydrofluorocarbons		
HFC 125	0	51%-65%
HFC 134a	0	24%-29%
HFC 143a	0	72%-76%
HFC 152a	0	2.6%-3.3%

Reproduced from Friends of the Earth, London, *Ozone Protection Campaign* '"H" CFCs: The Chemical Industry's New Ozone Destroyers', Briefing Sheet, June 1990.

overemphasizing the development of close variants of the current chemicals'.[55] The initiatives by Du Pont and ICI are not necessarily enough. Du Pont, which supplies 25% of the global market, announced on 24 March, 1988, that it would work towards the eventual total phasing out of CFC production. But as we have seen, the substitutes it offers should be viewed with caution. ICI and Du Pont have a near monopoly on substitutes worldwide and have strong vested interests. Self-restraint and voluntary reduction policies by industry may achieve the desired end in certain cases, but globally they are not enough. The driving motive of private industry is profit, and this can come into direct conflict with the value of environmental protection where governments have failed to set

[55] ibid, p.3.

adequate standards. Several governments have been slow to act to restrict CFC and HCFC production because of worries over loss of revenue and jobs involved in a switch to alternatives. They cannot always give priority in their decisionmaking to environmental interests. The trade in CFCs is very lucrative. The UK, for example, is the biggest producer of CFCs in Europe, and it is also the biggest exporter. In 1988 it exported over 45,000 tonnes to 117 countries.[56] The early findings of the European Arctic Stratospheric Ozone Experiment have prompted ICI to maintain that it is doing its best to produce completely safe alternatives to CFCs.[57]

Bromine is an even more effective ozone destroyer than chlorine and it is long-lasting in the atmosphere. It is contained in halons which are used for fire fighting. Halons were developed by US army engineers at the end of World War II to fight fires in tanks and armoured personnel carriers.[58] Like CFCs, they immediately gained popularity because they are non-toxic and can be used with sensitive equipment. They are used now in hand extinguishers and also in 'total flooding systems' designed for enclosed areas such as museums, computer rooms and bank vaults.[59] In the countries of the former USSR they are also used in fire-fighting equipment for nuclear facilities. The Nordic countries have again taken the lead in pressing for international regulation to stop the production of halons. However, the USA, the former USSR, Japan and the EC have so far resisted these attempts.

There has been great resistance from industry and certain governments to an international ban on methyl chloroform, which UNEP calculates was responsible for 13% of the ozone-destroying chlorine emitted into the atmosphere in 1985. According to the United Nations Technology Review Panel Report, substitutes already exist for 90-95% of its uses as an all-purpose solvent.[60] Dow Chemicals, which as the largest producer supplies 40% of the world market, has launched a campaign to get its customers to write to US Senators pleading that restrictions would harm their own businesses. ICI urged similar action in the British context.[61] Fear of job losses is raised to lend ammunition to the cause of big

---

[56]Greenpeace, Air Pollution Briefing, op.cit.
[57]BBC Six O'Clock News, 7 April 1992.
[58]Shea, op.cit, p.21.
[59]ibid.
[60]Friends of the Earth, 'Methyl Chloroform - Ozone Destroyer', *Briefing Sheet*, Ozone Protection Campaign, FOE, London, June 1990.
[61]ibid.

business. The industry, having accepted that regulation would come, fought to delay complete phase-out of production until the middle of the twenty-first century. However, as scientific evidence became overwhelming, it gave up the fight. Following the pattern established with CFCs and HCFCs, the EC and Japan have dragged their feet while others, such as Sweden, decided to ban methyl chloroform from 1994. ICI has announced total closure of methyl chloroform production, virtually on the same timetable as Sweden. As with all these harmful chemicals, what is important from an environmental viewpoint is not just to ban local production and consumption but also to ban trade.

6.4 What is being done: ozone diplomacy

Widespread public international discussion of the ozone problem dates back to the mid-1970s following the publication of the article by Molina and Rowland. Two conferences were held on the ozone issue in 1977 and 1978 in Washington and Munich respectively; both were characterized by much lip-service but little firm action. Organized by UNEP, their attendance was supposedly international; however, the northern countries were well represented while the developing countries were under represented. (The latter were limited by lack finance and many were not conversant with the issues. This situation has been improved by funding channelled from bodies like the ODA in the UK through UNEP to bring representatives from developing countries to meetings. Also the Montreal Protocol budget does the same thing).

The first conference revealed a general reluctance by the developed countries to reduce CFC production and consumption significantly. While reductions had taken place since 1974, and more especially since 1978 mainly due to the bans on CFC usage in aerosols which had come into force in Canada, the USA and the Scandinavian countries, there was growing evidence that the gradual growth in the use of CFCs for other purposes would soon nullify this.[62] Without further control, this could happen indefinitely. The Europeans, who had made little effort to reduce their emissions, used the argument of scientific uncertainty to justify their position.

Armed with a Coordinating Committee on the Ozone Layer Report indicating a 2% reduction in the ozone layer, UNEP convened the second international government-level conference in Munich in 1978. This

---

[62]German Bundestag, op.cit, p.199.

meeting took a slightly stronger line, despite continued scientific uncertainties, and urged substantial reduction in the use of CFCs in aerosols. The Conference recognized the threat to human health if ozone depletion continued, and suggested that bans on use might be necessary if convincing scientific evidence were forthcoming.[63] Two distinct approaches were beginning to emerge: outright bans, as favoured by the US, versus production caps favoured by the EC.

The trend at the international level towards much talk but little real action continued in 1981 with EC approval for the introduction of instruments for the exchange of scientific, technical, socio-economic and statistical information on CFCs, and the implementation of measures to reduce the release of CFCs in the fields of refrigeration, foamed plastics and solvents. Still there was no European ban on CFCs in aerosols; the only target set by the EC had been the 30% reduction on 1976 figures of CFC usage in aerosols by the end of 1991, and production capacity caps on CFC F-11 and F-12.

Interest in the ozone issue waned in the early 1980s as scientists made a downward revision of their estimates of ozone depletion, and the recession meant that environmental concerns receded in domestic political arena. Despite this, UNEP pressed ahead with efforts to negotiate an ozone convention which would set out broad principles. The hope was that this might be accompanied or followed by a protocol outlining specific targets which signatories would be obliged to meet. The process began in January 1982, and after much political disagreement finally came to fruition in March 1985.

The Vienna Convention for the Protection of the Ozone Layer

The Vienna Convention for the Protection of the Ozone Layer was signed on 22 March, 1985, by twenty one states, as well as by the European Community. Most Latin American, North American, and European Community countries signed. In August 1988 the Convention came into force, after being ratified by the required twenty states. It provided for cooperation in research, observations and exchange of information. While the hope had been that the Convention might be accompanied by a protocol setting out regulatory controls, this was not to be. A dispute had emerged in the negotiations between two groups of countries, the Toronto group (composed of Canada, the US, Finland, Norway and Sweden), and the EC. Each group had proposed that the first protocol to

---

[63]ibid, p.192.

cover CFCs should reflect the policies already adopted by countries within that group. Thus the Toronto group wanted a worldwide extension of a ban on non-essential uses of CFCs as aerosol propellants, with the stated intention of producing an immediate reduction in CFC releases. The EC on the other hand wanted a total production capacity limit on the grounds that non-aerosol use of CFCs was growing.[64] In the ensuing conflict, disagreement between the two blocs ensured that no protocol was adopted at the time of the adoption of the Convention in 1985. Nevertheless, the Convention represented a significant step forward in international cooperation on environmental matters. In the words of the Report to the German Bundestag:

The Vienna Convention has set an international precedent in two respects. To begin with, it has been possible for the first time to define a framework for a global agreement on cooperation in the struggle to control environmental pollution. Secondly, it is an attempt to use an international agreement to predict a problem in order to prevent it, instead of having to eliminate its effects; in other words: for the first time, there has been a breakthrough at international level for the principle of prevention.[65]

It represented the first international agreement, in principle, to tackle an environmental problem while the science of the matter was still contentious. While the Convention fell short of setting specific reduction targets and other obligations, it was important for creating a framework for cooperation on research, monitoring and exchange of information. The stated objective of the Convention - to protect human health and the environment against the harmful effects of human activities that result from changes in the ozone layer - was vague, but it was significant nevertheless as the first step to unified international action on the ozone issue. The rules laid down in the Vienna Convention allowed for protocols which would specify the Convention in greater detail. While the agreement was international in nature, the majority of states party to it were developed countries (excluding former centrally planned economies). The absence of major developing countries like Brazil, India and China represented a real weakness in the Convention and flagged up future problems.

---

[64]For this debate, see 'The Ozone Layer - Implementing the Montreal Protocol', *House of Lords Report*, 17th Report, Session 1987-88, Paper 94, HMSO, July 12th, 1988, p.7.
[65]German Bundestag, op.cit, p.259.

At the time of the signing of the Vienna Convention, the findings of the British Antarctic Survey had not yet been published; that came two months later. However, government officials must have been aware of the results that were shortly to be made public. Nevertheless, the lack of conclusive scientific evidence relating the ozone problem to CFC emissions gave large company lobbyists more leverage and increased the pressure of industry on government to take a moderate stand.

The publication of Joe Farman's findings relating to the existence of the Antarctic hole stimulated greater public and governmental concern in the industrialized countries on the issue of ozone depletion. The arguments in the scientific community died down. The USA and the former USSR agreed to extend an environmental cooperation agreement signed in 1972 for a further five years, and this included cooperation on research into ozone depletion.[66] An Ozone Trends Panel was established in 1986 by NASA, UNEP and the WMO, to monitor trends in the ozone level in the stratosphere from 1969 onwards. In a previous section we outlined the findings of the scientific surveys and experiments carried out in 1986 and 1987. These supported the idea that chlorine concentrations resulting directly from the emission of CFCs into the atmosphere played the major role in formation of the Antarctic hole. The impetus for a protocol to accompany the Vienna Convention gathered momentum over these few years, and by September 1987 the international community - or least, part of it - was ready for greater regulation of CFC emissions.

The Montreal Protocol

The negotiations which led up to the signing of the Montreal Protocol were protracted and difficult. They were shot through with conflicts between different countries and between governments and the scientific community. There was great tension between the scientific community which pressed hard for a very tough stand on CFCs, and the main negotiators.

Inter-state conflict focused on the level of cut required. The US and Canada took a much tougher stand than the EC countries. It has been suggested that the EC/US conflict became highly personalized between Brinkhorst and Benedict. The US representative was particularly critical of the UK and France, who were responsible for holding up the EC commitment, portraying them as being more interested in short-term

[66]*Keesings Record of World Events*, Vol.XXXIV (1), January 1988, p.35678.

profit than environmental protection. The US was calling for a 90% reduction in CFC emissions. The UK did not see the need for any cuts. The stand adopted by each of these countries may have been heavily influenced by the position of their respective industries, as well as by the users. Historically, of course, the US had shown itself more willing to act to protect the ozone layer; yet on this occasion their strong position may well have been fortified by the fact that Du Pont was to about to announce (later in September 1987) the successful development of substitutes over which it would have a monopoly. Du Pont was conceivably set to dominate a world market devoid of CFCs. Within the EC itself there was much bad feeling over the UK's perceived intransigence on the level of cuts. Even within some countries, such as the UK, there was much bureaucratic wrangling over the issue. China and India did not even attend the negotiations; understandably from the viewpoint of their respective domestic development imperatives, they were expanding their CFC production capacity rather than considering cuts.

Despite all these problems, the Montreal Conference of 14-16 September resulted in a compromise, and a protocol was signed on the last day. It was driven by political and industrial imperatives rather than science. The negotiators did not wait for the announcement of the latest NASA scientific reports which were due just days before the treaty was signed. John Gribbin has suggested that some of the main negotiators, for example the British, were keen to exclude input from scientists and keep decisionmaking in the hands of politicians.[67]

The Montreal Protocol on Substances that Deplete the Ozone Layer was signed by 24 states and by the EC on September 16, 1987. It came into force on the target date of 1st January, 1989. (The condition - that it had been ratified by at least 11 states representing at least two-thirds of global consumption of CFCs and halons - had been fulfilled the previous month). It contained specific targets in its provisions, unlike the Vienna Convention which had outlined general principles. These targets included:

1. A 50% cut in the consumption of five CFCs (CFC-11, CFC-12, CFC-13, CFC-14 and CFC-15) by 1999, using 1986 as a baseline. This would be achieved in three stages: by 1990, the consumption levels of these CFCs were to be frozen at 1986 levels; by 1994, there

---

[67] J.Gribbin, *The Hole in the Sky*, Corgi Books, London, 1988, p.135.

should be a 20% reduction of the 1986 levels; and finally by 1999 there should be a further 30% cut of 1986 base levels.

2. Halons should be frozen by 1992 at 1986 levels.

Certain exceptions were allowed. For example, production ceilings for CFCs and halons could be exceeded to cover domestic needs in developing countries and for the sake of industrial rationalization between signatories. Also, developing countries were given an extra ten years grace period to comply with all measures if their annual per capita consumption of CFCs and halons was below 0.3kg. A clause also allowed countries with state-run economies which had started building production facilities before signing the agreement to arithmetically increase their 1986 production and consumption figures.

Restrictions were imposed on trade with non-signatories. One year after the Protocol enters into force, imports of controlled substances from non-signatories would be prohibited. Signatories could export to non-signatories, but these exports had to be counted as part of the exporting countries' consumption volumes of the controlled substances as of 1993.[68]

The Protocol provided for a four-yearly revision in accordance with available scientific, environmental, technical and economic information, starting from 1990. This was important, in that even though the 1987 Protocol had serious shortcomings, it offered a mechanism for stricter rules in the future.

Almost immediately after the ink was dry, criticisms were voiced which accused the Protocol of not going far enough. Moreover, the fact that it was agreed upon a few weeks before NASA's latest scientific findings on the extent of the Antarctic hole were publicized raised some suspicions. Gribbin has described the Protocol as 'a masterpiece of fudge and compromise, so full of loopholes that it is hard to see what effect it will have in the long term.'[69] Environmental groups such as Greenpeace and Friends of the Earth were highly critical of the Protocol, as were many political parties in Scandinavia and Europe.

The obvious criticism was that the CFC and halon reduction targets did not go far enough. Apart from this, the Protocol was rightly accused of not covering all CFCs and other chemical ozone depleting substances.

[68]German Bundestag, op.cit, p.265.
[69]Gribbin, op.cit, p.135.

HCFCs, which by 1987 had become popular with the CFC manufacturing companies as a substitute, have an ozone depleting potential of 2-10% of the CFCs regulated under the Protocol. Moreover, both they and the substitute HFC have global warming potentials. Methyl chloroform, the fifth biggest destroyer of the ozone layer, contributes more to chlorine loading in the atmosphere than CFC-113. Yet while the latter was classified as a controlled substance under the Protocol, the former initially was not.[70] Carbon tetrachloride was also not covered until the 1990 amended Protocol.

The Protocol gave the impression of making special concessions for developing countries; yet this is questionable. Greenpeace saw it as being of particular benefit to northern economies and as serving the interests of industry rather than the environment,[71] in that developing countries provide a very lucrative export market for chemical manufacturers. The 10-year grace period given to developing countries has been interpreted as benefiting northern exports to the developing world as CFC production was to be kept in the hands of the developed. By omitting to provide for technology transfer, the Protocol ensured continued developing country dependence on the North not only for CFCs but also for substitutes. Moreover, research and the development of alternatives was left in the hands of industry. This contrasted sharply with research to meet traditional security challenges, where government was (and is) a major sponsor. Yet this massive non-military challenge to human welfare and potentially to the survival of life on earth was left to be met by the efforts of private industry.

Compliance with the Protocol was to be based on trust; and as with most international legal agreements, there were no international enforcement powers. Verification would be extremely difficult. All signatories were obliged to report to UNEP on their progress towards reduction targets. The government committees which were to compile the reports relied on the honesty and knowledge of the industrial sector. So there existed a verification problem even at the national level. By its very nature, the Protocol, in common with so many other international agreements, lacked teeth when it came to enforcement.

---

[70]Greenpeace International, '50% More production: the Failure of the Montreal Protocol', Greenpeace, Amsterdam, June 1990, p.5.
[71]ibid, p.10-11.

Interim meetings: Hague, London, Helsinki, Noordwijk

No date had been decided for the first four-yearly review conference. In 1988 the conclusive nature of the scientific evidence lent urgency to the review, and this was scheduled for 1990 - just three years after the Montreal Protocol. In the interim, however, several international meetings were held at which the Protocol was discussed. The Hague meeting in October 1988, attended by government officials, scientists and industry, made an informal review of the Protocol in light of the very significant scientific evidence published since September 1987. (See back to section on scientific findings). The Conference concluded that the target for CFC reductions should be raised to 85% or more by 1999. Interestingly, the UK, which had argued against the necessity of any reductions in CFC emissions prior to the 1987 Protocol, did a U-turn and supported the new goal. While some commentators attribute this change of policy to the influence of Sir Crispin Tickell in convincing Mrs Thatcher of the global importance of environmental problems, MacKenzie attributes it to the awakening interest of British business in the move over to production of substitutes. Hence, she remarks 'it now makes business sense to save the ozone layer'.[72] She cites Mostafa Tolba, Executive Director of UNEP, who drew parallels between governments' motives now and at the time of the Protocol:

> The difficulties in negotiating the Montreal Protocol had nothing to do with whether the environment was damaged or not ... It was all who was going to gain an edge over whom.

Likewise, his comments at the Hague conference indicated that the development of alternatives made a reduction in CFC production - even a total phase-out - good business practice.

Following their June ratification of the Montreal Protocol, in November 1988 the EC Commission called for the 'virtual elimination' of CFCs ostensibly in the light of new scientific evidence. In February 1989, EC Environment Ministers agreed to ban all CFCs by the year 2000, and to make an 85% cut as soon as possible.[73] This proved to be a big step forward.

---

[72]D.MacKenzie, 'Now it Makes Business Sense to Save the Ozone Layer', *New Scientist*, 29 October 1988, p.25. The author would like to thank Suman Natarajan for drawing this article to her attention.

[73]*Keesings Record of World Events*, Vol.XXXV, Bristol, March 1989, p.36540.

From 5-7 March, 1989, the UK, in association with UNEP, hosted an international conference in London on 'Saving the Ozone Layer'. According to the British government, the aim of the London Conference was to show how reductions in emissions of CFCs could be achieved in practical terms by use of existing alternatives and by new products and technologies under development. It was particularly concerned that reduction in some areas should not be offset by growth of use of CFCs in others. Ministers from the developing and the developed world were invited, as well as representatives from industry and international organizations.

It became clear at the London Conference that the issue of equity would have to be addressed if major developing countries were to be brought on board the Montreal Protocol. The Chinese government had announced in early 1989 that it could no longer afford to import CFCs, particularly CFC-11 and CFC-12, at world market prices, and therefore it would have to expand its domestic production facilities.[74] China set clear terms for desisting from this course of action and joining the Protocol.

Firstly, China insisted that the developed countries which had released most CFCs into the atmosphere would have to make the greatest cuts in production before developing countries would join a global ban on the ozone-depleting gases.[75]

Secondly, China insisted that the special needs of developing countries be addressed in the Montreal Protocol in a way in which they themselves felt was appropriate. The special exemption in the Protocol which allowed developing countries to postpone implementation of the agreement for ten years if their per capita consumption was below 0.3kg per annum, was regarded as a limitation on their industrial expansion. It contrasted sharply - and negatively- with the 1986 production level limit put on developed countries. Dr Liu Ming Pu, head of the Chinese delegation, said that the Protocol should allow developing countries to base their CFC production and consumption on their level of economic development, their specific needs and progress in finding safe substitutes. He remarked that most of the stresses that developing countries might inflict on the environment resulted directly from their poverty. He contrasted China's annual CFC production of 20,000 tonnes

---

[74] 'Chinese Bring Chill to Backers of Ozone Protocol', *New Scientist*, 11 February 1989, p.28.
[75] J.Ardill, *The Guardian*, 7 March 1989.

per annum with the US total of 300,000 tonnes and the Soviet figure of 130,000 tonnes. He pointed out that China, with its 1.1 billion population, would potentially suffer most from the effects of ozone depletion, even though it produced only 2% of the world's CFCs and related gases. The developed world, on the other hand, accounted for 80% at least.

Thirdly, Dr Pu advocated the creation of an ozone layer protection fund, financed by the major producers and consumers of CFCs. If the developed countries wanted the developing countries to suspend CFC consumption, then it must fund the poor countries to do so. He also suggested that the rich countries, on account of their wealth alone, could afford to protect the environment while for poor countries environmental protection was a luxury beyond their means:

> The developed countries have produced environmental problems of grave magnitude. They took advantage of cheap energy in the past to accumulate wealth, which they can now use to manage the environment ... The developing countries face expensive energy (costs) and cannot accumulate wealth to protect the environment.[76]

The Chinese delegation echoed the ideas of other representatives, such as President Daniel Arap Moi of Kenya, who, as host to the UNEP in Nairobi, gave the opening address. Moi called upon the northern industrialized countries to 'bear the burden of conserving the global ozone layer equitably with the less developed countries.'[77] He called for international trade agreements that 'reward equitably' all countries which ratify and implement the Vienna Convention and the Montreal Protocol.[78]

The equity theme was also voiced by the Indian Minister of the Environment and Forests, Mr Ziul Rahman Ansari. The Indian delegation raised the issue of the injustice of a northern monopoly on the technology for production of CFC substitutes. Clearly, without the support of key developing countries that are potentially massive CFC consumers, the Montreal Protocol will have little effect. Aware of this, Dr Mostafa Tolba called at the close of the conference for the establishment of international mechanisms to compensate countries which forgo the use of CFCs in the interests of international safety.[79]

---

[76]'China Attacks Unfair Ozone Protocol', *New Scientist*, 11 March 1989, p.26.
[77]*Keesings Record of World Events*, Vol.XXXV, No.6, Bristol, p.36785.
[78]Jones, *The Independent*, 6 March 1989.
[79]Radford, *The Guardian*, 8 March 1989.

The London Conference provided plenty of examples of the conflict between national interest and international interest which characterizes so many international discussions and negotiations. The west persisted in telling the developing countries what to do, but refrained from offering a real material or technological incentive to influence their policies. The USSR, for its part, at that time had persistently argued that complete phasing out of CFCs would result in impoverishment of the developing countries, and that the west would have to bear responsibility for this. Its opposition to a radical cut stems at least partly from its desire to continue using home-produced CFCs in its domestic market. The former USSR also opposed a complete ban on halons, particularly since they are used in the fire control systems of its nuclear power stations.[80]

By the end of the Conference, in addition to the thirty states which had already signed the Montreal Protocol, thirty-four others had announced their intention to sign or to give serious consideration to signing. (Importantly, the latter group included China and India). If they were all to go ahead, their accession would mean that 92% of CFC production would be covered by the Protocol, compared to the 82% at the outset of the Conference.

The first official gathering of the parties to the Montreal Protocol took place in Helsinki, on 2-5 May, 1989. This Conference proposed a set of amendments to the Montreal Protocol which would be finalized at the first four-yearly review conference to be held in London, 1990. The Helsinki Conference issued a declaration of intent to stop production and use of CFCs by the year 2000.[81] While this was not legally binding, it was an important symbolic act and was indicative of the way the international mood regarding CFCs was developing. Representatives of seventy-nine states signed: thirty-six were parties to the Protocol already, while forty-three, including China, were not. There was also a declaration regarding halons and other ozone depleting chemicals which had not been covered by the Protocol.

Great disagreement arose at Helsinki over the establishment of a fund to help developing countries acquire technology for the production of CFC substitutes. While the principle of financial aid and technology transfer to developing countries was unanimously accepted, there was opposition to the proposed instruments for achieving this. The UK and

[80]Wright, *Times*, 7 March 1989.
[81]*Keesings Record of World Events*, Vol.XXXV, No.6, p.36785.

the US in particular argued against the developed countries making available new funds, and instead suggested that such a fund should utilize aid already committed for other purposes. China and India would not accept this. However, it was agreed that a working group should be established to look into ways of helping developing countries, including 'adequate international funding mechanisms which do not exclude the possibility of an international fund'.[82]

In November 1989, a Ministerial level Conference on Atmospheric Pollution and Climate Change was held in Noordwijk, the Netherlands, and one of the issues addressed was the funding mechanism to help developing countries phase out consumption of CFCs. McKinsey and Co had undertaken a study of the cost of complete phase-out of CFCs in the developing world, and this was published as an appendix to the Noordwijk Conference. It estimated that 80% of developing countries' consumption of CFCs could be replaced at relatively low cost in the 1990s, but that the remaining 20% would be far more expensive to replace. It suggested that $550-700 million per annum would be needed to accomplish the phase-out - a sum far in excess of any new funds that were likely to be forthcoming from the developed countries. It suggested also that the funding mechanism should be managed by the World Bank which had experience in the disbursement of multilateral aid and took an integrated economy perspective.[83] Such a proposal does not seem to take into account the doubts which many developing countries have concerning the competence of the World Bank, and the lack of enthusiasm with which they could therefore be expected to view this suggestion. Moreover, the suggestion contained in the report that the developing countries should wait until the northern market had fully accepted substitutes before making the switch indicated that there would be no technology transfer to the developing countries.

London Review Conference of Montreal Protocol

From 20-29 June, 1990, the first official review of the Montreal Protocol was convened in London. Its aims were twofold: to amend the targets for CFC reductions and to look at the possibility of controls on other ozone depleting substances; and to achieve a wider adherence to the

[82]*Keesings Record of World Events*, Vol.XXXV, May 1989, pp.36672-3.
[83]McKinsey and Co., 'Protecting the Global Environment: Funding Mechanisms', Appendices, Ministerial Conference on Atmospheric Pollution and Climatic Change, Noordwijk, The Netherlands, November 1989.

Protocol, by persuading developing countries who had not yet joined to do so. The scene was set for some major political disagreements between developed countries over the first goal, and between the developing countries and the developed, particularly the USA, over the second.

The main argument between developed countries concerned the speed at which CFC production should be phased out. While the Conference finally decided on total phase-out by the year 2000, a breakaway group of countries including some Europeans and Scandinavians had pressed for a 1997 deadline.[84] The former Soviet Union, the USA and Japan found this totally unacceptable. The amended Protocol said that CFCs should be phased out by the year 2000, with intermediate cuts of 50% compared with 1986 levels by 1995, and 85% by 1997. However, it was agreed that the implementation of CFC controls would be reviewed in 1992, rather than at the next four-yearly review due in 1994. This might offer the opportunity for quickening the pace of reform. The Conference also set the target of a total phase-out of halons by 2000, and phase-out of carbon tetrachloride by the same date. The year 2005 was set as the target for phase-out of methyl chloroform. These targets were, in effect, commitments. No legal controls were set on the production and use of HCFCs.

The main political debate at the London Conference concerned the incentives to be given to developing countries to join the Protocol.[85] Technology transfer and the establishment of a multilateral fund to help developing countries make the transition to environmentally-friendly CFC substitutes received most attention. The UK, previously intransigent, had already conceded under pressure from the EC that new money would have to be forthcoming via a new funding mechanism from the North to the South, rather than simply diverting aid already committed for other purposes to the environment. It was only on the eve of the Conference, however, after receiving a personal plea from Prime Minister Thatcher, and under pressure from US companies such as Du Pont who feared trade barriers from countries participating in a new funding mechanism, that President Bush agreed to reverse US policy. He

---

[84] A.Travis, 'Patten Seeks EC Ban on CFCs', *The Guardian*, 3 July 1990.

[85] For a full summary of the debate on these issues, see UNEP, *Report of the Second Meeting of the Parties to the Montreal Protocol on Substances that Deplete the Ozone Layer*, UNEP/Ozl.Pro.2/3, Nairobi, 29 June 1990.

then lent his support to the creation of new funds to be disbursed via a new multilateral mechanism.[86]

Discussions during the Conference revealed massive differences of opinion on the institutional disbursement of new funding and on the transfer of technology to the developing countries. Maneka Gandhi, the then Indian Environment Minister, took a very firm line, saying that technology for the production of ozone friendly substitutes had to be forthcoming for her to recommend that her government sign the Protocol - especially since India had only recently installed some very expensive American CFC production plants. Moreover, the technology had to be transferred free.[87] She indicated that India would accept an interim three-year package of £23 million sterling if the developed world promised to provide to the developing world £350 million for switching over to new technologies.[88] China indicated that it would need £14 million over the next three years to begin phasing out CFC production.[89] On the question of free transfer of technology, which it would be difficult for western governments to force upon companies, a compromise was finally reached which said that:

> ... if developing countries like India had problems gaining the technology to make CFC alternatives and so found it difficult to meet their obligations to phase out CFCs, then a meeting of the Montreal Protocol nations would be convened to assess this.[90]

The amount of money involved could be argued to be trivial. Had states like China and India decided to pursue the 'polluter pays' principle, then they would have canvassed for compensation for past emissions of CFCs by rich countries far in excess of the £350 million which they are demanding as the price of not producing CFCs. Paradoxically, they may be reducing their claim on Northern funds by linking payment to technology transfer. They might get more by making the simple property rights claim that they should be compensated for past emissions by the rich. If they were to receive proper compensation on this score, it would exceed many times over the cost of new technology in this area.

---

[86]*International Herald Tribune*, 14 and 18 June, 1990.

[87]*The Independent*, 29 June 1990.

[88]*Daily Telegraph*, 25 June 1990.

[89]*The Guardian*, 21 June 1990.

[90]*The Independent*, 30 June 1990.

On the question of administering the multilateral fund, the US preferred using the World Bank, while the developing countries wanted an elected Executive Committee representing the developed and the developing countries. The US said that such a committee would only be acceptable to it as the largest potential donor if it were given the special status of a permanent seat. The Group of 77 (a loose coalition of developing countries) took great exception to what they saw as US efforts to dominate the Conference by such conditions. The Mexican representative, speaking on behalf of the Group of 77, said that 'it was unacceptable that one country should have such an advantage over others'.[91] A Chinese representative called for the US to treat other countries as equal partners: 'We the developing countries are certainly not willing to accept environmental colonialism in whatever form it may appear'.[92]

Eventually it was agreed that a multilateral fund would be set up to help developing countries meet the extra cost of using substances and technologies that do not harm the ozone layer. It would be administered by an executive committee composed of seven developing and seven developed countries, and this committee would meet for the first time in September 1990 in Montreal, Canada. Day-to-day administration would be delegated to the UNEP, the UNDP and the World Bank. (In this context, the fund is now administered as part of the GEF - see Chapter 3 for more details). Contributions to the fund would be expected from parties to the Protocol whose per capita use of ozone-depleting substances exceeds 0.3kg per annum. The fund was expected to reach a total of US$160 million over the first three years. This figure would be increased to up to US$240 million if India and China acceded to the Protocol.[93] Very sensitive issues such as the criteria to be applied in prioritizing applications to the fund were to be left for the Executive Committee.

6.5 Assessment

Environmental groups such as Friends of the Earth and Greenpeace have been highly critical of the amendments put forward at the London review.

---

[91]*Financial Times*, 22 June 1990.

[92]*Financial Times*, 23 June 1990.

[93]Minister Environment Canada, 'Multilateral Fund to Protect the Ozone Layer', Release: PR-HQ-090-54, 2 November 1990.

They argue that published scientific data shows that an immediate 100% cut in ozone depleters worldwide is necessary to protect the ozone layer.[94] Even if this happened, it would take sixty years for chlorine concentrations in the atmosphere to come back down to their 1985 level. Moreover, that level is itself unacceptably high, as that is the level at which the Antarctic hole exists.[95] The 1990 Protocol, by allowing ten years for abolition of CFCs, permits unacceptable chlorine loading. In the period 1930-86, 15.6 million tonnes of CFC 11 and 12 were manufactured; the 1987 and 1990 Protocols allow an additional 8 million tonnes of production between 1987-2000.[96] Furthermore, the manufacture of other ozone depleters, such as HCFCs and methyl chloroform, is still permitted, and the global warming potential of some such substitutes has been ignored. There is no adequate provision for technology transfer to the developing countries. The Protocols are weakened by the fact that non-signatories include India.[97]

It is true that all these weaknesses exist. Yet one wonders what else could have been achieved, given that countries by their very nature usually pursue self-interested policies. Perhaps in this context the surprising thing is what has been achieved, and the fact that the Protocols exist at all. Moreover, within the normal frame of reference of international negotiations, the achievement is outstanding for the relative diplomatic haste by which it has been characterized. The loopholes in the Protocols are probably prerequisites for their very existence. Environmental concerns - however serious - are only one of a number of factors which policymakers, be they from the developed or the developing countries, take into consideration when formulating public policy.

Whatever its limitations, the Montreal Protocol and the process that resulted in it show what the international community of states can achieve in terms of policymaking even in the absence of scientific certainty. Having acted in accordance with the precautionary principle,

---

[94]They base this on the US Environmental Protection Agency data.
[95]Greenpeace, 1990, op.cit, p.3.
[96]ibid, p.3.
[97]Indeed India had still not signed by September 1991, when that country's Environment Minister, Kamal Nath, said that the conditions governing aid to developing nations to help them develop alternatives to chloroflourocarbons potentially infringed his country's sovereignty. See 'India Refuses to Sign Ozone Layer Protocol', *The Independent*, 21 September 1991.

that community then showed itself to be capable of reacting to the growth of scientific knowledge by developing and adjusting commitments at a relatively rapid pace. Scientific discovery fed into the policymaking process.

By its very nature, the movement towards international regulation of a global issue is difficult, and verification is almost impossible. The Montreal Protocol and the London amendment indicate small steps in the right direction. Critics will say 'too little, too late'; political pragmatists will say 'be grateful for small mercies'. While the ozone layer has not yet been saved, it is quite remarkable that the political community of states is making a relatively hasty effort to arrest its demise.

Forests play a vital role in sustaining life on earth from the micro level up to the macro.[1] Tropical forests are the most diverse ecosystems on the planet. The relationship between tropical forests and climate is not yet fully understood. At the national level, forests are an important economic resource. For example, export-logging provides foreign exchange, and other forest products, such as medicinal plants, have considerable potential in this regard. At the local level, forests are crucial for livelihoods. They impede hazards such as water flow and soil erosion. They provide fuel, fodder, food, thatch, building materials, medicines and living space. Forests may also have cultural or spiritual significance for local communities.

The fate of millions of people around the world depends on sustainable use of forests. There is a strong case for ranking this as the most important immediate environmental and developmental challenge the 1990s.

The fate of forests is affected by policies and activities on many different levels, and any efforts to manage them sustainably must take them all into account. Our major concern in this chapter is tropical deforestation. More so than any other environmental problem addressed in this section of the book, the problem of tropical deforestation depends for its management not simply on the formulation of international conventions and the behaviour of a select group of multinationals and governments - though these are important - but on the attitudes and actions of individuals at the grassroots level.

---

[1]For the most wide-ranging and up-to-date collection of discussions of the issue, see N.Myers (Guest Editor), 'Tropical Forests and Climate', special issue of the journal *Climate Change*, Vol.19, Nos.1/2, September 1991.

7.1 The rate and extent of forest destruction

The term 'tropical forest' is generally used here to refer to tropical rain forest and tropical monsoon (seasonal) forest. In the former, rainfall is well distributed throughout the year, whereas in the latter there is a regular dry season. Taken together, these are known as tropical moist forests.[2] All moist forests have a closed canopy, and so are also closed forests. However, other forests, such as dry thorn forests, may also have a closed canopy, and are sometimes included in the term closed forest, but are not tropical rain forest. 'Open forest' or 'woodland' generally refers to vegetation types with less than 40% tree canopy cover.[3] Of course, there are grey areas where one type merges into another, and this has resulted in some differences in the results of various researchers.

The House of Commons Environment Committee uses a simpler and more general definition:

> We consider tropical rainforests as those areas of forest between the Tropics of Cancer and Capricorn with an annual rainfall of over 1,500mm (60 inches) and a warm, essentially frost-free climate not showing strong seasonality.[4]

The term deforestation means different things to different people. Myers suggests that for people with interests in the hardwood timber trade, deforestation refers to the removal of forest stands of commercial value. On the other hand, for people concerned with non-timber values such as biomass stocks and species diversity, the status of entire forest ecosystems is important. Myers uses the term deforestation to refer to 'the complete destruction of forest cover through clearing for agriculture of whatever sort ... It means that not a tree remains, and the land is given over to non-forest purposes.[5] Forests can suffer from degradation as well

[2]M.Collins and Sayer (eds), *The Conservation Atlas of Tropical Forests, Vol.I. Asia and the Pacific*, Macmillan, London, 1991. A more technical definition of tropical forests is: 'evergreen or partly evergreen forests, in areas receiving not less than 100 mm. of precipitation in any month for two out of three years, with mean annual temperature of 24-plus degrees C., and essentially frost-free; in these forests some trees may be deciduous; the forests usually occur at altitudes below 1300 meters (though often in Amazonia up to 1,800 meters and generally in Southeast Asia up to only 750 meters); and in mature examples of these forests, there are several more or less distinctive strata', N.Myers, *Deforestation Rates in Tropical Forests and their Climatic Implications*, FOE, London, 1989, pp.4-5.
[3]ibid.
[4]House of Commons Environment Committee, Third Report, *Climatological and Environmental Effects of Rainforest Destruction*, HC 24, March 1991, p.xii.

as destruction, and this is often the case when they are logged. Myers' definitions are similar to those suggested by the FAO and UNEP, who regard deforestation as a change in land use from forest to non-forest purposes, and degradation as changes in the site, or the tree stands, or both, but not amounting to an overall land use change.[6]

An up-to-date official global forest inventory is badly needed. The last official assessment of the scale of tropical forests was undertaken by the FAO in 1980 and published in 1981. Another should be published in 1992 or 1993. The 1981 FAO report estimated that tropical forest covered 1,935 million hectares (approximately 7.5 million square miles). Of this, 1,200 million hectares (or 4.5 million square miles) were closed forest, with the rest being open tree forest. It also stated that government indicators suggested that tropical deforestation rates were unlikely to increase much in the foreseeable future. Recent evidence suggests that this assessment was wrong and that the rate of deforestation has accelerated considerably.

From the mid to late 1980s, several conflicting assessments were publicized. The most recent, and large-scale assessment was conducted by Dr Myers on behalf of Friends of the Earth. His results were published in December 1989.[7] (Another is in hand, in the form of a BP-sponsored IUCN project).[8] While caution has been expressed about them in certain quarters, they provide the most up-to-date, comprehensive and well-researched compilation available by far, and thus they are relied upon very heavily in this section.[9]

Myers' findings are largely based on remote-sensing data from satellite imagery, side-looking radar and aerial photography,[10] although such

---

[5]Myers, 1989, op.cit, p.5.

[6]See K.D.Singh, 'Letter to the Editor', *Forest Ecology and Management*, Vol.24, 1988, p.312.

[7]Myers, 1989, op.cit.

[8]Collins and Sayer, op.cit, for Vol.1 (Asia and the Pacific); Vol.2, (Africa), forthcoming 1992; Vol.3, (the Americas) - in preparation.

[9]Of course there remains disagreement regarding some of the findings eg. P.Fearnside, A.Tardin and L.Filho, 'Deforestation Rate in Brazilian Amazonia', (Instituto de Pesquisas Espaciais and Instituto National de Pesquisas da Amazonia), National Secretariat of Science and Technology, Brazil, August 1990. Also K.D.Singh, op.cit. This is all the more reason why an official global survey is urgently needed.

[10]On remote sensing, see N.Myers 'Tropical Deforestation and Remote Sensing', *Forest Ecology and Management*, Vol.23, 1988, pp.215-25; and T.Stone and G.Woodwell 'Shuttle Imaging Radar. An Analysis of Land Use in Amazonia', *International Journal*

methods have not been used everywhere where forest exists. The database on Zaire, for example, is poor. Remote-sensing is widely regarded as the best method of determining deforestation rates, and Myers estimates that a global assessment on this basis would cost only $3 million.

Dr Myers conducted a country-by-country review of the 34 countries which make up 97.3% of the biome. Collectively, Myers indicates that they are losing 138,600 square kilometres per annum. Additionally, the forty-odd other tropical forest countries not considered in his study are reckoned to be deforesting at the same rate, adding another 3,600 square kilometres of forest destroyed each year. The total for the biome is therefore 142,000 square kilometres of tropical deforestation per year. This amounts to 1.8% of remaining forests which total 7,783,500 square kilometres.[11] This stands in stark contrast to the deforestation total for 1979 which was estimated by the FAO and by Myers at 75,000 square kilometres.[12] Myers concludes that over the past decade, there has been a 90% increase in the annual deforestation rate. This may well be the case. Some, however, believe that the early FAO statistics may have been incorrect. The WRI, in a report prepared in collaboration with UNDP and UNEP, remarks that:

> It has been suggested that what seems like a soaring deforestation rate is simply caused by the fact that the new surveys are more accurate and thus reveal old deforestation that had not previously been detected. It is also possible that the new studies show accelerating deforestation.[13]

The majority of deforestation is concentrated in a small number of countries. Figure 7.1 shows which countries account for most of deforestation in the late 1980s. Figure 7.2 indicates which countries house the remaining tropical forest stocks. Myers estimates that Brazil, Indonesia and Zaire are undergoing a combined annual deforestation

of Remote Sensing, Vol.9, No.1, 1988, pp.95-105; G.M.Woodwell, et al, 'Deforestation in the Tropics', *Journal of Geophysical Research*, 1987, Part 92, pp.2157-2163; and R.Nelson et al, 'Large Scale Forest Resources Assessment Using Landsat and Air Photos', *Journal of World Forest Resources Management*, 1989, Part 4, pp.21-36.

[11]Myers, 1989, op.cit, p.43.

[12]See N.Myers, *Conversion of Tropical Moist Forests*, Report to the US National Academy of Sciences, National Research Council, Washington DC, 1980.

[13]WRI, in collaboration with UNEP and UNDP, *World Resources 1990-91*, New York, June 1990, p.105.

Figure 7.1 Tropical deforestation in the late 1980s: 10 leading countries

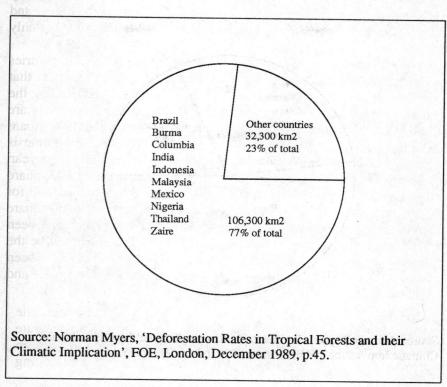

Brazil
Burma
Columbia
India
Indonesia
Malaysia
Mexico
Nigeria
Thailand
Zaire

Other countries
32,300 km2
23% of total

106,300 km2
77% of total

Source: Norman Myers, 'Deforestation Rates in Tropical Forests and their Climatic Implication', FOE, London, December 1989, p.45.

total of 66,000 square kilometres, or 46% of the total. These three countries between them have 52% of tropical forest stocks. It is noteworthy that since the publication of the Myers/FOE report, the arrival of Collor, as the President of Brazil, has resulted in government initiatives to stem deforestation in Amazonia. Whereas Myers proposed a deforestation trend figure for Brazil of 50,000 square kilometres, the current figure seems more like under 20,000 square kilometres. However, several other countries, such as Vietnam, the Philippines, Burma, and Bolivia, are revealing deforestation rates higher than those

Figure 7.2 Tropical forest stocks

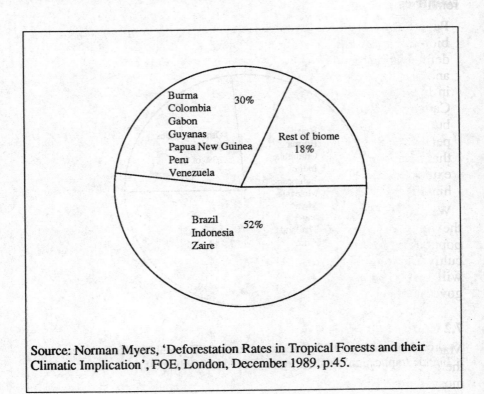

Source: Norman Myers, 'Deforestation Rates in Tropical Forests and their Climatic Implication', FOE, London, December 1989, p.45.

estimated for them by Myers. Thus the overall biome-wide annual deforestation figure of 142,000 square kilometres still stands.[14]

The spatial picture of deforestation is very uneven. Myers stresses that while the annual deforestation rate is currently running at approximately 1.8% of the global total of remaining tropical forest stocks, this does not necessarily mean that all forest stocks will be eradicated in another 38 years. Disappearance of all tropical forests could conceivably come sooner; or it could take longer. The future is uncertain. Current patterns and trends of deforestation differ between different geopolitical

---

[14]For these revised estimates, see N.Myers, 'Tropical Forests: Present Status and Future Outlook', *Climate Change*, No.19, 1991, pp.3-32.

regions.[15] Highlighting the configuration of current trends, Myers remarks that:

> Patterns and trends of deforestation are far from even throughout the biome. In Southeast Asia it is likely - supposing that present deforestation persists unvaried - that little forest will remain in another 20 years' time outside of central Kalimantan and Irian Jaya in Indonesia, and in Papua New Guinea. In West Africa except for Cameroon, hardly any forest will survive by the end of the century, but in the Zaire Basin there is prospect that a sizeable tract could persist for several more decades. In Latin America it is difficult to see that much forest can last beyond another two decades except for an extensive bloc in western Brazilian Amazonia and one in the Guyana hinterland.[16]

We cannot be sure that these trends will be simply extrapolated onto the future.[17] This will be dependent on a range of factors such as population growth, political responses to the problem of the shifted cultivator, logging policies plus a host of other factors. These of course will also differ over regions, and the political choices made by governments will be crucial.

7.2 Causes and explanations of deforestation

Many of the causes and explanations of deforestation are common across the globe. However, the emphasis may vary from region to region. The most significant factor worldwide is the permanent conversion of forest to agricultural land. Also important are rising demands for fuelwood and other forest products in areas where the immediate resources are insufficient, and also logging. Development projects in some cases result in deforestation. Greenhouse warming feedbacks and acid rain may contribute to deforestation. These immediate causes are symptoms of the underlying global economic and demographic structures.

Conversion to agricultural land

Friends of the Earth states categorically that: 'Agricultural expansion constitutes the single largest contributory factor in tropical

---

[15]Myers, 1989, op.cit, pp.43-7.
[16]ibid, p.1.
[17]ibid, pp.63-74

deforestation'.[18] There are few who would argue with this position. The reasons for agricultural expansion are many. Population growth is important, but of course it is ultimately the carrying capacity of the land, coupled with government policies, which determines how far population growth encroaches on forests. What matters is not simply population densities, but the ratio of agricultural land to forest. FOE reminds us that in some countries where population growth rates are average for the region, the rate of deforestation is high. Thailand is cited as an example. It is estimated to be loosing 8.4% of its forests annually, while its population growth rate is 1.6% per annum. This could be due to a relatively low ratio of forest to agricultural land to begin with. In other countries where population growth is high, this may be reflected in speedy deforestation, as is happening in Nigeria and Côte d'Ivoire.[19] Yet for others where population growth is high, deforestation may be fairly low for the region, with Bolivia being an example of this. In Bolivia, the ratio of agricultural land to forest is small, so rapid growth in the former will have only a moderate effect on forest cover. The picture, therefore, is highly differentiated, and while there may be general trends, there are no hard and fast rules. Each area where deforestation is occurring needs to be examined on its own merits, and then assessed in terms of the overall global impact. A high population growth rate in a state with a small population may result in far less damage to forests than a low growth rate in a country with a large population.

The role of slash-and-burn agriculture in deforestation is of great importance. Myers suggests that slash-and-burn cultivation accounts for over half of all deforestation, and that this proportion is likely to increase. He claims that slash-and-burn farming is the main cause of deforestation in Colombia, Ecuador, Peru, Bolivia, Nigeria, Madagascar, India, Thailand, Indonesia and the Philippines, and probably also in Mexico, Brazil, Burma and Thailand. Myers laments the fact that the shifted cultivator remains a forgotten figure, even though he represents an estimated 300-500 million people - or perhaps one-tenth of the world population.[20] With 80% of the world's projected population of 8 billion

---

[18]See FOE memorandum, in HC 24, op.cit, p.54.
[19]FOE, op.cit, p.55.
[20]Myers, 1989, op.cit, p.68.

people expected to be living in tropical forest countries in 2030, the outlook for the forests is extremely worrying.[21]

The traditional shifting cultivator practised a form of migratory farming which incorporated long fallow periods, thereby enabling the land to regenerate.[22] Where truly shifting cultivators remain, it has been shown that in general they do not form a threat to forests.[23] Indeed, Chin remarks that:

> Shifting cultivators know better than anybody else that their system of cultivation depends on the successful regeneration of the forest. In most shifting cultivation systems, there are specific practices to ensure that a forest fallow successfully develops.[24]

However, the 'shifted' cultivator[25] of today is not local to the forest area, neither is he familiar with such farming techniques. Consequently the land use practices which he pursues are inappropriate and result in the destruction of large tracts of forest.[26] The movement of such cultivators to the forest may be spontaneous, due especially to inequitable land tenure patterns in so many countries. It may also be planned and encouraged by the government as has been the case in the Indonesian Transmigration Programme.[27]

Typically in developing countries, land tenure patterns disadvantage the majority of the peasant population. Three-quarters of people in developing countries depend on agriculture for their livelihood, yet most of these do not own their own land. Landless people are incredibly vulnerable economically, socially and politically. Comparing the situation in different continents, Durning remarks that skewed land ownership is worst in Latin America, which suffers from the colonial

---

[21]ibid, p.66.

[22]On the impact of the traditional shifting cultivator, see S.C.Chin and T.H.Chua, 'The Impact of Man on a Southeast Asian Tropical Rainforest', *Malayan Nature Journal*, No.36, 1984, pp.253-269.

[23]See for example, S.C.Chin, 'Deforestation and Environmental Degradation in Sarawak', *Wallaceana*, Vol.49/9, 1987, p.7.

[24]ibid, p.7.

[25]see J.Westoby, *Introduction to World Forestry: People and Their Trees*, Basil Blackwell Ltd, Oxford, 1989.

[26]For a biological assessment of regeneration following slash-and-burn, see C.Uhl, 'Factors Controlling Succession Following Slash-and-Burn Agriculture in Amazonia', *Journal of Ecology*, No.75, 1987, pp.377-407.

[27]See A.J.Whitten, 'Indonesia's Transmigration Program and Its Role in the Loss of Tropical Rain Forests', *Conservation Biology*, Vol.1, No.3, October 1987, pp.239-246.

legacy of Spanish and Portuguese rulers establishing vast plantations. In that region, 1% of landlords own over 40% of arable land.[28] In the mid 1970s in Brazil, for example, 60% of rural households were landless, with another 10% being near-landless. The situation today is probably worse, as population has risen and there has been no real land reform. Indeed Myers estimates that 5% of Brazilian farmers occupy 70% of land today, and the situation is becoming more skewed as each year 1.7 million people are entering the job market, and only half of them perhaps finding sufficient employment.[29] The situation in South Asia is a little better, with 62% of Bangladeshi and 53% of Indian agricultural households being landless or near-landless in the late 1970s/mid-1980s period.[30] Land ownership patterns in Africa are moderated by collective tribal holding arrangements and the fact that land is less scarce anyway.

Many official government programmes have either directly or indirectly resulted in migration by peasants to the forest. The Indonesian Transmigration Programme is probably the most well-known.[31] This moved over one million people in the period 1983-88 from the fertile but densely populated islands of Java and Bali to the forested outer islands of Kalimantan, Sulawesi and Irian Jaya, was partly funded by the World Bank and the Asian Development Bank. The World Bank has also provided funding for the Brazilian Polonoroeste programme, which developed the infrastructure of Brazil's north-western region. Landless peasants flooded into the area, but the poor quality of the soils meant that they had to move further and further into the forest to find new productive land.[32] This trend was exacerbated by the absence of training and extension advice, together with random selection of colonized areas. Malingreau and Tucker have shown how in the south-eastern Brazilian Amazon, the building of all-weather roads directly resulted in the influx of peasants.[33]

---

[28]A.Durning, 'Ending Poverty', in L.Brown et al, *State of the World*, 1990, Unwin/Hyman, London, 1990, p.141.

[29]Myers, 1989, op.cit, p.66.

[30]Durning, op.cit, p.142.

[31]A.J.Whitten, Indonisia's Transmigration Program and Its Role in the Loss of Tropical Rain Forests', *Conservation Biology*, Vol.1, No.3, October 1987, pp.239-246

[32]See P.Fearnside, 'Deforestation and International Economic Development Projects in Brazilian Amazonia', *Conservation Biology*, Vol.1, No.3, October 1987; and J-P.Malingreau and C.Tucker, 'Large-scale Deforestation in the Southeastern Amazon basin of Brazil', *Ambio*, Vol.17, No.1.

[33]Malingreau and Tucker, op.cit, pp.49-55.

Large-scale agriculture also contributes to forest loss, both by utilizing forest land for ranching[34] and also by utilizing the best land outside the forest for cash crop production, thereby giving a push to the migration of peasants into the forest. With the increasing burden of debt repayment, the necessity of utilizing fertile land for export crop production to earn foreign exchange is clear. In many countries, the best land is in the hands of wealthy elites who want to increase their wealth by the production of cash crops for export.

In Central America, forest loss can be related directly to the development of cattle ranching for beef exports to meet the demand of the North American market.[35] In the Brazilian Amazon, the main cause of deforestation has been clearing for pasture by Brazilian entrepreneurs who develop huge ranches simply to take advantage of fiscal incentives such as zero tax rates for agricultural income and subsidies.[36] Indeed, Repetto has commented that: 'Because of the subsidies ... uneconomic projects have been extremely lucrative for the private entrepreneur able to use all available incentives'.[37]

FOE argue that apart from beef production, several other types of agricultural production for export markets threaten forests. Drawing on work done by Myers, they cite the example of cassava production in Thailand for livestock feed for the EC.[38] Small farmers in the eastern and north-eastern parts of Thailand grow the crop at the expense of the natural forest which is cleared. FOE state that: 'Similarly, natural forest

---

[34]Although the area deforested through commercial ranching has actually declined a little in the 1980s. The big increase is in the expansion of the shifted cultivator phenomenon. Myers, personal communication, 7 October 1991.

[35]J.Nations and D.Komer 'Rainforests and the Hamburger Society', *Environment*, Vol.25, No.3, 1983; B.Dewalt 'The Cattle are Eating the Forest', *Bulletin of the Atomic Scientists*, Vol.39, No.1, January 1983; H.J.Leonard, *Natural Resources and Economic Development in Central America: A Regional Environmental Profile*, IIED/Transaction Books, New Brunswick and Oxford, 1987, N.Myers and R.Tucker 'Deforestation in Central Amreica: Spanish Legacy and North American Consumers', *Environmental Review*, 1987, Part 11, p.55-71; N.Myers, 'The Hamburger Connection', *Ambio*, Vol.10, 1981, pp.3-8.

[36]S.Hecht and A.Cockburn, *The Fate of the Forest*, p.98. See also A.Hurrell, 'Commentary: the Politics of Amazonian Deforestation', *Journal of Latin American Studies*, Vol.23.

[37]R.Repetto, *The Forest for the Trees: Government Policies and the Misuse of Forest Resources*, World Resources, Washington DC, 1988, p.79.

[38]FOE, HC 24, op.cit, p.56; and N.Myers, 'Economics and Ecology in the International Arena: the Phenomenon of "Linked Linkages"', *Ambio*, Vol.15, No.5, 1986.

in Amazonia has been, and continues to be, cleared for the establishment of soya bean cultivation, the produce of which also supports European agricultural practices'.[39]

In India, the Green Revolution, backed by World Bank funding and expertise, resulted not only in massive increases in food production but also in the creation of millions of additional landless labourers in the Punjab alone. Mechanization of agriculture left them without employment, and therefore without the means to purchase the extra food that was grown.

Fuelwood and other forest products

The energy crisis in the developing world is a major spur to accelerating deforestation, and in the context of population growth, this factor will become even more significant. A major cause of deforestation is the need for fuelwood for energy, either in its raw state or after conversion to charcoal. Postel and Heise remark that: 'More than two thirds of all Third World people rely on wood for cooking and heating'.[40] Yet the data on this matter is inadequate.

Africa depends most heavily on fuelwood. For example, even in oil rich Nigeria, in the early 1980s 82% of energy demand was met from wood. In Tanzania, the figure was 92%; in Kenya, 71%, in Malawi 93%. In Asia the reliance is lower, except for Nepal where wood supplies 94% of the energy demands. In Latin America, too, reliance on wood is not so marked.

Demand for fuelwood comes not only from rural dwellers, but also from towns. Across the developing world this has resulted in belts of deforestation around the urban areas. Postel and Heise suggest that working class urban families spend 20-40% of their meagre incomes on the purchase of wood or charcoal.[41] Unlike the rural dwellers, who have the fallback position of using animal dung or crop residue for energy, town dwellers have no alternative but to spend increasing proportions of their income on wood.

The FAO has estimated that even in 1980, around 1.2 billion people were meeting their fuelwood needs by cutting wood faster than it was

---

[39]FOE, HC 24, op.cit, p.56.
[40]S.Postel and L.Heise, 'Reforesting the Earth', in *State of the World 1988*, Worldwatch Institute/Norton & Co. Ltd, New York and London, 1988, p.87.
[41]S.Postel and L.Heise, *Reforesting the Earth*, Worldwatch Paper 83, Worldwatch Institute, Washington DC, April 1988, p.18.

being replaced.[42] It predicted that by the year 2000, the number of people with insufficient wood or over-cutting wood would double to 2.4 billion - over half of the projected population of the developing countries.

Clearly there is a need to increase fuelwood supplies and where possible reduce demand. The latter could be done by technological applications such as the use of more efficient stoves. The former could be done not only by forestry practices such as afforestation and better coppicing techniques, but also at a much broader level, by structural policy changes for example in land reform or population policies.[43] The challenge ahead is enormous.

Any discussion of the fuelwood problem would be incomplete without a mention of the specific problem facing Africa. With its very high population growth rate, the land is unable to sustain the demand for fuelwood. The arid woodlands of Africa, with their low growth rate, are being decimated. Repetto remarks that:

> In Africa's Sahelian/Sudanian zone ... consumption now exceeds natural regeneration by 70% in Sudan, 75% in northern Nigeria, 150% in Ethiopia, and 200% in Niger'.[44]

Fuelwood supply is thus a major inhibiter to the regeneration of forests.

Concerning other forest products, the search for fodder, both by free-ranging cattle and by peasants to supply tethered animals, while it is difficult to quantify, is another notable cause of forest destruction.

Commercial logging

Commercial logging undoubtedly results in deforestation and degradation; yet in terms of overall destruction, it is not the primary cause of forest loss. According to a report sponsored by the World Bank, the UNDP and the WRI, commercial logging was estimated in 1985 to affect five million hectares of tropical forest annually.[45] During the 1980s, the area affected by commercial logging hardly expanded, even though the overall deforestation rate expanded by 89%.[46] However, it remains

---

[42]See FAO, *Fuelwood Supplies and the Developing Countries*, Forestry Paper 42, FAO, Rome, 1983.
[43]Postel and Heise, April 1988, op.cit, p.18
[44]Repetto, op.cit, p.5.
[45]WRI, *Tropical Forest: A Call to Action*, Report of an international task force convened by the WRI, the World Bank and the UNDP, Washington DC, 1985.
[46]Myers, personal communication, 7 October 1991.

important because of the damage it is responsible for, because much of it takes place to satisfy a voracious demand for tropical hardwood by a relatively small group of countries, and because logging roads open up access for migrants to follow, thereby making access into the forest easier. The question of commercial logging raises the temperature of debate in a highly emotive manner.

FOE has stated the opposing views on commercial logging succinctly:

... logging as it is currently conducted is almost wholly a 'mining' operation, whereby the timbers preferred for international markets are extracted unsustainably causing, in most cases, direct serious and long-term environmental damage, including species extinctions and disruption of soil, hydrological and climatological functions. The benefits of the industry largely accrue to a relatively small elite of wealthy, often urban business people, and foreign interests, whilst rural peoples suffer many of the disadvantages. The disruption of local forest economies caused by the timber industry perpetuates an environmentally destructive development model, one manifestation of which is the expansion into logged areas of shifting agriculture.

The countervailing view posits that the direct environmental impact of logging is minimal and reversible; the trade affords employment opportunities and economic development, contributing to national economic development (including, implicitly, the ability of developing nations to embark on forest conservation programmes), and the stabilisation of rural populations. Commercial exploitation of timber also confers a tangible value on the forest resource, thus providing an incentive for conservation, without which conversion to non-forest land-uses would occur. It is held that, by encouraging rapid secondary vegetative growth, logging makes a net positive contribution in ameliorating global warming.[47]

There are elements of truth in both positions. What can be said with certainty is that almost without exception, the commercial logging which has been carried out to date has been undertaken in an environmentally harmful, economically unsustainable, and socially destructive fashion. The most blatant case is in South East Asia, where many hardwood stands have been exploited in a markedly unsustainable fashion.[48]

---

[47]FOE, in HC 24, op.cit, p.56.

[48]M.Scot, 'The disappearing forests', *Far Eastern Economic Review*, 12 January 1989, pp.34-38. For a detailed analysis, i n particular of Japan's tropical timber trade and its

Japan has been the world's major tropical timber importer for two decades. Ninety-six per cent of these imports in 1987 came from three places; the Malaysian states of Sarawak and Sabah, and Papua New Guinea. In the 1960s and 1970s the Philippines and Indonesia were major suppliers of tropical timber to Japan. In the Philippines the resource has been so degraded that commercial forestry for the export market has virtually disappeared. Palawan, the country's largest remaining area of tropical forest, is being plundered.[49] In Thailand the government has finally acted, but too late following the destruction of villages in flash floods in 1988.[50] The same Thai loggers who have done a good job of decimating their own countries' forests, when met with a ban on logging activities in 1988, moved their operations to the Thai Burmese border. Burma possesses 70% of the world's supply of teak and it is exploiting this resource in an effort to keep its ailing economy afloat.[51] Thai loggers have been followed by companies from Hong Kong, Taiwan and Singapore who undertake joint ventures with Burma. China is also thought to be involved. In Vietnam the challenge has different roots; it has been estimated that 2.2 million hectares of forest were affected by bombing, land clearing, napalming and defoliation during the Vietnam war. More recently population growth is taking its toll; as forest cover shrinks the tribal peoples slash-and-burn agricultural techniques become less sustainable. Inevitably logging for export also plays a role.[52]

The greenhouse effect feedbacks and acid rain

Myers notes that certain atmospheric and climatic sources of deforestation are possible.[53] Early in the next century, for example, acid rain, which is usually thought to be a phenomenon of temperate zone forests in Europe and North America, will probably be an increasing threat to tropical forests. Forests in southern China have already been

environmental impact see F.Nectoux and Y.Kuroda, *Timber from the South Seas*, WWF, 1989.
[49]J.Clad and N.Vitug 'The politics of plunder; Palawan's forests appear doomed in power struggle', *Far Eastern Economic Review*, 24 November 1988, pp.48-52.
[50]P.Sricharatchanya 'Too little too late: Thai Government finally decides to preserve forests' *Far Eastern Economic Review*, 12 January 1989, pp.40-41.
[51]R.Matthews 'Cash starved regime courts an ecological disaster', *Financial Times*, 21 June 1990.
[52]E.Kemf *Month of pure light; the regreening of Vietnam*, The Women's Press, London, 1990.
[53]Myers, FOE 1989, op.cit, p.69.

affected.[54] Regarding climatic feedbacks Myers cites research in Brazilian Amazonia by Salati and Vose indicating that deforestation itself could generate climatic feedback effects that in turn could result in forest degradation on a broad scale. Much more research is needed on the effects of such a drying out process,[55] and the role of the forest in water recycling and retention generally. Possible greenhouse effect feedbacks could also affect tropical forests. Again much more work is needed on this, for the implications are potentially enormous. Forests and woodland cover about a third of the land surface of the world, and the socio-economic implications of possible effects of climate change on forest management, policy and land-use are enormous.[56]

Minerals exploration and production

The exploration for and production of minerals (including hydrocarbons) is becoming an important problem in some places. It is carried out both by domestic migrants (as in the case of gold diggers in Amazonia), government enterprises and by multinational companies. In the case of the latter, there has been much publicity recently about the adverse environmental effects of some of their exploration and production methods. The case of British Gas in Ecuador is an example. The company argues that well-managed exploration and production can have a minimal impact on local communities and ecosystems, and moreover, that it can offer opportunities for economic development in rainforest areas without the deforestation impacts associated with agricultural development. The debate on this has only just begun.

7.3 Results of deforestation

The results of tropical deforestation range from destruction of habitat for local tribes, flora and fauna, to potentially huge losses for the human race (for example in terms of lost medicinal potential of extinct species of plant) and climatic effects. Thus the spectrum of those affected ranges from individuals, through tribes, countries, regions to humankind.

---

[54]J.Galloway, 'Atmospheric acidification...projections for the future', *Ambio*, 1989, part 18, p.161-166.
[55]Myers, FOE 1989, op.cit, p.71.
[56]P.Duinker 'Climate Change and Forest Management, Policy and Land Use', *Land Use Policy*, April 1990, pp.124-137.

Loss of habitat for indigenous forest dwellers

Coupled with the associated import of disease, loss of habitat has resulted in the decimation of forest tribes in many parts of the world. The most notorious examples come from the Brazilian Amazon, where the plight of the Yanomami Indians has achieved international coverage, and Sarawak, where the fate of the Penan Indians has received international attention due largely to the efforts of Bruno Manser.[57] In both cases indigenous support groups campaigning for their protection find themselves up against entrenched vested interests. Externally, NGOs and prominent individuals from abroad campaign for a recognition of the rights of these groups.

Loss of species diversity

We cannot even begin to estimate the value of losses inherent in species reduction itself and also in lost potential for pharmaceutical remedies and other chemical processes, as well as agriculture. It has been suggested that the commercial value alone of drugs, medicines and pharmaceuticals manufactured from startpoint materials of tropical-forest plants is in the order of $22 billion a year in 1990.[58] For Wilson, the loss of biodiversity is in a sense the most important consequence of environmental damage because the process is *wholly irreversible*.[59] He argues that while countries are aware of their material and cultural wealth, they fail to recognize the value of their biological wealth and in doing so make a serious strategic error, for this is a source of untapped material wealth. He suggests that less than one-tenth of one per cent of naturally occurring species are exploited by mankind. Forests contain a treasure trove of untapped resources, yet we are destroying these very resources even before we have assessed their full potential. He gives the example of the rose periwinkle which provides two alkaloids extremely important in the treatment of cancer. The plant originated in Madagascar, where five other species are found, not one of which has been properly assessed for its potential scientific and commercial properties and one of which is already bordering on extinction. Over the past few decades, it is reasonable to assume that we

[57]S.Mills, 'Alone in the Longhouse', *BBC Wildlife*, September 1990, pp.617-620.
[58]See N.Myers, *The Primary Source: Tropical Forests and Our Future*, W.W.Norton, New York and London, 1984.
[59]E.O.Wilson, 'Threats to Biodiversity', *Scientific American*, September 1989, pp.60-66.

have lost at least 1,000, and possibly as many as 2,500, plants endemic to Madagascar due to deforestation. Forest loss extends far beyond timber.

Loss of export resources

It should be of concern to governments that badly managed deforestation results in a future loss of export revenue. Unless forests are harvested sustainably then a country may witness the transference of activity to neighbouring countries. This is already evident in South East Asia where unsustainable deforestation has resulted in immediate gain at the expense of medium and long-term loss. Thus depletion of the forest resource in Thailand simply resulted in the transference of the activity to Burma and Laos. Moreover the value of forest resources extends far beyond timber, and the loss of biodiversity represents future commercial losses for the country.

Watershed problems and downstream developments

Like so many other aspects of the deforestation issue, the question of how far the process contributes to watershed problems and downstream developments remains a highly contentious one and there is room for much more research. Moreover, again as with so many other issues, what holds true for one region of the world at a particular time may not be true across the globe. Caution therefore is required. Local connections between land use, soil and water are relatively easy to establish compared with regional connections. This is nowhere more the case than in South Asia, where the connection between deforestation high in the Himalaya of Nepal and India and flooding in the plains of Bangladesh remains a matter of intense debate. The high international profile of this particular example, and the possible fate of half a billion people (ie. one-tenth of the inhabitants of our planet) who live on the flood plains, indicate that it merits closer examination.

Conventional thinking on this matter suggests that the actions of peasant farmers high in the Himalaya are responsible for flooding in the Bangladesh delta. Massive population increases in the Himalaya have resulted in pressure being placed on forest cover to meet the increased need for subsistence farmland and fuel and fodder.[60] Early estimates

---

[60]For a thorough presentation of the debate, and a critique of convention views, see J.D.Ives and B.Messerli, *The Himalayan Dilemma: Reconciling Development and Conservation*, Routledge, London and New York, 1989.

suggested that half the forest reserves of Nepal were decimated in the period 1950-80. In 1979, the World Bank published a report in which it claimed that by the year 2000 no accessible forest would remain in Nepal.[61] Deforestation would be accompanied by further soil erosion, and the vicious circle set up would require further deforestation to build terraces for cropland. The downstream effects of this process would be horrendous. Massive build-ups of silt would be carried by the monsoon rains flowing with increased ferocity onto the flood plains below. Deposition of this silt would further exacerbate flooding. The terrible floods in Bangladesh in the late 1980s have been offered as proof of the validity of this theory by its proponents.

The World Bank prediction does not stand up to scrutiny, and doubt has been cast on downstream repercussions as well. Don Gilmour, of the highly respected Australia-Nepal Forestry Project, remarks that: '... the projected vision of no forests in the hills ... cannot seriously be contemplated'.[62] He claims that while some areas have undergone widespread deforestation in recent decades, other parts have increased their tree cover by the independent actions of small farmers working outside of government activities. Carter and Gilmour claim that such increases have yet to be acknowledged by the government and aid agencies involved in forestry.[63] The suggestion is that there are entrenched interests in government and funding bodies in perpetuating the apocalyptic vision which results in massive inflows of aid and a proliferation of jobs for highly-paid international bureaucrats.

A similar argument is presented by Ives, once a supporter of the conventional orthodoxy. He believes that the conventional thinking on population, deforestation, soil erosion and downstream implications was the product of outsiders who did not spend enough time in the region or really monitor local developments to provide hard evidence to back up their theory. He suggests that deforestation was well advanced in the central Himalaya by 1750, and by early this century all potential arable

---

[61] World Bank, *Nepal: Development Performance and Prospects*, Washington DC, 1979.

[62] D.A.Gilmour, 'Not Seeing the Trees for the Forest: A Re-Appraisal of the Deforestation Crisis in Two Hill Districts of Nepal', *Mountain Research and Development*, Vol.8, No.4, 1988, p.343.

[63] A.S.Carter and D.A.Gilmour, 'Increase in Tree Cover on Private Farm Land in Central Nepal', *Mountain Research and Development*, 1989, Vol.9, No.4, p.381.

land in the Middle Mountains of Nepal was deforested.[64] He suggests also that peasant farmers, often portrayed as ignorant, understand their land and its needs, and that in traditional farming systems tree cutting and the conversion to terraced agriculture may conserve the soil more effectively than leaving the forest in its original state. Low vegetation protects soil from erosion more than tall forest cover (though the latter behaves as a more effective sponge controlling the rate of water release). The arrival of farmers may actually *reduce* soil loss on a hillside. This is especially the case where the slopes are prone to landslips.

The implications for downstream developments are clear. There is no guarantee that reforestation in the Himalaya will reduce the risk of flooding on the plains of Bangladesh and India. Ives states that:

> No clear link has been established between changes in land use in the mountains and changes in the flows and transfer of sediment in the Ganges and Brahmaputra on the plains. It seems highly probable that the plains often flood simply because of the torrential rainstorms there, rather than because of natural or artificial events in the hills. Even if large scale reforestation in the mountains reduces the flow of monsoon water locally, the effects would be hard to detect on the plains.[65]

He cites research undertaken by the International Centre for Integrated Mountain Development in Kathmandu, which concludes that if all cultivable and grazing land in the Nepalese Middle Mountains were to be reforested, the flow of water might be reduced locally by 35%, but the effect on the flow of the Ganges would be about 3% only. The conclusion in this particular case, therefore, is that the effects of reforestation are local rather than regional. Moreover, the Himalaya, geologically a very young and active region of the world, are undergoing continual earth movements, and it may be the case that soil erosion results more from this activity than from deforestation.

Monsoon floods are not new in Bangladesh; the number of people affected by them is new. Pearce reports that when the British colonists arrived in 1757, they reported seeing thousands of kilometres of embankments, part of a routine flood control system built in the Mogul

---

[64] J.Ives, 'Floods in Bangladesh: Who is to Blame?', *New Scientist*, 13 April, 1991, pp.34-7.
[65] ibid, p.37.

period of two centuries before.[66] The British abolished the local taxes operated by feudal landlords to maintain the system, which fell into disrepair. Routine flooding has always been a mixed blessing. As well as destroying lives and homes, it renews the soil with moisture, silt and algae. Record crop yields followed the floods of 1987 and 1988. Without silt deposition, there would be no Bangladesh; after all, the country is built on the delta formed by the rivers Ganges, Meghna, and Brahmaputra.

What is clear from the Himalayan example above is that the relationship between deforestation, soil erosion, land use and flooding is far from clear, and undoubtedly generalizations should be avoided. Even in the case of Nepal, to claim that the country is undergoing rapid deforestation does not hold true throughout the land. Moreover, certain areas where it is ongoing relentlessly at the moment, such as in the low-lying Terai, fail to capture the attention of donors, media or government,[67] while areas where it is not occurring stand publicly accused by officialdom. Precise effects on the locality are much easier to establish than regional implications, and throughout much of the world the data is simply not available to arrive at definitive conclusions. More research is needed.

Effects on local and regional weather

Climatologists are not yet able to answer definitively the question of how far tropical deforestation affects climate, but it seems likely that some linkages exist. Research in the 1980s in areas such as the Côte d'Ivoire, India, the Panama Canal area and Malaysia suggested that forests play an important part in local climatic workings, notably on rainfall.[68]

Tropical deforestation may also affect regional and even global climate patterns. Work on the Amazonian Basin suggests that much of the moisture there is generated by the forest itself: it is transpired by plants into the atmosphere, and within a few days is precipitated back onto the forest as rainfall. Large-scale deforestation of Amazonia could result in

---

[66]F.Pearce, 'The Rivers that Won't Be Tamed', *New Scientist*, 13 April 1991, p.39.

[67]This was drawn to the author's attention in an interview with Don Gilmour of the Australia-Nepal Forestry Project in January 1991.

[68]N.Myers, 'Tropical Deforestation and Climatic Change', Paper for Conference on Climate and the Geo-Sciences, Session on Climate, Environment and International Security, Louvain-la-Neuve, Belgium, May, 1988, p.1, available from the author.

a self-reinforcing process of desiccation.[69] Without further research we cannot know whether such a phenomenon is occurring, or is likely to occur, in other large tracts of tropical forests such as that existing in Zaire. Looking beyond a regional context, there is some evidence to suggest that the severe tropical storms which have hit the Caribbean and the Gulf of Mexico can be traced to large quantities of moist air originating from the Central African tropical forests.

In the face of so much uncertainty, what we know for certain are the implications of, for example, diminished rainfall on the carrying capacity of the humid tropics generally - and by implication, for the two billion inhabitants thereof. Loss of cultivable land and forest products such as food, fuelwood and building materials will be devastating. Myers stresses the need to diminish uncertainty by extensive research, and also the importance of cautious decisionmaking now geared towards risk-reduction.

Contribution to greenhouse warming

The release of carbon dioxide into the atmosphere through deforestation has been estimated to be substantial, and hence its potential contribution to the greenhouse effect may be significant. However, this remains a matter of debate. Some theorists believe that as a one-off release, the significance will be diminished. Mature forests have an almost zero net carbon fixation rate. They are effectively closed systems recycling within themselves, rather than being the 'lungs of the earth'. In the short term what is planted may be more productive, and in any case scrub regeneration will fix carbon dioxide at a greater rate than mature forest (see Chapter 5).

7.4 Remedial action underway

International institutional framework

The Tropical Forestry Action Plan. On its establishment in 1985, the Tropical Forestry Action Plan (or TFAP) was hailed by governmental aid and lending agencies as the answer to the crisis of tropical forests which

---

[69]See J.Lean and D.A.Warrilow, 'Simulation of the Regional Climatic Impact of Amazon Deforestation', *Nature*, Vol.342, 23 November 1989, p.411-13. Also, R.E.Dickinson, 'Predicting Climate Effects', *Nature*, Vol.342, 23 November 1989, pp.343-44.

were fast diminishing. It was presented as a global forest conservation and development programme which would increase the flow of forest aid to US$8 billion over five years, halt the destruction of tropical forests and facilitate sustainable use of forests. However, from the outset there was an inherent tension, for while some lenders saw it as a mechanism to harmonize forestry aid, NGOs plus some intergovernmental lending agencies saw it as a vehicle for addressing the fundamental causes of deforestation. This tension resulted in the adoption of the Plan being held up until 1987, and it has affected its orientation ever since.[70] Recently the TFAP has come under strong attack not only from NGOs but also from certain governments and from an independent review team. The worst criticisms label it a 'loggers charter', and see it as a plan for forestry rather than for forests.[71]

Knowledge of the institutional evolution of the TFAP is imperative for understanding the current situation. Inter- and intra-agency bargaining has been central to its development, with negative results. We must go back to the mid-1980s when the need to do something about tropical deforestation was articulated by a group of experts who were concerned that the previous ten years of forestry aid had done little to halt deforestation. These included independent consultants, such as Norman Myers, and individuals affiliated to aid and lending agencies such as Chuck Lankester of the UNDP and John Spears of the World Bank. At that time the FAO responded that there was no significant problem. The organization was on the defensive, and declined the invitation to participate in the planning for the TFAP. It had been in charge of tropical forestry for several decades, and to have admitted the existence of a problem would have been to cast doubt on its own competence. The World Bank, the UNDP and the World Resources Institute (WRI), a Washington-based NGO, decided to go ahead anyway. The FAO then decided to set up its own Tropical Forestry Task Force, which came up with parallel conclusions and recommendations.

The TFAP came to be known formally as the product of joint efforts by the World Bank (its principal funder), the UNDP, the FAO and the WRI, although as indicated above, this is not an entirely accurate picture. The FAO was given the lead role, and was charged with the implementation of a plan. Since then it has coordinated the TFAP from its forestry

---

[70]See F.Pearce, 'High Stakes in the Rainforest', *The Guardian*, 19 October 1990.
[71]ibid.

department. This has had a critical effect on the shape of the activity. For whereas representatives of some of the other funding agencies, including the World Bank, had argued that at least half of the budget should be devoted to non-forestry activities aimed at supporting subsistence agriculture outside of forested areas, the FAO decided to stick to funding strictly forestry activities and dropped the agricultural dimension. The strategic emphasis of the plan, therefore, did nothing to tackle the root cause of tropical deforestation - the problem of the shifted cultivator. Thus an absurd situation has developed, whereby the basic cause of deforestation has received virtually no funding.

To understand the attitude of the Forestry Department within the FAO, we need to look at the institutional context in which that Department operates. Traditionally, forestry has taken a back seat in the FAO, enjoying less than 5% of the agency's budget at least since the mid-1970s. Moreover, this proportion has since declined steadily. Hence the Forestry Department is in a position of extreme institutional weakness relative to the FAO's Agriculture Department, some members of which have been known to favour removal of forests for extra croplands. This throws some light on the reluctance of the Forestry Department to channel funding into agriculture. Given this, the mistake was ever to have assigned the implementation of the Plan to the FAO in the first place; that action sealed its fate.

In the hands of the FAO's Forestry Department, the aim of the TFAP has been to provide a broad strategy within which national plans can be developed. Governments request help from the FAO, after which national forestry plans are drawn up.[72] To date, well over 80 countries, representing over 85% of all tropical forests, have expressed an interest in the TFAP and are at some stage of the seven-phase procedure for drawing up National Forestry Action Plans (NFAPs). At least forty major national and international aid agencies have channelled funding through the TFAP, and forestry aid has grown to US$1 billion per annum - twice the figure for 1985.[73] Some independent analysts have questioned how the money is spent. Pearce, for example, suggests that one-third of this money has been used on industrial forestry (ie. felling trees for wood

---

[72]For these and further background details, see D.Lewis 'The Billion Dollar Question Marks' *The Guardian*, 8 June 1990.
[73]ibid

pulp, plywood etc), one-third on agro-forestry, 9% on conservation and none on addressing the real reasons for deforestation.[74]

The TFAP highlighted five priority areas: forestry in land use; forest-based industrial development; fuelwood and energy; conservation of tropical forest ecosystems; and institutions.[75] The list in theory provides a fairly comprehensive approach to forest management, although it fails to address the fundamental reasons for deforestation which lie outside of the forest sector. Yet analysts have been hampered in their assessments by the secretive manner in which the FAO deals with NFAPs.[76] However, a group of NGOs have managed to obtain completed plans for nine countries: Cameroon, Colombia, Ghana, Guyana, Nepal, Papua New Guinea, Peru, the Philippines and Tanzania. Examination of these plans against developments in those countries has facilitated evaluation of the importance assigned to the priority areas, to provide critiques of the TFAP, and of its implementation via NFAPs. With the limited exceptions of Tanzania and Papua New Guinea, the prognosis for NFAPs was not good.[77]

In 1990, the criticism of the TFAP which had been building up over a few years came to a head. It ranged from the fairly negative report of the WRI, an author of the TFAP in 1985, to the more critical assessment of environmental NGOs such as Friends of the Earth,[78] and World-Wide Fund for Nature,[79] to the damning critique offered by the World Rainforest Movement (WRM).[80] There was a common belief that the original Plan contained many flaws, and also that its implementation was deficient. The WRI review stated that the TFAP was:

---

[74]Pearce, op.cit.

[75]FAO Forestry Department, 'Tropical Forestry Action Plan', *Unasylva*, 152, Vol.38, 1986/2, pp.1-36.

[76]See for example L.Lomen and M.Colchester 'Paved with Good Intentions: the TPAP's Road to Oblivion', *The Ecologist*, Vol.20, No.3, May/June 1990, p.92.

[77]For full assessments of these nine NFAPs, see Colchester and Lohmann's book, op.cit, and for summary reports, see their article, 1990, op.cit.

[78]FOE, 'Special Briefing - The Tropical Forestry Action Plan', April 1990.

[79]WWF, 'Reforming the Tropical Action Plan - A WWF Position', September 1990.

[80]M.Colchester and L.Lohmann, *The Tropical Forestry Action Plan: What Progress?*, The Ecologist/The World Rainforest Movement, Sturminster Newton, UK, and Penang, Malaysia, 1990.

... in need of a recommitment to its basic principles and goals, a new institutional framework, more systemic monitoring, and a more open and accountable management structure'.[81]

That an original architect of the Plan should take this stand is particularly significant. In conception and implementation the Plan had not lived up to expectations.

Outlining criticisms frequently voiced by NGOs, Colchester and Lohmann remarked that:

... [the Plan] had been developed in almost complete isolation from local peoples, with minimal consultation with NGOs and with the provision of very limited information to the general public. The TFAP was criticized as a top-down prescription that paid little attention to the needs and rights of forest dwellers. The Plan failed to address the root causes of deforestation, instead blaming the poor as the main cause of destruction. The plan was too much focused on the forestry sector alone and placed undue emphasis on the financing of classical forestry projects to develop commercial forestry and industrial forest-based enterprises. Too little attention and money was directed at conservation schemes and protected area management.[82]

The criticisms of the WRI, while not the most damaging, are extremely important simply because it helped draw up the TFAP in 1985. That an original architect should take such a stand means that the other authors have to take more notice than perhaps they otherwise would of other NGO critiques. The WRI report states that the original TFAP failed to address the major causes of deforestation which lay outside the forest sector:

... deforestation is largely driven by forces outside the forestry sector and by policy decisions, development planning priorities, and programs beyond foresters' control.[83]

The WRM report explicitly identifies the causes of the problem as poverty and landlessness, and indeed the FAO, in a reply to an Open Letter from the WRM, conceded that 'It is true that the TFAP is mainly focused on forestry but the main causes of deforestation are poverty and

---

[81] R.Winterbottom for WRI, *Taking Stock: The Tropical Forestry Action Plan After Five Years*, WRI, Washington DC, June 1990.

[82] Colchester and Lohmann, *The Tropical Forestry Action Plan*, op.cit, p.5.

[83] WRI, op.cit, p.24.

landlessness'.[84] Acknowledging the significance of the wider context, the WRI suggested that the TFAP be viewed in the:

... larger context of ... population stabilization, debt relief, agrarian reform, trade and macroeconomic policy reforms, biological diversity, conservation, and global warming strategies.[85]

The WRI report makes another central criticism repeated more forcefully by the other NGO assessments: that the TFAP failed to stress the rights and needs of forest peoples. It stated that:

to date the planning process has essentially been an extension of development assistance planning and negotiation, in which the only legitimate players are aid agencies and national governments.[86]

Moreover, it sees the TFAP as failing to anticipate the tension between local and national perceptions and goals, instead equating the local with the government position. Yet governments often fail to protect the rights of indigenous local forest dwellers. The IUCN, UNEP and the WWF, in their recent guidelines on forest management, have identified the involvement of local people as essential.[87] The role of the FAO in this context has been severely criticized by a wide spectrum of opinion. It has been seen as authoritarian and secretive by NGOs, with its failure to consult and involve local communities and NGOs in planning or implementation being a subject of particular concern. Its behaviour has also been the subject of concern of governments. Mrs Lynda Chalker, British Minister of Overseas Development, expressed reservations about the FAO's role and the need for institutional reform.[88] Indeed the perception of the FAO as anti-democratic and secretive extends far beyond the forestry sector, and has been repeated in many other contexts.[89] This is significant as it indicates that if the FAO is to continue to play a central role in administering the TFAP, then its whole outlook and modus operandi needs to undergo fundamental revision if the causes of deforestation, and forest management, are to be addressed effectively.

---

[84]Cited in Colchester and Lohmann book, op.cit, p.91.

[85]WRI, op.cit, p.30.

[86]ibid, p.25

[87]IUCN, UNEP, WWF, Caring for the Earth, Switzerland, 1991, p.131.

[88]HC 24, March 1991, op.cit, p.113.

[89]See for example, G.Hancock, *Lords of Poverty*, Mandarin Books, London, 1991.

Some critiques went as far as to suggest that the TFAP encouraged deforestation by promoting the expansion of commercial logging which often opened up forests to settlers. The FOE report noted that:

... this promotion of the expansion of commercial logging under the TFAP is in fact a recipe for accelerating deforestation, on balance. In some countries, in some cases, the TFAP may have had a net beneficial effect in conserving forests - but overall, not.[90]

FOE and WRM felt that all international funding for the TFAP should be stopped until certain conditions had been met. The Plan should be restructured to check deforestation and to promote genuinely multi-disciplinary and cross-sectoral planning so that alternative views and needs to those of forestry departments be taken into account. After all, the causes of deforestation, and hence the remedies, lay outside of the forest. Existing National Forestry Action Plans should be revised, for their narrow sectoral focus on forestry omits important cross-sectoral issues which have a real bearing on the future of forests.[91] They should be much more bottom-up rather than top-down documents. Logging operations under the TFAP should be massively scaled down. There should be freedom of information regarding the TFAP. The aims and the institutional mechanisms of the TFAP needed to be reformed, and there should be greater accountability. The WWF called for an independent TFAP secretariat, and an independent and on-going review of national plans. More recently, the FOE has called for far-reaching reforms to meet the need for an international mechanism to coordinate global responses to tropical deforestation. It suggested the establishment of an international steering committee responsible for guiding the TFAP. Membership would include representatives of governments and non-government bodies, scientists, private enterprises and multilateral development institutions.[92] The committee should be serviced by a multi-disciplinary, independent secretariat and the decisionmaking process should be open and accessible. Mounting criticism provided a stimulus for a mandate for an independent review group composed of three people, including the former Swedish Prime Minister, Ola Ullsten. After deliberating for five months, it reported in May 1990. Its position was cautious. While admitting that the Plan had run into trouble, it

---

[90]FOE, in HC 24, op.cit.
[91]WRI, op.cit, p.21.
[92]FOE, in HC 24, op.cit, p.62.

recommended transformation rather than abolition of the TFAP. Having identified the three basic aims of the Plan as halting forest destruction, forest conservation and their sustainable development, it added a fourth aim of environmental protection. In judging the TFAP against the yardstick of these goals, this review team came up with more conservative findings than the NGOs. For example, it saw no necessary contradiction between conservation and sustainable forest management. By contrast, the WRM report questions the very idea of sustainable logging:

> In terms of tropical forests, sustainable use includes not just maintaining timber resources and conserving biological diversity, but also maintaining the ecological functions of forests such as soil quality, hydrological cycles, climate and weather, downstream fisheries, as well as maintaining supplies of other forest products ... essential to the livelihoods of local people. Logging, which inevitably simplifies forest ecosystems, can never be sustainable in such terms.[93]

However, the independent report did criticize the implementation of the TFAP, and made various recommendations. For example, it suggested that the TFAP should become a long-term programme aimed at conservation and sustainable development of tropical forest resources in the interests of the inhabitants of the countries concerned and the global community. It advocated the appointment of a director, to be funded jointly by the FAO and the donor community. It called for new guidelines to be drawn up with NGO consultation to define objectives, set standards for sustainable development, and devise a planning procedure with which all participants in the TFAP must comply. It also advocated preparations for an International Forest Convention covering tropical and temperate forests. Commenting on the proposals, Ullsten remarked that:

> In the long run, the disappearance of forests is a political problem. These issues touch on national sovereignty. We cannot impose our views on how we believe forests should be husbanded, we can only convince and advise.[94]

---

[93]Colchester and Lohmann, *The Tropical Forestry Action Plan*, op.cit, p.13.
[94]D.Lewis and J.Vidal, 'UN Proposes Full Forestry Convention', *The Guardian*, 15 June 1990.

Some NGOs, however, such as the WRM, feel that the independent review skirts the issues and fails to address the most pressing problems. It is seen as treating tropical countries as if they were

... monolithic political entities, thereby obscuring critical conflicts of interest within these countries which are a major cause of forest loss ... The Review conflates the interests of the inhabitants and governments' of tropical countries ... (yet) it is the marginalisation of the rural poor by the development process, and the expropriation of their lands and resources, which is one of the main engines of forest destruction.[95]

The Houston Summit of the Group of Seven in July 1990 backed the findings of the independent review. Thus the forces opposing the TFAP and its administration by the FAO were gathering momentum. There were rumours both that the US might withdraw funding, and also that the World Bank might do likewise.[96] These appear to have been groundless.

The findings of this report were discussed by the FAO's Committee on Forestry in September 1990. Several of its suggestions were accepted. Firstly, the need for NGO involvement in drawing up guidelines for implementing the TFAP at country level was acknowledged. Secondly it was agreed that the TFAP should not fund commercial logging projects without rigorous environmental safeguards. Thirdly, a country capacity project should be set up to enable developing countries to undertake effective policy and planning processes for the forestry sector.[97]

Yet the possibility of reforming the management structure of the TFAP met with a cold response from the FAO which was keen to maintain its position of influence. It was reluctant to share the reform process with the original co-founders of the Plan. Nor did it relish the idea of an independent steering committee to coordinate the Plan. It accused the independent review of failing to understand the internal workings of the FAO. Given the secrecy involved, that is hardly surprising. Several governments, however, including the British, supported the need for improvements in the management structure of the TFAP. In November 1989, the same month that Prime Minister Margaret Thatcher had promised a £100 million forestry initiative of extra British aid, the bulk

---

[95]Colchester and Lohmann, *The Ecologist*, op.cit, p.99.

[96]F.Pearce, 'High Stakes in the Rainforest', *The Guardian*, 19 October 1990.

[97]HC 24, op.cit, p.113.

of which would be channelled through the TFAP mechanism, Mrs Chalker had told the FAO that some of the NFAPs encouraged deforestation.[98] She had supported an independent review. The persistent refusal of the FAO's Director-General Edouard Saouma to accept any dilution of his organization's authority concerning the TFAP might result in the collapse of the TFAP.[99]

Certain divisions arose between industrialized and developing countries at the September 1990 FAO meeting. One disagreement was over the establishment of a special fund to help developing countries with their forestry plans. This had been proposed by the review group. The developing countries were in favour, while the developed were against this. Without the financial backing of the latter, the fund will not get off the ground.[100] Another disagreement arose over Ullsten's idea of an international forest convention covering temperate and tropical forests. Many developing countries were suspicious that a code of conduct for forest conservation and use, based on the notion that the forests are essential to the well-being of the whole world, would result in policy imposition by richer countries. A Brazilian delegate was reported to have told the meeting that such a code would be 'wholly inappropriate'.[101] Mr N.Prasad, an Indian delegate, argued that a forest convention should not be considered in isolation from the broader issues of greenhouse gas emissions and climate change, and that once the context was thus broadened, the contribution of the developing countries was very small.[102] Governments are working in spring 1992 towards a statement of principles in the UNCED preparatory committees, for agreement by world leaders in Rio in June 1992. The hope is for an agreement to negotiate a legal convention on forests thereafter.

Many governments and NGOs have concluded that reform of the TFAP is the only practicable solution at present. Some NGOs, however, have had doubts about whether this is in fact possible. Time will tell.

The International Tropical Timber Organization. The International Tropical Timber Organization (ITTO) was set up in 1986 as an inter-state forum for the producers and consumers of tropical timber. It began operational activities in 1987. It comprises 48 member countries: 22

---

[98]F.Pearce, 'High Stakes in the Rainforest', *The Guardian*, 19 October 1990.
[99]Pearce, ibid.
[100]J.Madeley, 'Planning for Greener Forestry', *Financial Times*, 4 October 1990.
[101]ibid.

developing country tropical timber exporters, and 26 developed country consumers. It grew out of the International Tropical Timber Agreement (ITTA) which was signed in 1983 and came into force in 1985. Following more than a year of discussions, its executive body, the International Tropical Timber Council (ITTC), decided at its first meeting in July 1986 to set up headquarters in Yokohama, Japan. Also, it elected Malaysia's Deputy Director-General of Forestry, Dr Freezailah bin Che Yeom, as ITTO's Executive Director. These decisions reflected the fact that Japan was the world's largest importer of tropical timber products, while Malaysia was the largest exporter.[103]

The ITTO is fairly unique among IGOs, with the Chairmanship of its Council and three Permanent Committees alternating between the developed and developing countries, its voting structure reflecting a partnership of equals, and the equal contribution to the ITTO's administrative budget. It is also somewhat unusual in that it encourages conservation NGOs and timber trade associations to attend ITTO meetings as 'active' observers. They are also invited to take part in various Working Groups and Expert Panels.

The aim of the ITTO is to 'promote the expansion and diversification of the international trade in tropical timber' (ITTA, 1983), and also to 'maintain the ecological balance of the (timber producing) regions concerned' (Article 1(h), ITTA). In contrast to many NGOs, Dr Freezailah argues that the ITTO is not simply a commodity organization, but rather a global development organization in tropical timber which is concerned with the latter both as a resource and as a commodity.[104] Its mandate extends to sustainable forestry and conservation issues. Indeed, sustainable forest practices are in the interests both of producers and consumers. Critics of the ITTO identify an inherent tension between the two objectives of conservation and utilization of tropical forests through sustainable management, and hence see the mandate of the ITTO as being essentially flawed.[105] Supporters, however, see the organization

---

[102] ibid.

[103] *Keesings Record of World Events*, Vol.XXXIV, October 1988, p.36248.

[104] Dr Freezailah, 'The First Four Years of ITTO's Activities', Opening Statement of Executive Director of the ITTO at ITTO's Satellite Session, 25 September 1991, held in conjunction with the Tenth World Forestry Congress, Paris, paragraph 9.

[105] See for example, Friends of the Earth, 'Memorandum', in HC 24, Session 1990-91, March 1991, HMSO, p.63.

as being very young and undergoing constructive change, thus exhibiting potential.

The ITTO's 48 member states account for over 95% of the international trade in tropical timber, and 85% of tropical forests. NGOs have a voice in the organization. Indeed, FOE, which has official observer status at the Council and Committee meetings, has praised the Executive Director for his willingness to work with conservation groups.[106] Many countries include representatives of conservation NGOs, as well as representatives of the timber trade, in their delegation. The UK delegation, for example, at the time of writing is composed of two administrators from the ODA (one of whom leads the mission), two forestry advisors (one a consultant), one representative of the Timber Trade Federation, and one representative of conservation NGOs.

As with the TFAP, criticism by NGOs has been strident. FOE, for example, has criticized the Organization for promoting trade at the expense of conservation. However, defenders of the ITTO point to the list of projects in the pipeline, and highlight how they contrast with ongoing projects which they admit suffer from certain defects. The ITTO project cycle also came under attack in 1990 by donors who recognized that its reform was essential. The ODA, for example, financed two consultants to assess the project cycle, and to come up with suggestions for improvement. A number of reforms subsequently came into effect in July 1991. Of particular concern has been the poor quality of documentation reaching the ITTC from submitting governments, the lack of environmental and social impact assessments and the general lack of appraisal and monitoring of projects. Unlike multilateral development banks where project appraisal is done in house, the ITTO relies on governments to do the project appraisal themselves and to assemble documentation. Therein lies an important weakness.

One new idea now operational is that a technical panel should meet twice yearly before the main Council meetings to filter out unsatisfactory project applications or to advise how these might be strengthened. This panel met for the first time in February 1991 in Kuala Lumpur, and again in Yokohama in October 1991. It is to be hoped that its work will result in significant operational improvements. It will also, of course, have financial implications.

---

[106]FOE Memorandum, ibid, p.63

There are two types of funding of the ITTO. Firstly, all member states in principle contribute to ITTO's running costs. For example, in the case of the UK, the contribution to the ITTO's administrative budget for the financial year 1991 was assessed at US$98,602 out of a total US$3,173 million.[107] Secondly, there are voluntary contributions. When successful project proposals have been selected, the Council operates a system of pledging whereby donor countries literally pledge financial contributions to projects of their choice. A few donors, such as the US and Italy, rather than pledging to particular projects, pledge a particular amount. However, if nothing comes up which they wish to fund, they then enjoy the political prestige of having committed a certain sum without actually having disbursed it. FOE has noted that EC governments have generally offered 'unequivocal support for the principles and objectives of ITTO, and yet they have generally remained financially and politically uncommitted'.[108] In practice, Japan carries the weight of funding. As the largest importer, it has a clear interest in doing so. Japan would like the ITTO to develop into the lead institution in the area of forestry.

One of the main issues of contention in the ITTO has been conflicting attitudes to the idea of sustainable felling. The FOE would like to see an immediate ban on felling, especially for export. Representatives of the timber trade stress the importance of developing country sovereignty, and argue that if developed countries ban imports of their timber, the result will be effectively to remove value from the forest. Thus, poor countries will perceive themselves as being forced to cut down the forest to use it for more economically valuable ends such as agriculture.[109] The ODA takes a pragmatic line, arguing that it is both unrealistic and unnecessary to expect poor countries to give up what may well be one of their main foreign exchange earners. Hence the UK policy is to help developing countries manage their forest resources on a sustainable basis. Unlike FOE, the ODA believes this can be achieved through assistance in areas ranging from research, training, institution-building, conservation, afforestation, and the promotion of social forestry. FOE adopts a purist line, seeing the cost in terms of the quality of the product on the second and third generation of growth as being diminished, and a

---

[107] Personal communication from Dr Freezailah, 21 October 1991.
[108] FOE Memorandum, HC 24, op.cit, p.63.
[109] Morrell, HC 24, op.cit, p.42.

loss in terms of species composition. While these are fair comments, countries which are running to stand still in the present structure of the world economy, and which are faced with expanding populations and diminishing resources, must pursue politically realistic policies. Such purism for them is not politically feasible. Moreover, if they perceive developed countries telling them what to do within their own borders, via, for example, bans on timber imports into the EC as advocated by the Dutch, they may well accelerate deforestation to make best use of trees and of their investments before the commodity is robbed of its value. They may also become unwilling to cooperate on the value of biodiversity - something the developed countries are keen to promote. There is a bargain yet to be struck on the forestry issue.

By its own admission, the ITTO indicates that less than one half of one per cent of all logging areas are managed on a sustainable basis.[110] While this is a damning indictment of the intentions and/or effectiveness of the ITTO, any such institution is only as strong as its members allow it to be. It has already shown a certain degree of openness to change. It has responded to criticism from within and without. The ITTO has adopted 'Target 2000', by which time it hopes that all tropical timber entering international trade will come from sustainable managed forest sources. It is to be hoped that these developments can be built upon. It is in the interests of consumers and producers that this valuable resource is harvested sustainably.

NGO activity: debt-for-nature swaps. Protection of forests through debt-for-nature swaps represents an extremely innovative move by NGOs concerned to reduce developing country debt, itself a stimulus to deforestation, and simultaneously protect the environment. First proposed in 1984 by Thomas Lovejoy of the US World Wildlife Federation,[111] debt-for-nature swaps did not become a reality until 1987. Since then, several have taken place.

Recognizing that many debts will never be serviced, private lenders have developed means of trying to minimize potential losses from such loans. Thus a 'secondhand market' has evolved for developing country debt. Debt can be bought at large discounts off the face value. NGOs have sought to capitalize on this situation by purchasing blocks of

---

[110]D.Poore, *No Timber Without Trees*, Earthscan, London, 1989.

[111]A.Patterson, 'Debt-for-Nature Swaps and the Need for Alternatives', *Environment*, Vol.32, No.10, December 1990, pp.4-13.

developing country debt in the secondhand market at well below the face value, then trading or cancelling this debt with the state owing it in return for specified environmental action.[112] This may result in local currency being made available to a local NGO for conservation purposes, or it may involve public and private partnership in large-scale conservation and development schemes as was the case with the first ever debt-for-nature swap which took place between an American NGO and the Bolivian government in July 1987. In that particular case, the NGO purchased US$650,000 of Bolivian debt to a private bank at the discounted price of US$100,000, and then traded its face value for 'conservation payments-in-kind' with the Bolivian government.[113] A tropical forest land reserve of 3.7 million acres was set up.[114]

Several countries have now taken part in such swaps, for example Ecuador, Zambia, Costa Rica and Madagascar.[115] At present levels such swaps are a positive force for environmental protection, releasing funds into an area which otherwise would not enjoy them. In terms of debt reduction, they are of limited value since they merely scratch the surface of the debt burden of the countries participating in them. Moreover, were they to affect a larger proportion of overall sovereign debt, countries might be less inclined to take part in them, since swaps by their very nature carry conditions. The greater the proportion of debt swapped, the more extensive and stringent the conditions attached would be. Such infringements of sovereignty might be perceived as too high a price to pay for debt reduction, particularly if the government involved does not consider environmental protection a top priority. Ultimately, even if debt-for-nature swaps increased massively in scale, the real difficulty of keeping loggers, ranchers and shifted cultivators off forest land would remain.

---

[112]For an overview see S.Hansen, 'Debt for Nature Swaps: Overview and Discussion of Key Issues', Environment Department Working Paper No.1., Environment Department, World Bank, Washington DC, February 1988, p.3.

[113]Hansen, ibid.

[114]Professor Bob Rowthorn has commented that since the total area of tropical forest is about 7.8 square kilometres or 2,000 million acres, at the price paid to Bolivia it could all be purchased for US $50 million. Even at 100 times this price, it would still only cost $5 billion. This suggests that purchasing rainforest is very cheap.

[115]*Keesings Record of World Events*, Vol.XXXV, August 1989, p.36842.

National strategies

The area of 'national efforts' to alleviate deforestation is a rather grey one, since many of the measures undertaken have been planned or funded by external agencies such as the World Bank. However, since they are translated into government policy and fall under the authority and administration of the government, they are classified here as national rather than international. Such strategies often contain particular policies such as the development of agro-forestry or social forestry generally. Here we are concerned more with the strategy than the specific policy.

Environmental action plans. These are large-scale national strategies designed to promote growth and development while minimizing adverse impacts on the natural environment and therefore promoting economic sustainability. Several developing countries have adopted such plans, which have usually been developed with a greater or lesser degree of direction from the World Bank. In some cases there has been notable involvement by local NGOs in the discussions preceding national adoption of the Plan.[116]

The Mauritian case is not atypical. The World Bank was invited by the government in September 1987 to send a mission to produce a report on strategies for economic development with environmental management.[117] Having approved the report, the government, with the World Bank and the UNDP, sponsored an international conference in September 1988 to bring together representatives from public and private institutions, both Mauritian and international, and NGOs, to discuss the proposed Plan and other reports put forward by government agencies, international bodies and NGOs.[118] A Comprehensive Investment Programme supported the Plan. A donors' meeting took place in Paris in January 1989, and commitments of US$90 million were achieved.

The Plan sets out a broad strategy covering all important sectors of the economy with environmental implications. On the specific issue of deforestation, the Plan makes a number of observations and

---

[116]See for example M.G.Khalikane, 'The Environmental Action Plan Process: Some Lessons from Lesotho', AFTEN Technical Note, No.1, Environment Division, Africa Region, World Bank, Washington DC, March 1989.

[117]On the drawing up of the Plan, see S.V.Rathnam and K.Opsal, 'Environmental Action Plans: the Mauritian Experience', AFTEN Technical Note, No.5, Environment Division, Africa Region, World Bank, Washington DC, October 1989.

[118]For the Plan, see 'National Environmental Action Plan for Mauritius', World Bank, March 1990, Washington DC.

recommendations. Few areas of indigenous forest remain in Mauritius. Forest has been taken over by more vigorous, invasive exotic species such as guava and privet. This situation has been exacerbated by the introduction of monkeys and birds which spread the seeds of these exotics. Indigenous trees have not adapted to germination, having been eaten. Illegal logging for cooking puts pressure on remaining forest, as does forest clearance for deer ranching. The Plan recommends therefore that Crown lands with indigenous forest tracks should be declared as nature reserves and protected accordingly. Reforestation should concentrate on indigenous species. There should be some clearance of exotics. No further indigenous forests should be cleared for deer ranching. Conservation of indigenous flora by local and foreign groups should be supported.

Such plans have been developed for several countries, and they represent attempts to see the economy and the environment as an integrated whole. Multi-level participation from bottom up is as important to their eventual success as high levels of donor funding. We will have to wait a few more years before we can reasonably assess the success of these Plans in facilitating sustainable economic development.

Sustainable parks. The concept of sustainably managed forest parks has found best expression in the case of the Korup National Park in the Cameroon. Unlike many other such parks which serve the wants of foreign tourists, the Korup Park, created by Presidential decree in 1986,[119] is being developed as an integral part of a regional development programme.

The Korup Park enjoys special advantages which make its success as a sustainable forest more likely. Gartland and Momo remark that:

> Fortunately, the biological richness of Korup is matched by the poverty of its potential for extractive or agricultural uses.[120]

Lying in an inaccessible area, the park has grown up over granite which is unlikely to yield valuable minerals. The dominant trees have little value as commercial timber.

---

[119]For further details see J.Gadwohl and R.Greenberg Saving the Tropical Forests, Earthscan, London, 1988, pp.99-101.
[120]S.Gartlan and D.Momo, 'Korup: New Approach to Conservation', *IUCN Bulletin*, Vol.17, No.1-3, 1986, p.27.

Local people have been involved in all stages of development of the park, and it is well understood that they must benefit from its establishment if they are to protect it. Their education regarding the conservation aims of the park is vital. While some people will have to be resettled, a commitment has been made to keep them within their traditional ethnic heartland even if outside the park itself. New settlements will be provided with social services, and the essential food requirements of the people such as the bush beef previously hunted within the park will be met by special breeding programmes using traditional meat animals and also by the introduction of new animals such as rabbits. While the development of the park is still in the early stages, clear efforts are being made to ensure that local people develop a positive attitude to the park and that they do not perceive it as a source of grievance. These attitudes will need to be continually reinforced if the park is to succeed as a sustainably managed forest preserving unique fauna.

While the Korup Park has been heralded as a model for the rest of Africa, we have yet to see whether national parks can be managed sustainably in Africa and beyond. The special advantages of Korup have already been noted; unfortunately these are not universal. Parks will have to respond to the needs of local people if they are to protect the habitat and indigenous flora and fauna. This has been recognized in Nepal, where local environmentalists have called for the Sagamartha National Park to work with local people and not the exclusion of them. We have yet to see how well such ideas will take root in other areas of the world.

Local action. It is often the case that direct local action on the ground brings about the most positive results. It is not difficult to understand why: without the involvement, support and commitment of local people then efforts to halt deforestation are often ill-conceived and rarely stand a chance of success. Many a government has issued a moratorium on tree felling, only to find that illegal felling continues because of a local need for fuel and fodder. Where local people participate in forest management, success is more likely. Examples of spontaneous local action and action initiated by local NGOs proliferate. Perhaps the best known are the cases of the Chipko movement in India, and the rubber tappers in the Amazon.

The Chipko movement arose in the Indian Himalaya in direct response to threatened loss of livelihood since the forest was being put to the axe of external contractors. Locals, fearing loss of fuel, fodder, food and thatch, simply hugged the trees to prevent felling. 'Chipko' is Hindi for 'hug'. Far from being an orchestrated movement, the Chipko movement rather represents a mix of spontaneous local uprisings in response to perceived threat, and to actions encouraged by Gandhian sarvodaya or social worker-activists who worked to empower local people and help them fight for the viability of small-scale hill economies. Weber has written that:

> The movement aims to bring man back into living harmoniously with nature, to provide economic survival for the local hill people, to undertake reforestation work and to increase environmental knowledge and caring within the population at large. It is also a movement by hill women who are protesting the only way they can that, as forests disappear, they have to go even further to collect fuel for fires and fodder leaves for their animals.[121]

Weber suggests that the birth of the movement in the Uttarkhand region of Uttar Pradesh was no accident; here, 'environmental and economic factors came together with the right combination of personnel'.[122] In this very poor hill region, the forest was the only resource immediately exploitable, and increasingly this was coming under the hands of external contractors. There was no employment locally, so the men migrated to the plains to find work. Life was becoming ever more difficult for women as they had to travel further each day in search of fuel and fodder. The Gandhian tradition was strong in the area, with several sarvodaya workers active locally.

The latter made the connection between deforestation and poverty and saw the work of the axemen as being responsible for soil erosion, landslides and flooding. They called for small-scale forest-based industries to be developed in the hill regions, in other words, social forestry as the basis of community development. They called for the planting not of exotic fast-growing species such as eucalyptus and chir-pine on monoculture plantations, but rather the traditional mixed species local to the area, trees that would provide the local population with food, fodder, fuel, fertilizer and fibre rather than meeting the demands of industry on the plains.

---

[121]T.Weber, *Hugging the Trees: the Story of the Chipko Movement*, Penguin Books, Harmondsworth and Delhi, 1989, p.11.
[122]ibid, p.12.

The Chipko movement has inspired local protest and empowerment in other parts of India, most notably perhaps in Karnataka in south India where the Appiko movement has flourished.[123] There, efforts by the State Forestry Department to plant eucalytpus have been opposed, since they serve the interests of the rayon and pulp industry rather than contributing to the well-being of local communities.

The Chipko movement has also achieved international recognition, and has served as an inspiration to activists in other parts of the world who are worried by loss of livelihoods for forest peoples and the inappropriate nature of so much afforestation.

In Brazil, the efforts of the rubber tappers, led by union leader Chico Mendes, have played an important role in canvassing for the establishment of 'extractive reserves'.[124] The setting up of such reserves, based on recognition of usufruct rights,[125] is perceived as a direct assault on private ownership by local ranchers whose title to the land is of dubious validity anyway. The murder of Mendes in December 1988 by local ranchers who saw their interests being threatened brought the spotlight of the world's media onto their plight.[126] Such reserves have won external support from those concerned about climate change and species extinction, since they represent a sustainable way of harvesting the forest resource. The rubber tappers subsist by harvesting Brazil nuts and latex, growing food crops and raising livestock such as cows and oxen.

In an interesting alliance of former foes, the rubber tappers have been joined by Indians in formulating regional development strategies. Both groups depend for their survival on the forest, and the evidence suggests that the survival of the forest would be safer in their hands than in any others. With their intimate knowledge of the forest, they can work it in an ecologically- and economically-sustainable fashion. Entrenched interests of the landowning elite, however, remain a major obstacle.

---

[123]ibid, p.111

[124]C.Mendes, *Fight for the Forest: Chico Mendes in His Own Words*, Latin American Bureau, London, 1989.

[125]The right of enjoying others' property short of destruction and waste of its substance.

[126]S.Hecht and A.Cockburn 'Defenders of the Amazon', *New Statesman and Society*, 23 June 1989, pp.16-21.

7.5 Conclusion: what needs to be done?

The international instruments in place which deal with forestry, namely the TFAP and the ITTO, are inadequate and/or inappropriate for tackling the root causes of deforestation and, thereby, for turning the tide on this ecological, social and economic disaster. It is unlikely that the proposed statement of principles on forests, which is intended to be ready for signing by the UNCED conference in 1992, will represent a major step forward. There are too many conflicting interests at the international, national and commercial levels for real progress to be made. Indeed, even the definition of deforestation itself, and therefore what constitutes managed forestry, depends on the interest of the respective parties. As far as a convention is concerned, the objectives of different parties vary. For governments of certain developed countries, concern over the contribution of tropical deforestation to global warming may play the most important part. Biological diversity will be very important for some developed countries' governments. For environmental NGOs, biological diversity and the protection of indigenous peoples' lands may be uppermost. For the governments of hardwood exporting countries, access to markets will be crucial. What matters for the millions of shifted cultivators is immediate survival and then sustainability of their livelihoods.

It is clear that if deforestation is to be halted and reforestation or afforestation undertaken, then action is needed on various levels. The most important level is the local level: the problem of the increasing numbers of often landless peasants. If governments were to implement serious land reform and population policies, this would be a step in the right direction. As yet there are few signs of either of these occurring. Even if land reform were implemented, social forestry would still need to be promoted.[127] Indeed, social forestry may well be the key to progress on a global scale. The involvement of local landowners and community groups in tree- or forest-related activities to increase food production, employment, and fuel is crucial to protecting remaining forests. While indigenous forest dwellers possess the knowledge necessary for sustainable harvesting of the forest, shifted cultivators are a different matter. Even outside forest domains, social forestry is becoming increasingly necessary for sustainable development as populations

---

[127]H.Gregersen, S.Draper and D.Elz, (eds), *People and Trees: the Role of Social Forestry in Sustainable Development*, The World Bank, Washington DC, 1989.

increase and land degenerates. Social forestry is underway in many parts of the world, often promoted by local NGOs and sometimes by government. Examples range from the Majjia Valley windbreak project in Niger,[128] to sal tree protection schemes in Bengal, to the Yanesha Forestry Cooperative in Palcazu Valley, Peru.[129]

In Bangladesh,[130] the local NGO Proshika is playing a prominent role in helping raise the awareness of government, forestry officers and peasants regarding protection of sal forests on which the latter depend for their subsistence and cash needs.[131] Many experts have called for replacement of sal forests with fast-growing exotic species, yet such species would not provide the whole range of benefits for local peasants offered by the traditional sal forests. Proskika argues that sal coppice has rapid regenerative powers under protection. Therefore local management by user groups is essential. Proshika has a membership of over 300,000 landless agricultural labourers and artisans who are organized into groups to protect areas of regenerating sal coppice.

The idea of community forest management by user groups has been taken up elsewhere. In Nepal, where communities have been given the right to use the forest, they have had a clear incentive to police it, thereby preventing excessive logging and coppicing.[132] The involvement of adjacent village groups is considered essential, for there is little point in one group harvesting a woodlot in a sustainable manner if the grazing animals of an adjacent group then enter the woodlot.[133] One way around this problem is to feed animals in stalls, rather than allowing them to graze freely. To this end, buffalo have been introduced to replace cattle.

[128]ibid, pp.31-33.

[129]S.Postel and J.C.Ryan, 'Reforming Forestry', in L.R.Brown, *State of the World, 1991*, Worldwatch Institute, Norton & Co, London and New York, 1991, p.83.

[130]See ADAB Environment Advisory Group, 'Environmental Problems in Bangladesh: an NGO Perspective for Policies and Action', Dhaka, August 1990, available from Proshika.

[131]See C.K.Lai and S.I.Ali, 'Sal Forest Protection by Local Groups in Bangladesh: Towards Regenerating Degraded Forests', Paper presented to the International Conference on Sustainable Forestry, Indian Environmental Society, Delhi, January 1991.

[132]Nepal-Australia Forestry Project, 'Directions for Community Forest Management in Nepal', Seminar Series at the Institute of Forestry, Pokhara, September 1988, available from NAFP, Kathmandu, Nepal.

[133]E.Pelink P.K.Manandhar and R.H.Gecolea 'Forestry Extension: Community and Development in Nepal', *Unasylva*, Vol.36, No.143, FOA, Rome, 1984/1, pp.2-15.

A buffalo produces 4 litres of milk a day, compared with 0.5 litres for a cow. Also buffalo calves can be sold for meat, whereas the dominant Hindu religion in Nepal means that cows are not a useful cash commodity.

The importance of local or user-group management cannot be over-stressed. To this end, at the grassroots level, communication of the environmental message is essential. Peasants realize that they are placed in a no-win situation by the trade-off between immediate survival versus sustainable development. For many, a major problem is lack of access to knowledge, resources and organization that might be very beneficial. Dr Yagya Karki, Director of the international NGO Worldview International Foundation (WIF) in Nepal, believes that the way forward must be through appropriate educational techniques. WIF, which has branches in eighteen developing countries, specializes in promoting development through the media. WIF-Nepal has concentrated until recently on promoting rural health through videos and radio broadcasts. Having successfully completed a UNICEF-sponsored immunization project, a CIDA-sponsored women's development programme (Canadian Development Agency), and a WIF/UNICEF project on oral rehydration, WIF-Nepal has now lent its expertise in media-related development efforts to the promotion of environmental awareness. It is the first national WIF to move into the environmental field. Dr Karki has remarked that:

> In a country like Nepal, where the vast majority are illiterate, the audio-visual (video) method of communication can perhaps have the greatest impact in bringing knowledge to the largest number of people. Through entertainment it brings development messages, environment being one of them. WIF, as a non-governmental development communication organisation, sees the promotion of development through education as its primary role.[134]

All too often development projects have failed because they have relied upon culturally inappropriate methods of communicating the message. It is futile to produce fact sheets for dissemination in areas where the population is largely illiterate, yet this has been done on numerous occasions. Methods such as theatre and puppetry may have a far greater impact in villages throughout the developing world than any written message. Development workers, whether appointed by the government,

---

[134]Personal communication, 2 January 1991.

international aid agencies or local NGOs, must be sensitive to how best local people can learn, and to do this they must shed their own cultural biases and expectations. They need to work with local leaders and institutions that are respected by the villagers, such as church organizations, village committees, women's groups, traditional healers and elders.

At the national level, the possibilities for action are endless, and will depend on the particular concerns of respective governments. However, entrenched timber interests will place obstacles in the way of change. Reducing industrial demand for wood in the developed countries would not be too difficult, by such methods as reducing waste in the construction industries[135] and placing more emphasis on paper recycling. In timber-producing countries, more stringent rules regarding logging would slow the degeneration of old-growth forests and promote secondary growth in logged areas. The developed states of North America could set an example by protecting their own old-growth forests, such as in the US Pacific Northwest.

At the international level, complete overhaul of the TFAP is imperative, so that the interests of sustainable forestry and the livelihoods of millions of peasant cultivators are put first. The ITTO is still young and undergoing change, so while complete overhaul may be premature, the organization should be closely monitored to see if the policies it promotes really do strike a balance between conservation and utilization of tropical forests through sustainable management. The international economic structures of world finance and trade, and the implications of international debt, all push tropical country governments in the direction of greater immediate exploitation of the timber resource. Yet forests possess resources far beyond timber.

It is in the long-term interest of everyone that forests are managed on a more sustainable basis, and incentives must be created to that end.[136] An international moratorium on logging, which is in any event unlikely, would be impossible to police. What is needed most of all is education: of timber consumers in the developed world, and the producers and consumers in the developing countries. Social forestry is the best answer we have to ensure that forests do not disappear. It is naive to think that

---

[135]Postel and Ryan, op.cit, p.85.

[136]R.Repetto 'Creating Incentives for Sustainable Forest Development', *Ambio*, Vol.16, No.2-3, 1987, pp.94-99.

forests can be fenced off from the very people whose livelihoods depend on them; forests and trees must be used to meet those peoples' needs in a sustainable fashion. Local communities must be empowered to police forest areas themselves, and must be given incentives to use them sustainably. They must benefit from the right of access. This is possibly the greatest immediate environmental and developmental challenge of the 1990s, on which the personal security of millions of people around the world depends.

*The challenge for international relations and diplomacy is to take us
back from the brink of disaster by promoting the principle of global
sustainability over parochial state interest. This requires local
communities, grassroots organizations, governments, scientists,
diplomats, bureaucrats, IGOs, NGOs, and business to learn from each
other and to collaborate. The situation calls for unprecedented levels of
cooperation and billions of dollars, often in the face of scientific
uncertainty. Sir Crispin Tickell remarks, 'Uncertainty may be part of the
human condition. We must always look at the cost of doing nothing.'[1]
The established risks associated with inaction are huge; moreover their
potential is not fully understood. In essence, the international political
and economic systems must change, for they are a major part of the
environmental problem. At the national level, rich and poor countries
alike must face up to their respective responsibilities and adapt local
behaviour. Unless consumption is curbed in the developed countries and
population controlled in the developing, efforts towards sustainability
will be rendered impotent.*

There is no convincing evidence that the fundamental changes required
in the underlying political, economic and demographic structures to halt
environmental decline are occurring. Booth remarks that:

> While ecological problems are becoming more obvious, so too are
> the obstacles to solution. Progress is hindered by the nature of the
> international system itself and by prevailing ideas about economic

---

[1] See F.Pearce, 'The Green Diplomat: Sir Crispin Tickell', *New Scientist*, 21 March 1992,
pp.38-40.

progress. Unfettered capitalism and a self-help world are incompatible with the needs of global economic management. The latter directly threatens sensitive issues relating to sovereignty and standards of living.[2]

Nationalism is rearing its head in many parts of the world, and the number of sovereign states is increasing. Developments in the former USSR and eastern Europe may well give added impetus to the claims for sovereign statehood being made by peoples in other parts of the world. The current direction of transformation of the international economy, with the emphasis on liberalization as a spur to growth, is at odds with the requirement of environmental sustainability. Moreover the philosophy which informs it has enormous implications for conceptions of burden-sharing and general equity issues at the heart of the international environmental dialogue. Global population is not expected to stabilize until 2070, when it is expected to reach over 10 billion - more than twice the current number.

If traditional state interest is to give way to global vision, there must be some fundamental changes. The enormity of the nuclear threat to our planet did not result in global cooperation to rid the world of the danger. An effort was made to stop horizontal proliferation, but vertical proliferation continued apace. Can we expect the threat of environmental destruction to trigger global cooperation to rid the planet of this new danger? On the evidence of history, probably not. However, the nuclear threat did result in the development of management strategies by the two superpowers for dealing with crises. Perhaps that is the best we can hope for in the short-term with the environmental crisis: limited cooperative actions simply to ensure that the worst fears are not realized.

While transformation of the structures which have created the environmental crisis cannot be expected, it appears that there are possibilities for reform within the system. Indeed there are examples of successful reform, such as the Vienna Convention and Montreal Protocol regarding the problem of ozone depletion. While these do not add up to a final solution, they do suggest a way forward out of diplomatic deadlock. They also suggest that agreements can be updated to respond to growing scientific knowledge, or to growing perceptions of risk. Such

---

[2]K.Booth, 'War, Security and Strategy: Towards A Doctrine for a Stable Peace', in K.Booth (ed), *New Thinking About Strategy and International Security*, Harper Collins Academic, London, 1991, p.348.

responsiveness is essential, since environmental change itself is evolving. This reform amounts to edging away from the abyss, a necessary but not sufficient condition for meeting the challenge of sustainability. It represents a first, short-term response to a long-term problem.

Agreements over technical environmental issues should be easier to forge than agreements concerning fundamental transformation. Yet even these may escape us in some instances. The case studies reveal that the range of issues confronting us demands a flexible response; there can be no blueprint. Some issues lend themselves to regional solutions, others require the participation of a select group of countries, while others require a global response involving many different types of international actors. For some problems, grassroots involvement is the key. There are a few precedents, such as the Convention on Trade in Endangered Species, the International Whaling Agreement, the Vienna Convention and the Montreal Protocol to tackle the ozone issue, and the Basel Convention on Toxic Waste. However, some problems, such as climate change, present formidable difficulties for negotiators due to their magnitude, complexity, and the number and range of actors involved, each with different interests. A truly global agreement on this is as necessary as it is unlikely. Moreover, the immediate success of such an agreement would depend very heavily on a small number of countries which would therefore have disproportionate influence in that particular arrangement in the short-term.

While radical policies are unlikely in the short-term, over the medium- to long-term it is possible that the attitudes of governments may shift. For this to happen, public opinion in developed countries will have to change, for this largely dictates the political importance attached by their governments to respective questions. The promotion of change in the public's perception of environmental issues in these countries has to date been achieved largely by the activities of NGOs.

The three competing concerns of environment, development and security pose great medium- and long-term challenges for international environmental collaboration. Yet the fate of each is intimately connected to the fate of the others. What is required is a reduction of the focus on state actors, short-term perspectives, traditional security concerns such as borders and territory, and the separation of high politics dealing with matters of national security from low politics dealing with socio-economic matters.[3] A holistic approach[4] must take account of non-state actors and of levels of analysis other than the state, it must be long-term, and must work with an expanded conception of security based as much on socio-economic as on military/strategic factors. Environmental diplomacy, whilst acknowledging traditional inter-state concerns, must not be limited by them. It must aim at harmonizing environment, development and security concerns in a context of: rapid global population growth; a seemingly limitless appetite for consumption by the richer parts of the world; and the growing appetite of the developing countries, with all that entails for pressure on resources and political stability.

Despite short-term interest coalitions which straddle the North/South divide, that divide still reflects the major international division on the environmental crisis. Resolution of the crisis will be impossible unless that division is addressed. The perception of imposed economic policies and unfair debt leading to further social deprivation in already impoverished countries heightens international tension and reinforces a confrontational atmosphere in the international arena, thus lessening the possibility of negotiated agreements to tackle global environmental change.

With the passing of the Cold War and the opening of the former eastern bloc to western economic policy, the international economy has been truly globalized. The global homogeneity thus produced is lessening the options for discussion of different economic philosophies, and largely determining that the debate remains within the context of tinkering with the present system rather than transforming it. The opportunities for environmental improvement are being couched in terms of market instruments, such as tradeable emissions permits. At a general level, developing countries do not feel that their needs and interests have been well-served by this system, and in order to win them over, environmental agreements will have to address equity issues.

At the heart of the debate is the issue of who should pay for clearing up existing environmental damage, and for ensuring that further damage

---

[3] See C.Thomas, 'New Directions in Thinking About Security in the Third World', in Booth, op.cit.
[4] B.Buzan, *People, States and Fear*, Wheatsheaf, Brighton, 1983.

does not occur. The question of historic responsibility cannot be swept aside with the argument that people alive today in developed countries should not have to pay for the profligacy of their ancestors. After all, they are enjoying a standard of living achieved at the expense of past emissions of greenhouse gases which remain in the atmosphere today, and which will contribute to future global warming. Developing countries believe that the developed countries which have been responsible for most of the mess to date should pay the price of restoration and provide the finance and technology necessary for them to develop along a cleaner path. From the viewpoint of equity, developing countries do not believe they should be held back from further development when it is not they who have caused many of the problems in the first place. Regarding funding levels, the developing countries want new money, whereas some of the most powerful developed countries have preferred the transfer of aid already allocated for other purposes into the environmental area. On the question of mechanisms, developing countries are adamantly opposed to the channelling of new money in any way via the World Bank, including through the relatively recent Global Environment Facility. They express a lack of faith in the competence of the World Bank, which they see as having pushed economically and environmentally inappropriate policies. They are also critical of its lack of openness, accountability, and democracy in policy formation, implementation and assessment, and in allocation of funding. They fear environmental conditions to loans. Hence their call for new institutions based on new principles, with representation from all states concerned and also from local people affected by projects.

Not every problem in poorer countries is the result of harmful outside forces, and Southern states bear some responsibility for their environmental predicament. Misuse of agricultural land, rural overpopulation and urban pollution are particular problems. While the situation varies widely between countries and is often dependent on the stage of development, in much of the developing world the distribution of resources is heavily skewed. Such distribution patterns, which are in the control of local elites, have a profound impact on the environment. In their daily struggle for survival, the growing numbers of landless peasants must degrade their environment; they are offered no alternative. They realize that they are eroding tomorrow's base for survival, but they have no option. While the Northern countries have helped make the

South what it is today, and in this respect bear an historic responsibility, Southern elites must take responsibility for the environmental repercussions of the domestic maldistribution of land and wealth. It is the responsibility of local elites to reform domestic distribution patterns to the benefit of the majority. This would add weight to their call for a reversal of international resource transfers which currently flow in an absurd direction, from the South to the North. It would also further their call for democratization of international institutions.

Are environmental issues here to stay on the international agenda? It is widely believed that the nature and extent of global environmental change means that failure to act is likely to result in irreparable harm to our planet. Yet the imperative of urgent action implicit in such knowledge cannot alone explain the new place of these issues in international discourse. If it did, then we could confidently expect the environment to remain on the international agenda. Knowledge of the severe implications of other problems, such as the nuclear arms race, has not resulted in immediate, meaningful global action. Yet it has resulted in sustained interest. The current diplomatic profile of global environmental change derives largely from the activities of NGOs who took advantage of the political space provided by the fortuitous ending of the Cold War. Indeed the ending of the Cold War provided a crucial window of opportunity, without which the environmental cause would not have been promoted so successfully at the international level. This coincided with greater awareness on the part of international institutions such as the World Bank and various other branches of the UN of the links between economic development and environmental degradation, itself partly the result of NGO campaigning. NGOs are continuing their campaigning; indeed they are consolidating and expanding their role in discussion of public policy by developing sophisticated research capability. This, coupled with the bureaucratic and scientific networks that have developed in the environmental area, means that the environment is likely to remain on the international political agenda even if the immediate political circumstances of recession suggest otherwise.

In the longer term the importance of NGOs as international actors may be enhanced. The environmental crisis is not going to go away, and as politicians take decisions to meet short-term political requirements, environmental problems will intensify. Looking to the future it is likely that NGOs will build up their support base as the adverse consequences of environmental degradation become more obvious and affect the lives of voters in the richer countries.

Governments continue to be the most powerful actors in formulating environmental policy changes. They are also key agents in facilitating or obstructing the grassroots empowerment necessary for policy implementation. National interest is the prime catalyst of state behaviour. We must hope then, that governments perceive it to be in the interest of their respective states to cooperate to meet the global environmental challenge. As Ken Booth has remarked, 'We can only hope ... that the fear of ecological collapse will empower reason, and also the political will to act upon it.'[5] We must hope also that this happens in time.

---

[5] Booth, op.cit, p.348.